UNIX POWER UTILITIES

FOR POWER USERS

JOHN MUSTER, PETER BIRNS, AND LURNIX

MIS: PRESS

MANAGEMENT INFORMATION SOURCE, INC.

W9-CTO-353

UNIX™ Power Utilities for Power Users

Copyright © 1989 by Lurnix
1680 Shattuck Avenue
Post Office Box 10164
Berkeley, CA 94709
(415)849-4478

Published by Management Information Source, Inc.
1107 N.W. 14th Avenue
Portland, Oregon 97209
(503)222-2399

First Printing

ISBN 1-55828-000-6

Library of Congress Catalog Card Number: 88-29074

All rights reserved. Reproduction or use, without express permission, of editorial or pictorial content, in any manner, is prohibited. No patent liability is assumed with respect to the use of the information contained herein. While every precaution has been taken in the preparation of this book, neither the publisher nor the author assumes responsibility for errors or omissions. Neither is any liability assumed for damage resulting from the use of the information contained herein.

UNIX is a registered trademark of American Telephone and Telegraph Corp.
VAX and **DEC** are registered trademarks of Digital Equipment Corp.
Xenix is a registered trademark of Microsoft Corporation.
Modular Guides is a trademark of Lurnix.
Legos is a trademark of Interlego, A.G.

Acknowledgements

Although as senior authors we accept responsibility for the modules that constitute this book, the efforts of the following people while they were staff members at Lurnix were absolutely essential in the development and production of the work.

Scott Anderson	technical advising, editing
Mathew Atkins	technical advising, programming
Alice Brzovic	graphic designing, text processing
Dave Cottle	contributing author, technical advising, programming
Kevan Garrett	contributing author, graphic design, text processing
Eduardo Gutentag	contributing author, programming, advising
Carl Hallberg	text processing
Joan Heller	consulting
Iva Heuser	editing
Sue Hulley	editing
Peter Koch	text processing, editing
Shelley Louie	programming, text processing
David Lukas	programming, text processing
Rose Mucci	editing, text processing
April Ogimachi	editing, text processing
Aloke Prabhakar	technical advising, editing
Carl Pregozen	contributing author, technical advising
Patty Ratliff	contributing author, editing
Shahrokh Sadjadi	programming
Peter Shipley	programming, graphic design
Troy Smith	editing
Gretchen Stude	coordinating, text processing, editing
Beth Sumner	editing, text processing
Sharon Thompson	text processing
Connie Jo Tilford	text processing

On a personal note:

Catherine Muster, 1920-1988, was a teacher's teacher. In the early 1950's she developed a series of stand alone educational modules designed to challenge and meet the individual needs of her students in a mixed fifth and sixth grade class in the Canton, Ohio, public schools. The instructional modules made it possible for each student to work alone, in a small group, or individually with her, as it was appropriate. When each student completed a module, more were available that could be tailored to meet the student's interests and particular needs. "Assist each student, don't teach the class." The power of the approach was evident even to her son who visited the classroom during college vacations.

I am very grateful to the colleagues, co-workers and friends listed on the previous page who made developing this book a memorable, usually enjoyable, team effort. Thank you.

Of utmost importance to me while I worked on the completion of this project, was the affection, encouragement, understanding and support of my wife Catherine Cavette.

It is well known that collaboration can be a difficult task. Peter Birns and I worked together for several years: team teaching, starting Lurnix and developing the educational foundation for Lurnix Modular Guides, while maintaining a close friendship. I am grateful that we were able to do it, and that collaboration with Peter proved to be both very important and enjoyable for me. --JM

In addition to the acknowledgements listed on the previous page, I would like to offer my special thanks to my family. Growing up with them taught me the invaluable lesson that loving, while not always easy, is always important. I would also like to thank my friends, Ann Hildebrand and Dave Cottle, for growing with me as I worked on this book. Finally I would like to thank John Muster. As John's mother, Catherine Muster, demonstrated teaching at its best to John, John demonstrated it to me. Thank you John for being my friend, mentor, and collaborator. --PB

Table of Contents

Foreword   1

Module 1:
Effectively Using Power Utilities for Power Users   7

A: Using Self-paced Modular Guides.................................... 8
B: Interpreting the Style Conventions 11
C: Identifying the Formatting Conventions 12

Module 2:
Using Basic UNIX Utilities   15

A: Making a Test File 18
B: Counting Characters, Words and Lines in a File 19
C: Ordering the Lines of a File with **sort** 21
D: Identifying and Removing Duplicate Lines 27
F: Identifying the Lines That Are Unique 29
G: Identifying the Duplicated Lines 30
H: Comparing the Contents of Two Files 31
I: Translating Characters into Other Characters 34
J: Formatting a File with **nroff** 37
K: Removing a File's Formatting Commands 39
L: Obtaining One Word Per Line Output 41
M: Merging Files with **cat** 42
N: Searching Through Files with **grep** 43
O: Selecting Portions of a File with **cut** 45
P: Putting Lines Together with **paste** 47
Q: Combining Selected Lines with **join** 49
R: Editing from the Command Line with **sed** 50
S: Manipulating Data with **awk** 51
T: Locating Files and Printing Their Pathnames 53
U: Combining Utilities 54

Module 3:
Command Interpretation   59

A: Interacting with the Shell   62
B: Executing Utilities   65
C: Setting Up Input and Output with the Shell   69
D: Passing Arguments to Utilities   82
E: Stipulating Reading from Standard Input   86
F: Interpreting Filenames with the Shell   87
G: Preventing Interpretation of Single Characters   90
H: Evaluating Variables with the Shell   92
I: Setting Your Own Variables   94
J: Including Utility Output in a Command Line   96
K: Stopping the Shell from Interpreting Characters   100
L: Prohibiting Variable Evaluation   101
M: Issuing Commands with a Shell Script   104
N: Entering Long Command Lines   105

Module 4:
Using Regular Expressions   111

A: Using the **ex** Line Editor   114
B: Using Metacharacters in Searches   124
C: Using Metacharacters with Target Patterns   135
D: Using Special Replacement Pattern Characters   138

Module 5:
Global Searching and Printing   147

A: The Basic **grep** Command Line   150
B: Using Regular Expressions   155
C: Using **grep** with Other Utilities   160
D: Using **grep** in an Alias   162
E: Comparing **grep, egrep** and **fgrep**   164
F: Using Metacharacters with **egrep** and **fgrep**   165

Module 6:
Database Report Writing with awk   177

A: Creating and Defining a Simple Database File   179
B: Understanding **awk**'s Basic Usage   181
C: Printing Specific Fields   184
D: Creating and Using **awk** Command Files   188
E: Improving Program Readability   191
F: Performing Arithmetic Operations   196
G: Using the **printf** Function to Format Output   206
H: Using the **BEGIN** and **END** Patterns   210
I: Changing the Field Separator   213
J: Redirecting **awk**'s Output and Input   215

Module 7:
Stream Editing with sed   227

A: Creating Example Files   229
B: Using Line Addresses to Edit   230
C: Using Contextual Addresses   233
D: Giving **sed** Multiple Instructions   237
E: Adding Text to a File with **sed**   238
F: Reading and Writing Files   241
G: Exploring How **sed** Works   242
H: Executing Substitute Commands   248
I: Using Advanced Print Features   254
J: Grouping and Selecting Lines   255
K: The General Form of **sed** Command Lines   262

Module 8:
Manipulating Columns of Data   269

A: Creating Example Databases 271
B: Examining How **cut** Works 273
C: Using a Database File with Spaces as Delimiters 277
D: Selecting Specific Characters 278
E: Changing the Default Separator (Delimiter) 281
F: Putting Files Together by Column 285
G: Changing the Default Separator 289
H: Pasting Multiple Files 292
I: Summary of the **paste** Process 294
J: Pasting Standard Input 296
K: Changing the Separator for Multiple Files 297
L: Combining **cut** and **paste** 298

Module 9:
Using Relational Files with join   303

A: Increasing the Example Files 305
B: Identifying Relationships in Database Files 306
C: Combining Selected Records with **join** 307
D: Determining the Output Order 311
E: Creating Example Files with Colon Delimiter 313
F: Changing the Delimiter Character 314
G: Changing the Field to be Joined 319
H: Examining a Single File Design 324
I: Examining a Relational Database Design 326
J: Implementing a School Relational Database 327

Module 10:
Locating Files with find   **349**

A: Finding Files and Printing Their Full Pathnames   352
B: Using Multiple Selection Criteria   363
C: Performing Actions on Located Files   365
D: When **find** Complains   371

Command Index   **377**

Index   **389**

Foreword

The UNIX Operating System with its associated programs and languages has become a major field in computer science and information processing. This book is a set of Lurnix Modular Guides™ designed to assist you in mastering a wide variety of very powerful UNIX skills. After completing the exercises in this book you will be able to use many useful utilities including several of the UNIX Power Utilities or "little [programming] languages" as they were described by UNIX pioneer Dennis Ritchie.

System Requirements

These modules are designed to be used at a terminal connected to a computer running UNIX (System V, BSD 4.x, Xenix and most of the other flavors of UNIX).

Overview of Contents

If you have the ability to log on the system, create, move, copy and remove files, create and change directories, and issue basic shell commands, you will be able to complete the exercises in these modules.

If you are more experienced, you may be able to proceed quickly through part or all of Modules 2 and 3, and the introductory steps to several of the other modules.

Module 1: Effectively Using these Modules

- This first chapter is a description of our recommendations concerning effective learning. Suggestions are made for novice users, advanced users, and UNIX gurus, with interests in system administration, text processing and programming.

- Formatting conventions.

Module 2: Using Basic UNIX Utilities

- The UNIX system provides a large set of useful basic utilities that count lines, sort lines, remove duplicate lines, compare files, translate characters, and remove formatting commands. The first portion of this module is designed to assist the novice and intermediate user in mastering the basic utilities.

- The second half is an overview of the Power Utilities that are examined in detail in later modules. The utilities search files for strings, select columns from a file, put files together, join files, make editing changes, manipulate data in a database, and locate lost files.

Module 3: Command Interpretation by the Shell

- Mastery of the UNIX system's command interpreter is essential for using the Power Utilities. This module integrates two related topics: 1) a survey of how you use the shell to execute commands, redirect input and output, pass information, interpret special characters, substitute for variables, and run basic shell scripts; and 2) an investigation into how the shell interprets the commands you enter to accomplish those same tasks.

Module 4:   Using Regular Expressions with **ex**

- Special characters used with the editor for identifying places in a file for editing are also used in several other utilities such as **grep** and **awk**. The syntax of regular expressions is explored using the editor on example files.

Module 5:   Global Searching and Printing with **grep**

- The **grep** utility is used to locate files that have lines containing specific character strings. The utility can be used to identify which file contains specific text. The regular expressions explored in the previous module are employed in searches.

Module 6:   Database Report Writing with **awk**

- Database files consisting of line records that contain fields of information can be manipulated using the **awk** utility. Specific fields of records can be printed based on values in any field, record number, etc.

Module 7:   Stream Editing with **sed**

- Most editing changes are made with editors that work on a *copy* of the file. The stream editor, **sed**, makes changes *line by line* following the editing syntax of the **ex** editor.

Module 8:   Manipulating Columns of Data with **cut** and **paste**

- Characters and fields can be selected from a file using **cut**. Two or more files can be pasted together line by line using **paste**. This module is a step by step examination of using the **cut** and **paste** utilities.

Module 9:   Using Relational Files in a Database with find

- Database information can be stored in relational (multi-file) applications. The key to using multiple files is *joining* files based on values in specific fields. This module is an exploration of the **join** utility and relational database development.

Module 10:   Locating Files with find

- A well used system has files in directories in directories, etc. Locating a lost file can be time consuming. The **find** utility allows the user to locate files and make some alterations.

The modules in this book were developed to assist you in efficiently mastering several very powerful UNIX utilities that will help you solve a wide variety of computing problems.

The utilities can be used individually, in combination and in shell scripts to manipulate text, programs and data. The utilities can be used in specific applications, as mock-up experiments, and to solve specific problems in larger programs.

Our hope is that you will find working with these modules and the utilities both enjoyable and rewarding. Because development of the most educationally effective Modular Guides is our goal, we would appreciate your comments and suggestions.

The Staff at Lurnix

Module 1

Effectively Using
Power Utilities for Power Users

Introduction

The UNIX operating system is used on an increasing number and variety of computers today. Although UNIX performs the essential tasks of an operating system, it is also an extensive collection of programs or utilities. The modules in this book will assist you in using several very useful basic utilities and many of the UNIX Power Utilities.

Suggestions for Use

Objective A
Using Self-paced Modular Guides

Each module consists of hands-on exercises coupled with text that explains the concepts, relationships and pitfalls.

No two people using this book arrive with the same experience and knowledge. Users with very different backgrounds have employed these modules with remarkable success, but they use them in different ways. How you should best use the following materials depends on your level of experience.

Self-paced learning can be very effective, providing you use the resources well. Be certain to both *read* and *work* through the examples in the modules. From our experience, we have found that to learn computer skills well requires not only teaching one's mind but also "teaching one's fingers." Therefore, you will find these modules most useful if you sit at the terminal and complete each module step-by-step. If you do the exercises as well as read the material, you will see how the computer responds, you will experience the process, and you will be able to remember the specifics. Do each command or exercise on a terminal. Module 2 is a review of basic utilities as well as the Power Utilities explored in later chapters. This module assumes you are able to edit with the visual editor, create and change directories, plus move, remove, print, and copy files. If you are familiar with many of the basic utilities, you may want to explore only the parts of Module 2 that are new to you.

A tutorial book is useful for learning, but without excellent index and reference facilities it can be of limited value as a reference work for answering questions at a later time. Included with these modules are:

• Command summaries at the end of each module;

• A detailed Table of Contents;

• An extensive Index; and

• A Command Index which lists each command used in these modules and its page number.

After completing the modules, you will be able to return to appropriate explanations and command summaries using the indexes and table of contents.

People using these materials vary in ability level and interest areas. We offer the following suggestions to those with Novice, Experienced, and Guru ability levels and to those who are (or who want to become) Programmers, Text Processors and System Administrators.

Novice Users

Make sure you can do the prerequisites. If you are a little rusty with the editor, or fuzzy about directories, or out of practice in manipulating files, brush up with one of the UNIX introduction books, such as our companion, *Unix for People*, published by Prentice-Hall, 1985.

As you begin working on the next module, carefully complete each step at the terminal. Look back over each section after you finish the exercises. Avoid skipping sections. Many people find reviewing the command summaries at the end of each module helpful.

Experienced Users

Module 2 is an examination of many useful utilities such as **sort, uniq, tr** and a brief overview of the Power Utilities that constitute most of the remaining modules. Most experienced users are familiar with many of the basic utilities. If you are, leaf through the module stopping to complete only those portions that are new to you.

Module 3 is a brief look at how the shell interprets command lines entered by users. Skim through it and proceed until you find your level. Wade in until it is appropriate to swim.

Gurus

Many gurus report that this set of modules is helpful in two ways. They can answer users' questions by saying, "Work through this module, then ask me any questions remaining." They can also use these modules to review quickly or explore power utilities they haven't yet had a chance to master.

Programmers

Many data manipulation projects can be mocked-up using these utilities. Often their speed and power is sufficient to make programming in a higher level language unnecessary.

The utilities are also powerful aids in cleaning up code, comparing programs, locating program modules, etc.

Text Processors

Global editing, stream editing, file location, comparison of versions of text, creation of information files: all are assisted by these modules. For example, in the preparation of this book Power Utilities were used to create formations such as the Table of Contents and the Command Index Tables.

System Administrators

In addition to locating files and other system data, the Power Utilities can be used to create tables that are useful in identifying stale passwords, composing lists of users in groups, etc.

Many System Administration applications are included in the modules.

Objective B
Interpreting the Style Conventions

The following conventions are used in these modules:

- Each module begins with an **Introduction,** setting the stage for what you will do in the module. Read this section to see where the module fits into the scheme of things;

- A list of **Prerequisites** appears next. Make certain you satisfy each prerequisite before beginning the module;

- The **Objective** describes the general skills you will have after completing the module. Reading this section identifies the goals for the exercises;

- The **Procedure** section is last and includes a series of specific objectives with appropriate step-by-step actions for you to complete. Each portion includes appropriate explanations that you should read carefully.

Objective C
Identifying the Formatting Conventions

As you work through the exercises in these modules, you need to know which text is a command that you should enter, what represents the system's screen displays, and which paragraphs are our explanations. To make this clear we have adopted the following conventions:

- When we are instructing you to strike a specific key, for instance the Return key, we identify the key within a box, such as:

  RETURN

- When we are instructing you to type a specific command, for instance "ls," we indicate it in bold modern type, like this:

  ls

- Many commands consist of a command such a **vi** followed by filename, for instance "practice1". The command part is constant, but you can vary the filename depending on which file you want to edit. When we request that you type a word, character, or filename, that you can change when you use the command in another situation, we indicate it with a modern italic type:

    practice1

- The contents of a file to be entered, or a message appearing on your screen is displayed using:

    This is what appears on the screen.

Conclusion

The purpose of these modules is to present essential information and activities to assist you in mastering the skills needed to use the Power Utilities. Our goal has been to organize the content into the optimal order, appropriate step size, and clearest explanations that we could develop. Read the explanations, complete the activities, apply the utilities to your work. Have a good time.

Module 2

Using Basic UNIX Utilities

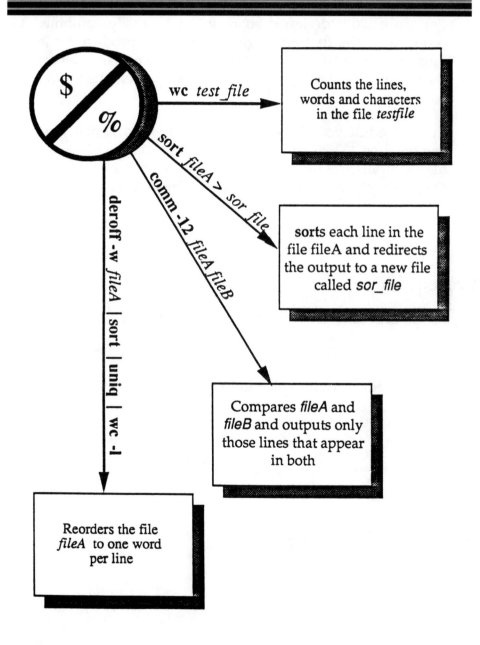

wc *test_file*

Counts the lines, words and characters in the file. *testfile*

sort *fileA* > *sor_file*

sorts each line in the file fileA and redirects the output to a new file called *sor_file*

comm -12 *fileA fileB*

Compares *fileA* and *fileB* and outputs only those lines that appear in both

deroff -w *fileA* | sort | uniq | wc -l

Reorders the file *fileA* to one word per line

Introduction

One of the prominent features of the UNIX system is its wide variety of powerful utility programs. You can use a utility to locate system information, manage files or the contents of files, and manipulate the output of other utilities. These basic utilities are usually designed so they can be easily combined to produce results that no single utility could produce by itself. This toolbox of utilities and the UNIX way of using several of them at once provide you with a set of powerful solutions to computing problems.

In this module you will use several utilities individually and in combination. This module is an examination of several useful file manipulation utilities, followed by a brief introduction to the power utilities that constitute the remainder of the book.

Prerequisites

Before beginning this module, you should be able to:

• log on to a UNIX system and issue basic commands;

• create, edit, move, copy and remove files.

Objective

Upon completion of this module you will be able to:

- count the words, lines and characters in a file;

- sort the contents of a file;

- identify or remove duplicate lines in a file;

- compare two files by identifying lines common to each;

- translate characters in a file;

- remove formatting commands from a file;

- search through files for a string of characters;

- select a portion of all lines in a file;

- put files together, one after another;

- put two files together line by line;

- join together, from two or more files, those lines that have a common value in the first field;

- make several editing changes in each line of a file by passing the file through a filter;

- manipulate the contents in a database file;

- locate "lost" files.

Procedures

Using Basic Filter Utilities

As you begin, if you are familiar with the utility, skim the text and read the summary. If the utility is less than familiar, log on and do the activities. Regardless, be sure to create each of the test files because several are used later with other utilities.

Many utilities accept information such as a copy of a file (input), perform an operation on the contents, then pass on the modified or transformed version (output). Such utilities are called filters. The first half of this module is an explanation of several filter utilities on the UNIX system. The second half is an overview of Power Utilities, many of which are also filters.

Objective A
Making a Test File

You will be using the following file as input for several exercises in this module. Use an editor to create a file named *test_file* with the contents

```
File: test_file
This is a file
you will use with several utilities
to demonstrate how they work.
chocolate
chocolate
And he said,
"Use a utility with agility to avoid futility"
++++
13100
13101
11223
12133
11223
++++++
(and increase ability)
++++
```

Objective B
Counting Characters, Words and Lines in a File with wc

B1   You can use a UNIX utility to count all the lines, words and characters in a file. Enter the command

      wc *test_file*

The output from the **wc** utility (that's **w**ord **c**ount, not water closet) consists of four fields:

      17   42   253   test_file

The four fields are:

Number of lines	*17*
Number of words	*42*
Total number of characters	*253*
Name of the file	*test_file*

B2   ## Counting Only Lines Using Options

Like most UNIX utilities, the **wc** utility works in optional ways. You can tell **wc** to limit the count to lines, words or characters. For example to request a count of just lines in the file, enter the command (with a "minus el" option)

      wc -l *test_file*

The **wc** utility with its **-l** (minus el) option produces a count of the total number of lines in *test_file*. It suppresses the count of total characters and words in the file.

Most options begin with a minus sign and are listed after the command name. You specify which optional form of the command you want by entering a *-flag* such as the -l you just used.

Enter each of the other options

> **wc -l** *test_file*   lines
> **wc -w** *test_file*   words
> **wc -c** *test_file*   characters

B3   Combining Options

More than one option can be used at the same time. Enter

> **wc -lc** *test_file*

Both the word count and the line count options were selected.

The **wc** utility is a filter. It takes input, counts the number of characters, words and lines in its input and then **wc** outputs each of the three totals. Options are available to have **wc** output the number of lines (**-l**), number of words (**-w**) and number of characters (**-c**).

Objective C
Ordering the Lines of a File with sort

Another filter utility sorts the lines of its input and then outputs the ordered results.

C1   Enter the following command to sort the file and have the output displayed on the terminal:

sort *test_file*

The resulting material is sorted:

"Use a utility with agility to avoid futility"
(and increase ability)
++++
++++
++++++
11223
11223
12133
13100
13101
And he said,
File: test_file
This is a file
chocolate
chocolate
to demonstrate how they work.
you will use with several utilities

In its basic form, **sort** arranges the lines of a file in alphabetic and numeric order by comparing the first character of each line. The sorting order is symbols first, then numbers, followed by upper and then lower case letters. This is the order (ASCII) that **sort** uses to sort the lines of a file unless you provide specific instructions to do otherwise.

C2 **Sorting in Dictionary Order**

The **sort** utility also has options. You can have **sort** ignore punctuation and other special characters, using only letters, digits and blanks in its sort. Enter

sort -d *test_file*

The dictionary sorted output is:

```
++++
++++
++++++
11223
11223
12133
13100
13101
And he said,
File: test_file
This is a file
"Use a utility with agility to avoid futility"
(and increase ability)
chocolate
chocolate
to demonstrate how they work.
you will use with several utilities
```

The *"Use a utility..."* line was sorted according to where the *U* fit into the scheme, not the quotation marks. Each line that begins with a special character is sorted by the first character in the line that can be sorted in dictionary order. Thus the special characters are ignored and the lines are sorted according to the characters that follow.

C3   Sorting Regardless of Capitalization

The **sort** program can be told to ignore the case (upper or lower) of the letters in the file when sorting, that is, to fold them into one. Enter

> **sort -f** *test_file*

C4   Reversing the Sort

The order of sorting can be reversed so that the line that would normally be output first is output last. Enter

> **sort -r** *test_file*

C5   Creating a Data File

The **sort** utility generally sorts lines based on the *first character* in each line, then the second, then the third, etc. There is an alternative. Many lines of data are composed of separate fields. Examine the following text.

```
0. Dyllis B. Harvey nurturer
1. C. Lyle Strand inventor
2. Mitchy C. Klein explorer
3. Marjorie M. Conrad teacher
4. Orin C. Braucher farmer
5. David A. Waas professor
6. Fred R. Reif physicist
7. Marge M. Boercker teacher
```

A field is defined as a group of characters (a word, a number, a series of letters, etc.) separated by some specified or default character. This character is often called the *field delimiter* or a *field separator*. The default field delimiter for **sort** is the space character. Each line in the above text consists of five fields separated by spaces: a number field, three names fields and a profession field.

C6   Create a file named *respected* containing the text displayed above. Each line contains the five fields of information (one line for each individual). Add one or two people you respect to the list using the same five-field format.

C7   **Sorting by Fields**

Sort the file according to last name (4th field) with the command:

   sort +3 *respected*

The +3 tells **sort** to skip the first three fields and base the sort on the *fourth and following fields*.

C8   **Using sort with a Different Field Delimiter**

The file */etc/passwd* on your system contains information about each user. Have **sort** sort the lines in the file by entering

   sort /etc/passwd

In the file that you used a few steps back, the fields were separated by white space. In the */etc/passwd* file the separator character is the colon. The third field is the user's unique identification number.

C9   To see how **sort** handles sorting by specific field with a file that does not use white space as separator, enter

> **sort +2** /etc/passwd

The results are not sorted by the third field because **sort** expects spaces for the delimiter. To request sorting by the third field with fields separated by the colon character, enter

> **sort -t:** +3 /etc/passwd

The **-t** option instructs **sort** to use a different character for the tab character or field separator. The new character follows the **-t** option.

C10   **Directing the Output of sort into a File**

Thus far the output of **sort** was sent to your terminal screen. You can have the output from a utility sent to a file, instead of your screen. Enter

> **sort** test_file **>** sor_test_file

The file named test_file is sorted and the output of **sort** is placed in a file named sor_test_file where it can be edited, manipulated or examined by other utilities.

Examine the sor_test_file using **more, page** or **cat**.

Although **sort** is a powerful and flexible utility, it only sorts lines. Once it sorts, it outputs whole lines, not just selected fields. Later in this module you will meet **cut** and **awk**, utilities that overcome this limitation. Another constraint of **sort** is that it cannot easily sort records consisting of multiple lines.

> **sort** rearranges all lines it receives as input into a variety of orders, which include: alphabetical (the default), reverse alphabetical (**-r** option), dictionary (**-d** option), and folded regardless of case (**-f** option). **sort** is also capable of sorting by fields using the **+***n* argument, where *n* is the number of fields **sort** is to ignore, sorting on the *n+1* field. The **-t***x* option changes the field delimiter to *x*, any character.

Objective D

Identifying and Removing Duplicate Lines with uniq

Often when sorting a file such as an index, the resulting file includes duplicate lines. The **uniq** program will assist in situations where there are several copies of identical lines.

The **uniq** utility compares each line in a file with the line that precedes it. If they are identical, an action is taken.

Look back at the *test_file* you entered earlier. There are several identical lines.

D1 Eliminating Duplicate Lines

To produce an output of single copies of the adjacent lines (i.e., additional copies are deleted), enter the following shell command line:

    uniq *test_file*

Examine the output:

File: test_file
This is a file
you will use with several utilities
to demonstrate how they work.
chocolate
And he said,
"Use a utility with agility to avoid futility"
++++
13100
13101
11223
12133
11223
++++++
(and increase ability)
++++

Output consists of one copy of all unique lines and one copy of all duplicated lines that were adjacent to each other. Duplicates have been discarded leaving one copy.

Objective E
Removing All Duplicate Lines

Are all the duplicates removed? Alas, the *chocolate* is gone, but there are two ++++ lines and two 11223 lines remaining. Because the **uniq** utility compares only *adjacent* lines, duplicate lines must be next to each other in the file to be **uniq**ed. One way to be certain all duplicates are adjacent is to first **sort** the file. Earlier you sorted *test_file* and called the sorted version *sor_test_file*.

Have **uniq** work on the sorted version by entering:

> **uniq** *sor_test_file*

Examine the output. The **sort** utility grouped all identical lines together, then **uniq** removed all but one of each set. This can be accomplished in one step.

Enter the following (the | is the "pipe," usually the "upper case" or shifted backslash key):

> **sort** *test_file* | **uniq**

In this case, after the contents of *test_file* were sorted, the output was sent to the input of **uniq**, which removed all duplicate lines.

Objective F
Identifying the Lines That Are Unique

In the file there are some unique and some duplicated lines. The unique lines alone can be selected.

F1   Enter the command:

> **uniq -u** *sor_test_file*

With this option **unlq** examines the contents of *sor_test_file* and outputs only the lines that appear in the file one time. The unique lines are all that are selected. All copies of the duplicate lines are discarded.

Objective G
Identifying the Duplicated Lines

To ignore the unique lines and choose the duplicates, enter the command:

unlq -d *sor_test_file*

It examines *sor_test_file* and outputs only those lines that are *repeated* (i.e., the output consists of the duplicate lines only). In this case, **unlq** prints a single copy of each line, no matter how often it was repeated in the file. Output consists of no copy of all unique lines and one copy of all duplicated lines.

The **unlq** utility accepts sorted lines as input, then outputs single copies of each line regardless of the number of times it was present in the input. Also, **unlq** outputs only the unique lines (**-u** option) or just the lines that are duplicated (**-d** option).

Objective H
Comparing the Contents of Two Files with comm

H1   Another utility compares two files, line by line, and identifies
      three categories: lines found in *fileA*, lines in *fileB*, and lines
      which were in both files. To examine the properties of **comm**,
      you need two files with their contents sorted. Create a file
      called *west* with the following contents:

           California
           Washington
           Oregon
           Nevada
           Utah

H2   Create a second file named *coast* and enter:

           Florida
           Washington
           Maine
           Oregon
           California
           Georgia

H3   To sort the files, enter:

           sort *west* **>** *sor_west*
           sort *coast* **>** *sor_coast*

Consider the following diagram which represents the lines in two files: *sor_west* and *sor_coast*. Some lines are the same in both files. Some lines are unique to each file.

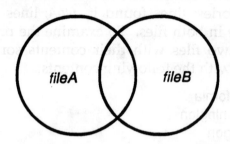

There are three groups of lines:

1   Lines found in *fileA* but not in *fileB* (western states not on the coast)

2   Lines found in *fileB* but not in *fileA* (coastal states not in the west), and

3   Lines found in both files (western states on the coast).

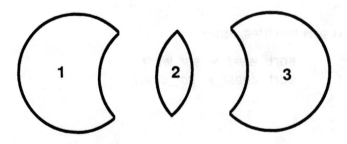

H4 **Identifying Unique and Common Lines**

To locate the common lines in the two sorted files, enter the shell command:

comm *sor_west sor_coast*

This command performs the comparison and then prints all three categories.

1   Only in *west*.   Nevada
                                     Utah

2   Only in *coast*.   Florida
                                     Georgia
                                     Maine

3   In both *west* and *coast*. California
                                     Oregon
                                     Washington

H5 **Selecting Unique or Common Lines**

To *suppress* the printing of lines found in *sor_west* but not found in *sor_coast* (section 1 in the previous diagram) include the number **1** as a flag in the command line.

comm -1 *sor_west sor_coast*

This command results in the printing of those lines found in *sor_coast* only and lines in both files (groups 2 and 3 above). Those lines found only in *sor_west* (group 1) are not printed, but suppressed.

H6   To list only those lines common to both files (select area 3, leave out groups 1 and 2), enter:

comm -12 *sor_west sor_coast*

With the **-12** flag the **comm** command suppresses printing of groups 1 and 2. Only those states in the west that are also on a coast are listed.

H7   Likewise a listing of western states not on the coast can be attained by entering:

comm -23 *sor_west sor_coast*

Suppress groups 2 and 3, select group 1.

The **comm** utility compares the contents of two files and reports a table indicating the lines unique to each file and the lines common to both. In addition, it can output only those lines common to both files (with the **-12** option), lines unique to one file (with **-1** or **-2** option) or lines unique to each file (with **-3** option).

Objective I
Translating Characters into Other Characters with tr

Another useful utility takes input from a file, searches for all examples of specific characters, and translates each into another specified character. The output is a translated version of the input file.

I1   **Translating Specified Characters**

To have a translation made, carefully enter the following:

   tr **"***13S***"** **"***G&n***"** **<** *test_file*

This command line includes the **<** redirection symbol to tell the shell to open the file *test_file* for input to the utility. A thorough examination of redirection is the focus of the next module.

As a result of **tr**'s efforts, all instances in the file of the number *1* became a *G*. Every *3* became a *&*, and each *S* character became a small *n*.

$$
\begin{array}{c|c|c}
1 & \text{-->} & \text{G} \\
3 & \text{-->} & \text{\&} \\
\text{S} & \text{-->} & \text{n}
\end{array}
$$

I2   **Translating a Range of Characters**

With the **tr** command you can also translate ranges of characters.

For example, enter the command

   tr **"***[a-z]***"** **"***[A-Z]***"** **<** *test_file*

The output sent to the terminal screen by default will be similar to the following:

```
FILE: TEST_FILE
THIS IS A FILE
YOU WILL USE WITH SEVERAL UTILITIES
TO DEMONSTRATE HOW THEY WORK.
CHOCOLATE
CHOCOLATE
AND HE SAID,
"USE A UTILITY WITH AGILITY TO AVOID FUTILITY"
++++
13100
13101
11223
12133
11223
++++++
(AND INCREASE ABILITY)
++++
```

This command instructs the **tr** utility to translate all lower case alphabetical characters [a-z] in *test_file* to upper case [A-Z].

The **tr** utility translates specific characters into other specific characters and ranges of characters into other ranges.

Objective J
Formatting a File with nroff

One of the utilities in UNIX that is used extensively in document preparation is the text formatter, **nroff**.

The **nroff** utility formats text according to commands that are embedded in the text. It is not a "what-you-see-is-what-you-get" operation but instead provides command driven formatted output. Because **nroff** is examined in detail in other books, it is our intention to briefly introduce it in this module.

J1   To examine what **nroff** does to a file, give it your *test_file* for input. You can have the output displayed on your screen, one screen at a time. On System V machines, use the **pg** utility and enter:

> **nroff** *test_file* **| pg**

On Berkeley machines, the utility is **more**, so enter:

> **nroff** *test_file* **| more**

Press the [SPACE] bar to reach the end of the file. On both systems, typing the letter [q] will return you to the shell before the end of the file if you prefer.

The output from **nroff** has a right justified margin; the lines have been joined and spaces were added. The output is "filled" and "left-right" justified. Interesting, but not enough to shout *Hold the Presses*.

J2   To see how **nroff** commands are executed, copy your *test_file* into
       a new file, *n_test_file*, with

>   **cp** *test_file n_test_file*

J3   Modify *n_test_file* to include the following lines identified by
       arrows:

```
.ce              ←
File: test_file
.sp 2            ←
This is a file
you will use with several utilities
to demonstrate how they work.
.in 5            ←
chocolate
chocolate
.in -5           ←
And he said,
"Use a utility with agility to avoid futility"
.nf              ←
++++
13100
13101
11223
12133
11223
++++++
(and increase ability)
++++
```

All **nroff** commands are placed at the beginning of the line and
are preceded by a period. An **nroff** command may take an
argument. Above, **.ce** and **.nf** are **nroff** commands; likewise,
.sp *2*, **.in** *5* and **.in** *-5* are each **nroff** commands with arguments.

J4   Format and view the file *n_test_file* by entering:

nroff *n_test_file* | **pg**

on System V machines. On Berkeley machines enter:

nroff *n_test_file* | **more**

Press the SPACE bar to reach the end.

In addition, you can have the output from **nroff** sent to a new file by entering:

nroff *n_test_file* **>** *formatted*

Examine the new formatted file.

> The **nroff** utility takes an input file that includes embedded formatting commands. It follows the formatting instructions and outputs a formatted version of the input file.

Objective K
Removing All Formatting Commands from a File

Formatting commands must be in a file when you have it formatted by **nroff**. However, when you want to use an **nroff** file in some other way, you may want to strip away those commands.

K1   Enter the command:

  deroff *n_test_file*

In this command line, the input to the **deroff** command is the file *n_test_file*.

The following output from **deroff** has blank lines where the **nroff** commands had been:

  File: test_file

  This is a file
  you will use with several utilities
  to demonstrate how they work.

  chocolate
  chocolate

  And he said,
  "Use a utility with agility to avoid futility"

  ++++
  13100
  13101
  11223
  12133
  11223
  ++++++
  (and increase ability)
  ++++

The **deroff** utility examines each line of the file. If the line is an **nroff** command, all the characters are removed. In effect, it removes all formatting instructions. For example, **.In**, **.sp** and **.ce** are eliminated in the output.

Objective L

Obtaining One Word Per Line Output

The **deroff** utility has an option that outputs each word from a file on a different line.

L1   Enter the command:

deroff -w *n_test_file*

The **-w** option tells **deroff** not only to strip off formatting commands, but also to remove all punctuation and place each word on a separate line.

As you can see from examining your screen, **deroff** is not intelligent enough in a case like this to leave the numbers untouched. They are removed. Indeed, **deroff** with the **-w** option does interesting things to a variety of punctuation marks, non-alphanumeric characters and numbers when embedded among alphabetical character strings. You may want to play around with it for your own amusement.

The **deroff** utility takes as input a file containing **nroff** formatting commands. The **nroff** commands are stripped. Where the commands were there are now blank lines (empty lines) in the output. An option (**-w**) instructs **deroff** to output one word per line.

Objective M
Merging Files with cat

Depending on your UNIX experience, you have probably used the **cat** command to examine the contents of a file by entering:

cat *filename*

The **cat** command (a shortened form of the word concatenate) is an excellent tool for combining files.

M1   In an earlier step you created the files *coast* and *west*. You can combine them into a new file called *states* with the following:

cat *west coast* **>** *states*

You now have 3 files: *west, coast* and *states*. Examine the contents of *states*. This new file consists of the contents of the first file followed by the second.

M2   The general form for using the **cat** command is:

cat *file1 file2* **>** *file3*

In this command, *file1* and *file2* are the files to be combined, the **>** is the "greater than" (the redirect symbol), and *file3* is the name selected for a new file to receive copies of the contents of *file1* and *file2*.

Procedures

Using Power Utilities

The remainder of this module is a set of brief introductions to the utilities **cut, paste, grep, sed, awk, join** and **find**. Each of these utilities is examined more fully in the remaining modules of this book. The following introduces the general functions.

Objective N
Searching Through Files with grep

N1   Almost all text editors provide ways to locate words or any group of characters (called a *pattern*) within a file. Or you can locate patterns in one or more files directly from the shell, without using an editor, by using the **grep** utility. Powerful uses of **grep** include quickly locating a pattern in a file or identifying which of many files contains a specific pattern.

N2   **Searching Files and Printing Lines**

The following is a basic **grep** command line. Enter it from the shell:

> **grep** *he   test_file*

All lines containing the pattern *he* in the file *test_file* are located and displayed on the screen.

The line containing the word *they* is displayed along with the line containing the word *he* because **grep** searches for regular expressions. When a person sees the regular expression *he*, the word "he" is thought of. When the computer sees this expression, it reads it as the letter *h* followed by the letter *e*. We see words and the computer sees two characters that may be part of the word "the," "they," "mother" and so forth.

From whence cometh the name **grep**? Elementary, Dr. Watson, elementary: **g**lobally search for **r**egular **e**xpressions and **p**rint them.

N3   Searching Through Multiple Files

The power of **grep** to search multiple files for a pattern is useful when you believe that you created a file with some known contents, but you cannot remember which of several files contains the text.

Select a word that you believe you entered in one or more of your files and enter the following command line substituting your selected word for *pattern,* and your file names for *file1* and *file2*:

grep *pattern file1 file2*

N4   Examining the grep Command Line Syntax

The basic command line is:

grep *pattern filename(s)*

where *pattern* is a regular expression and *filename* is the name of one or more files to be examined by **grep**.

> The **grep** utility is used to search through one or more files for lines containing a string of characters. It outputs the filenames and located lines.

Objective O
Selecting Portions of a File with cut

Data is often arranged in columns in a file. It's easy to obtain lines of data as output using **grep**, by targeting relevant data. Columns of information rather than lines can also be extracted from a file using the **cut** utility.

O1 ## Creating Example Database Files

With an editor, create a new file called *names.tmp*. Because **cut**'s default field delimiter is the `Tab` character, enter the following text with the fields separated by `Tab` characters, not spaces:

> 101 `Tab`Bill `Tab`Z.
> 102 `Tab`John `Tab`M.
> 106 `Tab`Mary `Tab`L.
> 107 `Tab`Santa `Tab`C.

O2 Create a second file called *numbers.tmp* and enter the following with characters separated by `Tab`:

> 101 `Tab`555-9136
> 104 `Tab`591-1191
> 105 `Tab`511-1972
> 106 `Tab`317-6512

O3 ## Selecting a Field from a File

The simplest use of the **cut** utility is to extract one field from a file. From the shell, enter the following command line:

> **cut** **-f2** *names.tmp*

The **cut** utility outputs the second field of the file *names.tmp*.

Bill
John
Mary
Santa

O4 To select the first field from the *numbers.tmp* file enter:

cut -f*1 numbers.tmp*

In the previous examples:

cut   is the command that executes the **cut** utility;

-f   is an option that specifies the extraction of **f**ields;

is any number that follows the **-f** option and indicates which field to extract. In the first example it was a *2* for the second field;

filename   is an argument that informs **cut** which file(s) to use as input.

The **cut** utility can be used on a file to extract fields, ranges of fields, characters and ranges of characters. Each field must be separated by a field delimiter.

Objective P
Putting Lines Together with paste

The **cut** utility cuts out selected data from a file; **paste**, as the name implies, is used to put things together. It is very useful when you want to put together information located in various files, or are one of the King's men working on the Humpty-Dumpty project.

P1   You can instruct **paste** to operate on the lines of two files. Enter the following:

> **paste** *names.tmp numbers.tmp*

The output will be:

```
101   Bill    Z.    101   555-9136
102   John   M.    104   591-1191
106   Mary   L.    105   511-1972
107   Santa C.    106   317-6512
```

The first line output by the **paste** utility consists of the first line of the first file combined with the first line of the second file. Then it combines the second line of the first file and the second line of the second file, and so on until the end of the file.

The **cat** utility places one file *after* the other; **paste** places them *side by side*.

For example:

cat *file1*

line1
line2
line3

cat *file2*

lineA
lineB
lineC

cat *file1 file2*

line1
line2
line3
lineA
lineB
lineC

paste *file1 file2*

line1   lineA
line2   lineB
line3   lineC

The **paste** utility connects lines from 2 to 12 files. Lines are connected in numerical order. The **paste** utility can also be used with different field delimiters.

Objective Q
Combining Selected Lines with join

Q1   The contents of two files can also be joined together based on
the data each file contains. Examine the contents of the
names.tmp and *numbers.tmp* files once again. Each file contains
a column of room numbers (101, 102,...) as its first column.

The objective is to create a joined file that has people's names
matched with their appropriate phone numbers. Clearly, the
field which could be used to join the two files is the room
number. Notice that in both *names.tmp* and *numbers.tmp* the
room numbers are the first field in the file.

To **join** the files, enter

> **join** *names.tmp numbers.tmp*

> 101 Bill Z. 555-9136
> 106 Mary L. 317-6512

Q2   The output is useful information, showing both name and
phone for each room number. This function of joining data
based on field value is the core of relational database operations.

> The **join** utility puts together, or joins, lines from separate
> files *if and only if* the lines are related to each other through
> the presence of an identical value in a specified field.

Objective R
Editing From the Command Line with sed

Suppose your caffeine addiction changed flavors; you want to replace the word *chocolate* with the word *coffee* at every instance where *chocolate* occurs in the file *test_file*. Without calling up an editor, you can make the substitutions.

R1   Enter the following:

> **sed** '/*chocolate*/**s**//*coffee*/**g**' *test_file*

This **sed** instructions in this command line are:

/*chocolate*/	locate all lines that have the word *chocolate* in the file *test_file*,
s//*coffee*/	substitute the word *coffee* for the target word located.
g	Make the changes globally (in case there is more than one instance of the target word on a line).

R2   To create a new, modified file, enter:

> **sed** '/*chocolate*/**s**//*coffee*/**g**' *test_file* > *coffee_test*

The output of **sed** is placed in a new file, *coffee_test*.

The **sed** utility takes an input line, makes whatever editing changes are requested, then outputs that line. It is a stream editor that uses the editing commands of **ex** line editor.

Objective S
Manipulating Data with awk

S1 Often data is stored in files in rows and columns (records and fields). The **awk** utility is designed to perform various actions on lines containing fields of data. The **awk** utility can be used to locate data in a database, modify it and perform computations. Thus it is particularly useful for information retrieval, data manipulation and report writing.

The name **awk** is derived from the names of the utility's authors, Aho, Weinberger and Kernighan.

S2 For this section of the module create a file called *food* and enter the following text. The fields are separated with multiple spaces to make them line up cleanly but one space is all you need for **awk** to work. One or more spaces serve as the default field delimiter for **awk**.

milk	dairy	2.00
hamburger	meat	2.75
cheese	dairy	1.50

S3 ## Selecting Lines and Printing Fields

The basic use of **awk** is to select a record based on the presence of a specified pattern and then to perform some action on the selected record. Enter the command:

awk *'/dairy/* **{ print $3 }**' *food*

This command line instructs **awk** to select each record containing *dairy* and performs the action of printing the third field (the price) of the selected records.

In this example the pattern used to select the lines was not printed in the output. If you want that field also, you must specify it.

The basic **awk** construction:

awk	is the command that executes the **awk** utility;
' '	are single quotation marks that surround the **awk** command so it is passed *as is* to the **awk** utility (more about this in the next module);
/dairy/	is the pattern used for selecting lines to be worked on;
{ print $3 }	is the action, identified by curly braces, performed on all the selected lines. The **{print}** statement is one of **awk**'s many possible actions. The **$3** is interpreted by **awk** to mean the third field in the selected record. All other records are ignored.
food	is the argument that specifies which file(s) **awk** is to read for input.

The **awk** utility locates records that are stored in rows and columns (records and fields) in files (databases). It modifies records, performs computations, and outputs selected fields.

Objective T

Locating Files and Printing Their Pathnames with find

Think of the name of a file located in a directory below your current directory. Ask the system to locate that file by entering:

find . -name *filename* **-print**

replacing *filename* with the name of a file you know is located below your current directory.

The functions specified in the above example were:

find   instructs the shell to execute the **find** utility;

.   is interpreted to mean the current directory. This is the starting point, hence **find** will examine not only the current directory, but also all of its subdirectories;

-name *filename*   instructs **find** to act on any file with the specified name;

-print   specifies that the full pathname of each occurrence of the file(s) matching the selection criterion should be printed.

The **find** utility searches for files with a specified name, starting from a specified directory and following through all of its subdirectories. It then prints the path to all files located.

Objective U
Combining Utilities

In several of the earlier exercises you had the output from one utility sent to another such as:

sort *filename* **| uniq**

This pipeline feature of UNIX is very useful and central to effective use of Power Utilities. Even basic utilities can become very versatile when properly piped.

It is sometimes instructive when examining your writing to know how many different words you are employing. Enter the following pipeline, substituting the name of one of your files for *filename*.

deroff -w *filename* **| sort | uniq | wc -l**

In this case, the file is the input to **deroff** which, because of the **-w** option, outputs one word per line. The output is piped to **sort**, which arranges the lines in alphabetical order. The sorted output is given to **uniq**, which discards all duplicate lines, leaving only one copy of each line (word). The output from **uniq** is sent to the input of **wc**, which, because of the **-l** option, counts the number of lines (unique words).

Conclusion

In this module you used a variety of UNIX filter utilities and employed basic versions of the Power Utilities. The utilities took input, made transformations (such as selecting, modifying or combining data), then output results. In later modules, you will explore more fully the capabilities of Power Utilities.

Summary of Utility Commands

COMMAND	FUNCTION
awk *pattern* {*action*} *filename*	Performs the *action* on all records in *filename* that contain *pattern*.
cat *file1 file2* **>** *file3*	Creates new *file3* with copies of the contents of *file1* and *file2*.
comm *file1 file2*	Shows the **comm**on lines in two files. Compares *file1* to *file2*.
cut *option filename*	Prints selected fields from *filename* as specified by *option*.
deroff *filename*	Strips a file of its **nroff** commands.
deroff -w *filename*	Places each word in the file on a line by itself.
find . -name *filename* **-print**	Locates named file (*filename*), then prints full path to the file. Search starts from current directory (.).
grep *expression filename*	Prints all lines in filename that contain the regular expression.
join *file1 file2*	Combines lines from *file1* and *file2* that contain common fields.
nroff *filename*	Acts on formatting commands embedded in *filename*.

Summary of Utility Commands (Continued)

COMMAND	FUNCTION
paste *file1* *file2*	Combines line 1 from *file1* with line 1 from *file2*, etc.
sed *command* *filename*	Executes specified **sed** editing *command(s)* on *filename*.
sort *filename*	Sorts the contents of the file *filename*.
tr "*string1*" "*string2*" < *filename*	Translates *string1* characters into *string2* characters.
uniq *filename*	Removes duplicate adjacent lines from *filename*.
wc *filename*	Counts words, lines and characters in filename.

Module 3

Command Interpretation by the Shell

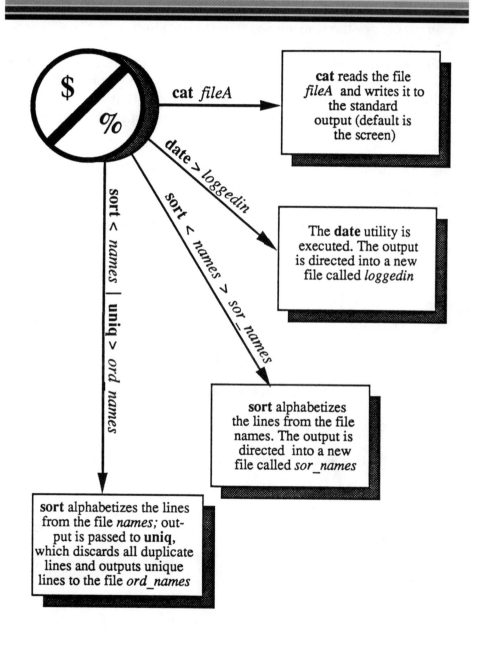

cat *fileA*

cat reads the file *fileA* and writes it to the standard output (default is the screen)

date > *loggedin*

The **date** utility is executed. The output is directed into a new file called *loggedin*

sort < *names* > *sor_names*

sort alphabetizes the lines from the file names. The output is directed into a new file called *sor_names*

sort < *names* | **uniq** > *ord_names*

sort alphabetizes the lines from the file *names;* output is passed to **uniq**, which discards all duplicate lines and outputs unique lines to the file *ord_names*

Introduction

On UNIX hundreds of utilities are available that accomplish many useful tasks. An essential utility is the command interpreter, or shell. On most systems, the two the shell programs available are the Bourne shell and the C shell.

Users enter shell command lines to instruct the shell and other utilities to do tasks. When you enter a UNIX command line, the shell reads the command line, interprets it and then executes the specified utilities, passing along appropriate information.

In this module you will examine what the shell and other utilities do after you enter a command line. Understanding the steps of command interpretation makes it easier for you to enter command lines to accomplish specific tasks.

Prerequisites

Before beginning this module, you should be able to:

• create, edit, move, copy, view and remove files;

• make directories and move around in the file system;

• use the utilities examined in Module 2.

Objective

Upon completion of this module you will be able to:

- issue commands to the shell to establish where utilities read their input and where they write their output;

- use the command line to pass information to utilities;

- use special characters to communicate with the shell;

- explain the steps the shell goes through as it interprets commands.

Procedures

The UNIX computing system is comprised of the Central Processing Unit, storage devices, working memory, connecting cables and software to run it all.

The software consists of the main scheduling program (the kernel), the data files located on secondary memory (both user files and system programs) and a series of user processes.

The kernel controls the CPU, other hardware, primary memory, and input/output to terminals, disk drives, etc.

The data files in memory consist of files created by users and executable versions of programs (utilities) that are available to users.

The shell is one of the utilities. It also serves as the interface between users and the other utilities.

One of the shell's primary functions is to read a command line issued by a user, examine the components of the command line, and then do what is requested. The following exercises begin with how the shell interprets simple commands and proceed to an investigation of how the shell works with complex command lines calling for programming, passing of information and interpretation of special characters.

Objective A

Interacting with the Shell

The basic way users communicate with the shell is to request execution of commands. If you have not issued the following commands several times before, log on and enter each from the shell. As you enter them, consider what steps the shell must be completing, and what activities the utility must be accomplishing.

ls -l

pwd

wc -l *filename*

For *filename* use a file in your current directory such as *test_file*.

who | wc -l

The process begins with the shell displaying a prompt. As you enter each of these command lines, a utility is started up or executed. The utility retrieves information from the system, or does work on either a file or the information provided by a previous utility. Output is then displayed on your screen.

A1   Examining Events Resulting from Issuing Commands

When you enter each of the commands, a series of specific events takes place.

ls   After the **ls** utility is executed, it locates the names of the files in your current directory and then formats a screen display of the listing of filenames. When **ls** is told to use the l (el) option, it operates differently, producing a long listing of the files in your directory. The output list is displayed on the terminal of the user who issued the command.

pwd   The **pwd** utility determines the absolute path to your current directory from the top of the file system. It sends the complete path to your screen.

wc -l   When you enter **wc -l** *filename*, the file is opened, its contents are examined by the **wc** utility, the number of lines in the file is computed and the result displayed on your screen.

who | wc -l   When the **who** utility is executed, it obtains information from the system concerning which users are currently logged on. The **who** utility creates a formatted output with a listing of the logged on users. That output is passed to **wc** which, because of the -l option, counts the lines. The count of users logged on (number of lines) is then output to your screen.

A2   **User View of Interaction with the Shell**

The commands you just entered demonstrate basic interactions with the shell:

- As soon as the user logs on, the shell displays a prompt such as: **%** or **$**, indicating that it is ready to receive instructions from you;

- You enter a command, and press ⬚Return⬚;

- The command is executed;

- The results of the utility's work (output) go to the terminal, and

- The shell displays another prompt.

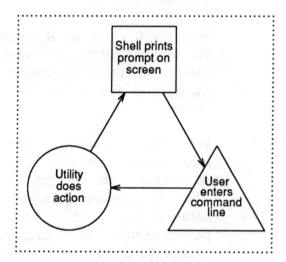

User Interaction with Shell and Utilities

To the user, a cycle of prompt, command and utility takes place.

In fact, a lot happens between your entry of a command line and execution of the utility: the shell must interpret the command line.

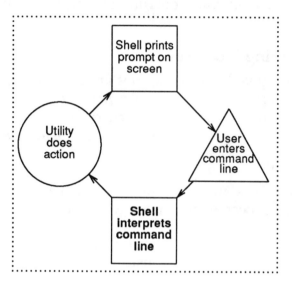

Shell Interprets User Issued Commands

The remainder of this module is an examination of the actions that occur after you enter command lines.

Objective B
Executing Utilities

In looking at the basic commands just executed, several questions arise.

- How does the output from the utility get back to the user's terminal?

- How does the utility get input from a file?

- How does the output from one utility become the input of another?

- How can several users run the same utility at the same time?

B1   **Examining Processes**

If a utility is doing work, files are being read, calculations are being performed, etc., then a *process* is underway. You can find out which processes are currently running that are associated with you. From the shell, enter the following:

>   **ps**

The **p**rocess **s**tatus command results in a listing of all currently running processes associated with you.

If you do not have two listings, a shell (**csh** or **sh**) and **ps** listed, try entering **ps -g** instead.

Fill out the following chart based on the output that is displayed on your screen:

PID	COMMAND

At the time you entered the **ps** command, probably two processes were running and were listed. You recorded two pieces of information for each process - A PID (which is pronounced "P. I. D." rather than "pid") and a COMMAND.

PID   The numbers in the PID column are Process IDentifiers. As each process is created on the system, it is assigned a **PID**, like customers entering a busy bakery. The numbering of **PID**s begins with 0. Thus if your **ps** process had 1207 as its

PID, it was probably the 1,208th process started on your system since the last time the system was restarted. Because the system has a maximum ID number, when this number is reached the numbering starts over again from the first number greater than zero not in use.

COMMAND   The items listed in the column labeled COMMAND are the names of the utilities associated with each of the two processes that were running. The **ps** is the name of the utility that you just entered to get the system to display the list of processes that you are running. The other process is your shell. The shell that interprets your commands is a currently running process.

B2 Starting Processes

All utilities reside in UNIX as ordinary files. The utilities that come with the system are located in one of the system directories, such as /bin, /etc or /usr/bin. Utilities are files located on the disk. Each contains instructions to be followed (or "executed") by the UNIX system. The user does not normally know (or care) what is actually in these files. UNIX follows the instructions in the file when the utility is being executed. What matters is whatever the system accomplishes by following the instructions.

When a user enters a command name (for example, **ps**, **sort** or **who**) the shell locates an executable file with that name, a *process* is started and the instructions in the utility file are read or *loaded* into memory.

Saying that a utility is doing something is another way of saying that the system is running a process that is following the instructions in the utility file.

Several users can be running the same utility at the same time because each is running a *different* process. Each process had a copy of the same utility file loaded when the utility was executed.

B3   Using Standard Files

Every time you instruct the shell to begin or **exec** a new process, the new process receives several essential pieces of information from your current shell: your user ID, your search path for locating utilities, your home directory and the *file descriptors* for three open files. These files are used to read in information (**standard input**), write output (**standard output**) and write error messages that are pertinent to the utility (**standard error**).

Whenever programs read or write files, they do not use filenames, but file descriptors (the file descriptors for standard input, standard output and standard error are: **0**, **1**, and **2**, respectively). These three file descriptors give the new process all it needs to know to be able to read input, write output and write any error messages.

For example, you just entered **ls -l**. A process was begun and the **ls** executable file was read or loaded. The process was told to operate with the **-l** option. When the process completed its work of determining the names of the files in your current directory, it wrote its output ("executed a write") to the *standard output* (file descriptor **1**). It did not write to your terminal; it wrote to the standard output. At that moment your terminal was connected to standard output. The system's resources manager (the kernel) sent the output to wherever the standard output was connected. Because the standard output is connected by default to the user's terminal, when **ls** wrote its output, it wrote to your terminal.

The last command you entered was **who | wc -l**. When **who** completed its work, it wrote to standard output, which the shell connected through a *pipe* to the standard input for **wc**. After **wc** counted the lines, it wrote its results to standard output which, for that process, had not been redirected so it was still connected to your terminal.

Redirecting input and output from the default (terminal) destination to files and other utilities is one of the functions of the shell.

Objective C
Setting Up Input and Output with the Shell

In three of the previous examples the command line included no instructions as to what the utilities should do with the information they either retrieved from the system or created when they did their work. The output from the utilities wound up on your terminal screen by default. In this section you will examine how to tell the shell to redirect standard output to files or other utilities.

C1   Sending Output to a New File

You can instruct the shell to have the output from a utility placed in a file instead of sent to your terminal. For example, as you enter the following command line, consider how a new file is created and how the output from **who** winds up in the new file. Enter:

```
who > logged_in
```

Examine the contents of *logged_in* with one of the usual:

pg *logged_in*

or

more *logged_in*

or

cat *logged_in*

In this case, when you entered the **who** > *logged_in* command line, you instructed the shell to:

who   execute the **who** utility;

>   redirect the standard output to a new file; and

logged_in   create a new file named *logged_in* to receive the output.

The shell interprets the symbol **>** as: *redirect the output of the utility to the filename that follows.* Instead of the default destination (terminal), the shell redirects the output of the utility to the named file. In fact, as the new process was started, the shell closed the file that is the terminal and opened the new file *logged_in*, assigning it the file descriptor **1**. When **who** wrote to standard output, it wrote to the new file.

Although the execution of such a command line appears to be fairly straightforward, the shell must do several things to make it happen.

C2   **Interpreting the Basic Command Line**

After you entered the **who** > *logged_in* command line the shell took several steps to interpret it.

- **Shell Divides Command Line Into Words:** First the shell divides the command line into pieces or words separated by spaces. In this case there were three words: **who**, **>**, and *logged_in*.

- **Shell Sets Up Redirection:** The **>** redirection symbol is employed in this command line. The user is requesting the shell to connect the standard output to a file.

- **Shell Creates Files:** A new file named *logged_in* is created and opened. It is assigned the file descriptor **1**. When the utility writes its output to standard output, it writes to the file.

- **Shell Locates Utility(ies):** All utilities on the command line are identified. In this case there is only one utility: the first word, **who**.

- **Shell Replaces Utility Names With Full Pathnames:** Most utilities are executable files located in one of the root directories. To execute them, the shell must first have each utility's absolute path. The shell searches through the directories where utilities are located (in the order set by your PATH variable) until it finds the utility (or does not find it, and tells you so).

- **Shell Executes Utilities:** With all the preliminaries completed, the shell starts a new process and passes the information including the input, output and error file descriptors. It then has the new process execute the utility.

When the shell interprets a command line it determines how the user wants the input and output redirected away from the terminal, as well as which utilities are to be executed.

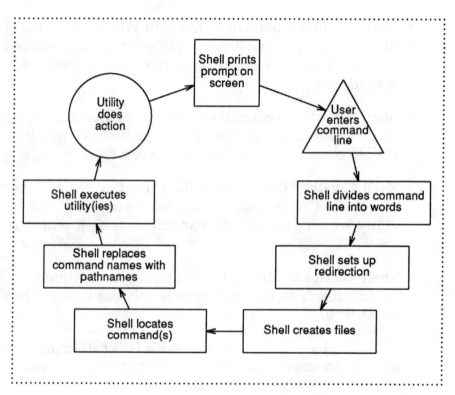

Shell Interprets Command Line

If the command line is more complex, the shell must take additional steps to properly interpret it. The other steps will be examined as you proceed.

C3   Redirecting Output to an Existing File

You used **>** to tell the shell to redirect output to a file. What does the shell do if the file named after the **>** redirection symbol already exists?

In the last step you created a file of current users named *logged_in*. Enter the following:

> **date > ** *logged_in*

Depending on which shell you are using and how your account is set up, the shell did one of two things. It either gave you a new prompt (all is completed), or it sent you an error message. If the prompt was displayed on the screen without an error message, then the old contents of the file *logged_in* were replaced with the output of the **date** utility. If the shell gave you an error message that the file exists, then no further action was taken by the shell.

If you are using the Bourne shell with its dollar sign prompt, the old file was replaced with the new one.

The C shell will also *clobber* the existing file unless a variable called **noclobber** is set. If **noclobber** is set, prohibiting you from clobbering files, the shell (a process itself) sends an error message to its standard error file descriptor. Standard error is connected to your terminal by default; hence you receive the message at the terminal.

C4   Adding Output to an Existing File

You can instruct the shell to take the output from a utility and add it to the *end* of an existing file.

Look at a listing of the files in your current directory. Pick a filename, any filename, for the following.

Enter:

date >> *filename*

Examine your file *filename* to see that a date stamp has been added as the last line.

The >> double redirect symbols are interpreted by the shell to mean: *redirect the output of the utility and add it to the end of the named file, thereby leaving its current contents intact.*

C5   Using Files for Input to Commands

For this section you will need a sample file. Use an editor and create a file named *years* with the following contents:

```
This is a file called
"years",
which contains names and a year
Mary 70
Pat 52
Suzi 48
Jack 54
Virginia 59
Bob 61
Dick 66
Bob 70
Bob 70
Marge 72
Harry 72
73 Bob Danny Steve
Harry 72
Greg Chuck 73
Pat 52
```

Many utilities work on a copy of the lines in files. They can sort the lines into alphabetical order, eliminate duplicate lines, etc. For this kind of utility to work, you must be able to specify the name of the file to be used as input. Enter the following:

    sort < *years*

The output from **sort** is displayed on your screen. The **sort** utility reads input and orders the lines into alpha-numeric sequence. The < redirect symbol tells the shell to locate the file *years*, open it, and connect it to the standard input. The shell closes the input file (terminal) and then opens the *years* file, assigning it the file descriptor **0** for this process. When the utility read from the standard input, it read the file *years*. The **sort** utility did not open the file, it just read from standard input.

In this command line, no output destination is specified. The standard output is not redirected. When the utility sends its output to standard output, the default connection (terminal) is still in effect.

C6   You can, in the same command line, tell the shell what file to connect to the standard input, and specify a file for connection to standard output. Enter the following command line:

    sort < *years* > *sor_years*

C7   Examine the contents of the *sor_years* file.

By entering this command line you instructed the shell to:

sort   execute the **sort** utility;

< *years*   open up the file *years* and connect it to standard input for the **sort** utility;

> *sor_years*   create a file named *sor_years* and connect the
                    standard output from **sort** to the new file.

Similarly, enter the following command line:

tr "[a-z]" "[A-Z]" < *years* > *cap_years*

C8   Altering the Order of Redirection in a Command

In the above command line, the input file **<** *years* was listed
first, and the output **>** *sor_years* entered second. Does it make
any difference? Reverse the order of the placement of the
redirection symbols and associated filenames in the command
line by entering the following:

sort > *2_sor_years* < *years*

C9   Examine the new *2_sor_years* file. It is also a sorted version of
the *years* file. The placement order of the input and output
redirection statements in the command line is not important.
Whatever file is to the right of the **>** symbol will be opened by
the shell if it exists and created if it does not. It is assigned a
file descriptor **1**. The file will receive the utility's output. Likewise, the file listed to the right of the **<** will be opened and connected to standard input (file descriptor **0**).

C10   Redirecting Output to Another Command

As you have seen, the output from one utility can also be used
as the input for a second utility. Enter the following:

who

The list of current users that **who** outputs is not in alphabetical order of login names. Now enter:

who | sort > *alpha_users*

C11   Examine the file *alpha_users*. It is a sorted list of the output from **who**. When you entered this command you told the shell to do the following:

who	start up the **who** utility, which produces a list of users currently logged on. Its output is written to standard output;
|	connect (or pipe) the standard output of the previous utility, **who**, to the standard input of the next utility, **sort**;
sort	start up the **sort** utility;
> *alpha_users*	open the file *alpha_users* and then connect the output of the previous utility, **sort**, to this new file.

The output from **who** was written to standard output, which the shell connected through a pipe to the standard input of **sort**. The output of **sort** was sent to a new file.

In most versions of UNIX the pipe uses a chunk of memory. The first utility writes to the memory and the second reads from it. It is essentially a temporary file in main memory.

C12 Comparing Redirection Symbols

You can tell the shell to redirect output with two symbols, the
> and the **|**.

Enter the following:

who | sort
who > *sort*

The **|** redirects the standard output of one utility to the stan-
dard input of *another utility*. The **>** redirects the standard output of a utility into a *file*. In the **who > *sort*** command line, you
told the shell to create a new file named *sort* and connect the
output of **who** to that new file. This is a legal filename, but, a
file named *sort* could lead to problems if your current directory
is included in the places the shell searches for commands. To
avoid that possibility, remove the new file with:

rm *sort*

C13 Examining the Default Output Destination

In this module you have been telling the shell what to connect
to each utility's standard input and output using one of the
> < >> | redirection symbols. If you do not give specific
instructions to the shell, the default connections will take
effect. For example, a few steps back you entered the following:

sort < *years*

In this command line you instructed the shell to open the file *years* and connect it to the standard input of the utility **sort**. When the command was executed, **sort** read from standard input. Because you did not specify what should be done with the standard output it was sent to your screen.

C14   As another example, enter the following:

    unlq < *years*

In this case, the shell opened the *years* file and connected standard input to it. The **unlq** utility read standard input then discarded all but one of any identical lines located next to each other. For instance, there are two *Bob 70* lines in the *years* file, but only one in the output. The output from **unlq** was sent to standard output which, because you did not tell the shell to redirect it, was connected to your screen.

C15   **Examining the Default Input Source**

You can also enter command lines that do not specify the utility's source of input. Enter the following:

    sort > *so_temp*

After pressing ⌈Return⌋, nothing happens. Clearly the output from **sort** is to be redirected into the new file *so_temp*, but where does **sort** read its input? Enter

    Hello
    This is some text
    2222
    abcedfg
    789
    ABCDEFG

Now enter

$\boxed{\text{Ctrl-d}}$

The shell prompt reappears.

C16 Examine the file *so_temp*.

By default, the standard input of **sort** is connected to the keyboard. Your terminal was the source of input for the **sort** utility. Each line you type is sent to **sort** until you send the end-
of-file symbol $\boxed{\text{Ctrl-d}}$, which indicated you are finished. The **sort**
utility then sorts the input lines and writes its output to stan-
dard output, which the shell had connected to your newly
created file, *so_temp*.

C17 **Specifying Neither Input Nor Output**

You can use the default standard input and output connections. Enter the following:

sort

Press $\boxed{\text{Return}}$. Neither input source nor output destination is
specified. Both are left at the default.

Enter some lines of text, then press $\boxed{\text{Ctrl-d}}$.

The lines you enter at the keyboard are sent to the utility for
input. After the utility completes its work, the output is sent to
your screen.

When the output destination is not specified, the utility's standard output is connected to the terminal screen. When the
input source is not specified, the standard input is connected to
the terminal keyboard.

C18 **Using Several Redirection Symbols**

You can use several pipes and redirect symbols in the same command line. Output can be passed from one utility to the next and then to another and so on. Enter the following:

sort < *years* | **uniq** > *ord_years*

C19 **Examining the Command Line**

When you entered the previous command line, you instructed the shell to establish input and output redirection, as well as to execute two utilities.

By entering this command line, you tell the shell:

sort	execute the **sort** utility;
< *years*	open the file *years* and connect standard input to that file;
|	connect the standard output of **sort** to the standard input of **uniq**;
uniq	execute the **uniq** utility;
> *ord_years*	create a file *ord_years* and connect the output of **uniq** to that file.

One of the shell's functions when it interprets command lines is to set up input/output redirection. Output is redirected into a file using the **>** character. Redirecting with a pipe | connects standard output to standard input of the next utility. Output can be appended to a file using **>>**. Standard input can be redirected from a file using the **<** character.

Objective D
Passing Arguments to Utilities

In this section you will enter command lines that provide information for utilities; this includes files to be read for input, options, and data.

D1   Telling the Utility Which Options to Use

The UNIX system consists of a large number of utility programs that accomplish many tasks. Most utilities can be told to function in slightly different ways. Everyone's friend, the **ls** utility, results in a listing of the names of the files in the current directory. You have also instructed **ls** to provide a long listing of the files by entering the following:

   ls -l

The **-l** option of the **ls** command lists the filenames as well as other information such as permissions, owner, size, and date of last change.

Another option to the **ls** command results in the listing of all files:

   ls -a

The housekeeping or *dot* files are listed along with the names of regular files in the current directory.

After the shell has interpreted the command line words that it recognizes, it passes to the utility whatever words remain. Most utilities interpret remaining words preceded by a minus sign as options.

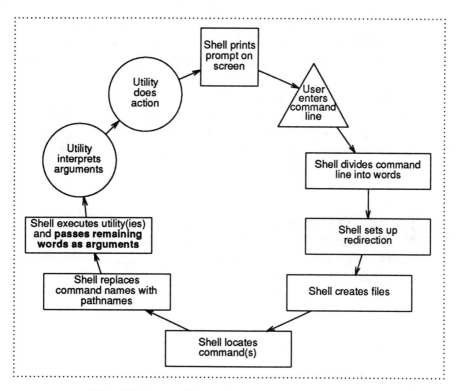

Shell Passes Remaining Words to Utility

D2 Informing the Utility Which File to Read

Thus far in this module, you have used the **<** symbol to connect files to the standard input. There is another way for the utility to get input. As you have seen, the shell passes all remaining words as arguments. Those arguments preceded by a minus sign are usually interpreted as options.

For many utilities, arguments that have no minus sign are interpreted as filenames to be opened and read for input. It is standard practice to enter commands like the following:

sort *years*

In this command line there is no redirection symbol. Instead of opening the *years* file and connecting it to the standard input, the shell gives **sort** the single argument *years.* Then **sort** interprets the word *years* as a filename. The file is opened and read by **sort**, not the shell. The result appears to be the same to the user. In both cases the file is read as input by the utility. When you use the **<** redirect symbol, you are instructing the shell to open the file. When you enter the filename as an argument, it is passed to the utility, which looks for and opens the file.

D3   The roles of the shell and the utility can be examined if we look at error messages generated by each. Both produce error messages when a non-existent file is requested. Enter the following where *xyz* is a non-existent filename.

   uniq < *xyz*

The usual error message from the shell results.

D4   Now try entering the filename as an argument rather than using the redirection symbol. Enter:

   uniq *xyz*

In this case, the error message is probably different. The *utility* failed to find the file so the *utility* sent its error message.

If you got the same message in both cases try **sort, cat, wc, more** or **pg**. The UNIX programmers are moving toward standardizing error messages of the shell and utilities, but usually one or two remain different.

D5 Passing Other Information to the **write** Utility

In addition to filenames, you can send other strings of characters to the utility for its use. What the utility does with the string it receives depends on the utility. As an example, enter the following where *login* is your own userid:

> **write** *login*

Enter a line of text and then press the RETURN key.

Write a few more lines to yourself, possibly explaining how much you enjoy your company, asking yourself out for lunch and a movie, then conclude by entering:

> Control-d

The **write** command is used to send messages to a logged in user. When the shell receives the command line **write** *login*, it executes the write utility and passes it the argument, *login*. The **write** utility interprets the string of characters *login* as the user identification, looks up what terminal port that login is using and sends its output to that user's terminal. It reads input from standard input, currently connected to your terminal.

D6 Passing Information and Redirecting Input

You can send one line at a time as you just did, or you can send whole files. Enter the following where *login* is your own *login*.

> **write** *login* < *years*

The utility sends the whole file to the login's screen, in this case your own, because: a) it receives one argument from the shell, which it interprets as the login of the intended user, and b) the shell redirects the standard input to the file *years*, which **write** then reads.

D7 **Passing Two Arguments to a Utility**

The shell simply passes arguments to the utilities. If there are two words left, two get passed. It is the job of the utility to figure out what to do with each. Enter the following:

   grep *an years so_temp*

The shell divides the command line into four words: the utility and three arguments. The utility is executed and the arguments are passed to it. The **grep** utility interprets the first argument as the string to be used in the search. The remaining arguments **grep** interprets as the name(s) of the file(s) to be searched. Therefore, each line that has the string *an* in the file *years* or in the file *so_temp* is output by **grep**.

The generic form of the command is:

   grep *string filename(s)*

The **tr** utility interprets the first two arguments as the target string and the translation string. The third and any remaining arguments are read as filenames. For instance:

   tr *"[A-Z]" "[a-z]"* **<** *years logged_in*

There are four arguments passed to **tr** in this command line: target and translation strings, and two file names to be opened.

Objective E
Stipulating Reading from Standard Input

When commands are used in a pipeline, it is sometimes necessary to specify where the standard input should be read. For instance, **comm** compares two files. One filename can be named in the command line, and the other could be the output from a utility in the same command line.

To explore how this works, first create a file of those who are currently logged on to your system by entering:

who > *old_who*

If you are on a large system, wait a few minutes. Hopefully, someone will log off or on. If you are on a small system, log off and then back on.

E1   You can compare the information that lists who is currently logged on with the file that lists who was logged on a few minutes ago. Enter

who | **comm** - *old_who*

The minus sign is interpreted to mean: *read from standard input.* The shell pipes the output of **who** to the standard input of **comm**. As usual, the **comm** utility examines two input files. In this case, one is read from standard input (from the output of **who**), and the other is opened and read (*old_who*).

In a pipeline you can place this minus sign at the location where you want standard input to be read.

Objective F
Interpreting Filenames with the Shell

Filenames can be created with common elements or numbers; these can be selected in groups using specific characters. As the shell examines each command line you enter, it looks for special characters. Some characters are interpreted as *wildcard* characters for expansion of a partial filename into a complete name. Others are used to select a range of characters for matching with filenames.

F1   **Expanding Filenames with Wildcard Characters**

For these exercises, create a new junk directory. Change directories into the new directory and create junk files with the following filenames (The contents are irrelevant, the filenames are all that matter).

chap	*chapter2*	*chapter5*	*summaries*
chapter	*chapter3*	*chapter5A*	
chapter1	*chapter4*	*index*	

You can obtain a long listing for a selection of the files by entering:

    ls -l *chap**

The shell expanded the ***** to be any number of any characters in a match with the current directory's filenames. Thus, it replaced *chap** with all the files that had a name beginning with *chap* followed by zero or more additional characters. The file named *chap* was therefore also selected. The selected filenames were passed to **ls** as arguments. The **ls** utility then produced its long listing about those files.

Another filename expansion character is more limited. Enter the following:

    ls *chapter?*

Neither *chapter* nor *chapter5A* was selected because the **?** character is expanded to be any one character—no more, no less.

As the shell interprets the command line it does not open files; it just creates a list of words that match the filenames based on the string of regular and expansion characters you entered, then passes this list as an argument to the utility.

After the shell sets up redirection, creates and clobbers files, it expands filenames.

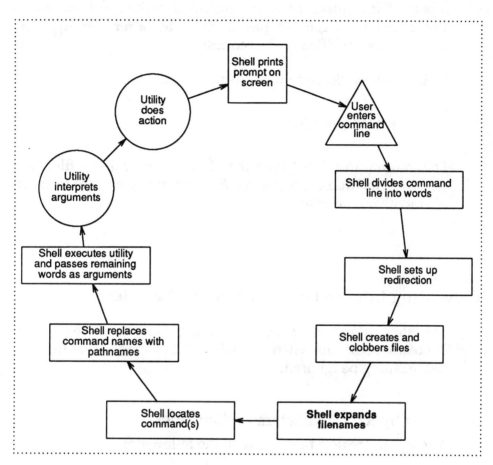

Shell Does Filename Expansion

F2 Selecting Filenames Within a Range

You can have the shell expand the filename argument to include all filenames with letters or numbers that fall within a specified range. For example, enter

wc *chapter*[*2-5*]

In this case *chapters 2, 3, 4* and *5* were selected, but both *chapter 1* and *chapter 5A* were not included in the word count report. The number *1* was not included in the specified range. The filename *chapter 5A* has a character after the number, which is not specified in the request.

To include *chapter 5A* in the selection, enter:

wc *chapter[2-5]* *****

This addition of the ***** tells the shell to expand the filename *chapter* to include the numbers: *2, 3, 4, 5* and then zero or more of any other characters.

Objective G
Preventing Interpretation of Single Characters

The shell interprets special meaning to several characters. There are occasions when you will want to specify that the special meaning be ignored.

G1   Using Special Characters in Filenames

Attempt to create a new file with the following:

echo *xxx* **>** *>test.file*

The **echo** command takes whatever arguments it receives and writes them to standard output. In this case the command requests that **echo** write *xxx* to standard output.

The shell is programmed to interpret the "greater than" arrow as the redirect symbol. It argues that it does not know what to do.

Tell the shell to view the second redirect symbol as an ordinary character with the following.

> **echo** *xxx* **>** *\>test.file*

Obtain a listing of your files with:

> **ls -l**

Attempt to remove the new file by entering the usual:

> **rm** *>test.file*

You can again remove the redirect symbol's specialness with a backslash.

The shell understands that the backslash means "interpret the next character literally, without special meaning."

G2 Issuing Long Command Lines

One valuable use of the backslash is as an aid in entering long or complex command lines.

When you enter the ⌷Return⌷ key at the end of a command line, a *newline* character is sent to the shell. It is the arrival of the *newline* character that prompts the shell to begin interpreting the line. You can hide the *newline* character with a backslash.

Enter the following two lines where *login_name* is your login:

> **who | sort | grep** *login_name* \
> **| tr "[a-z]" "[A-Z]"**

The ⌷\⌷ instructs the shell NOT to interpret the ⌷Return⌷ key (*newline*) that follows.

Objective H
Evaluating Variables with the Shell

An essential aspect of the UNIX operating system is its use of variables. Your current shell process knows the value of many important variables relating to your account. For example, enter the following:

echo $HOME

The value of the variable *HOME* is returned. Likewise, enter the following:

echo $SHELL

The absolute pathname of the shell program chosen for your account is displayed. The path for searching out commands that you enter can be examined with:

echo $PATH

In all cases the **$** precedes the variable name. The shell interprets **$**string to be: *find the current value of the variable string and place that value here*. The value of the **HOME**, **SHELL** and **PATH** variables were found, and their values placed in the command line. When the commands were executed, arguments were passed to the **echo** utility. The **echo** utility sends its arguments to standard output.

For another example, using a different utility, enter:

cd $HOME

After the variable was evaluated, the value was placed in the command line. The command line was then executed. Your home directory is now your current directory.

Confirm your current directory status by entering **pwd** or **ls**. As the shell interprets command lines, it substitutes variables.

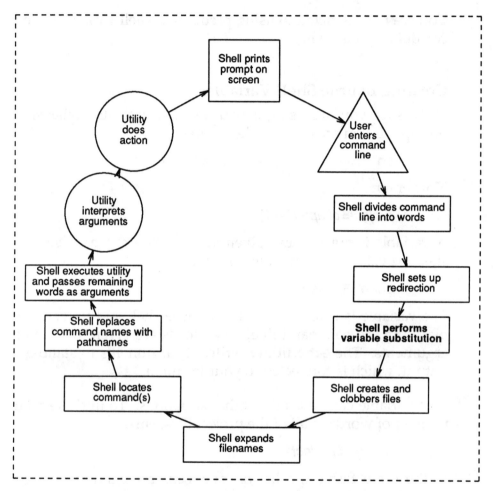

Shell Substitutes Values for Variables

Objective I
Setting Your Own Variables

You are not restricted to using predefined shell variables. You can define your own.

I1   **Creating Bourne Shell Variables**

Make sure you are using a Bourne shell with its dollar sign prompt. If you are in the C shell, enter:

sh

Now enter:

project=chapter[1-4]*

A variable is created and given values. You can now get the shell to evaluate the variables. Enter:

echo *$project*

The variable is evaluated by the Bourne shell and its value is placed in the command line. The words are given to **echo** as arguments. The **echo** utility writes its arguments to standard output, which is connected to your terminal.

This variable can be used in other situations. To find the total number of words in all of the project files, enter:

wc -w *$project*

In the same fashion, a list of logins for a committee can be created.

school="butch kaye jason amber brandon"

The variable *school* can be used to send mail easily to the whole committee:

mail $*school*

In interpreting this command line, the shell replaced the variable *school* with: *butch kaye jason amber brandon.*

As the shell interprets a command line, it identifies all variables and then replaces each with its current value.

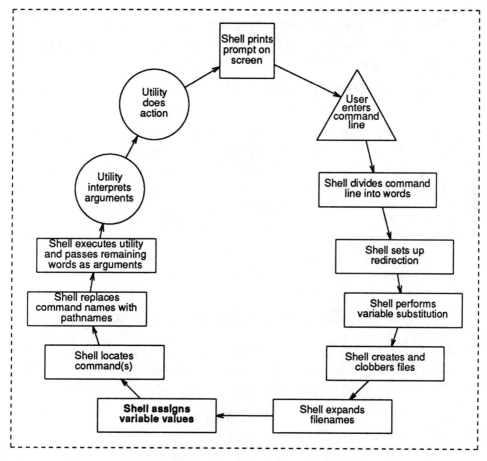

Shell Assigns Variable Values

I2   **Creating C Shell Variables**

At this moment you are probably in the Bourne Shell. If your default shell is a C shell and you started a Bourne shell a few steps back with a **sh** command, end that shell and return to the C shell with:

> ⌈Control-d⌉

If your default shell is the Bourne shell, start a C shell by entering:

> **csh**

The C shell does not assign variable values as part of the command line execution. From the C shell you set the value of variables using the **set** command. Enter

> **set** *project* = *"chap[1-4]*"*

The C shell expects spaces around the equal sign. The remaining steps of the previous section are the same. For instance, you can check the current variable values in your C shell by entering:

> **set**

Objective J
Including Utility Output in a Command Line

Utilities can be executed within a command line and the utility's output included in the command line itself. Enter the following, being careful to use *backquotes* around **pwd**:

> **echo** *You are in the `***pwd**`* directory*

When the shell finds the **pwd** command surrounded by backquotes, the shell executes another shell process (a sub-shell) to run the enclosed command. The output from the **pwd** is substituted in the command line and the `pwd` removed.

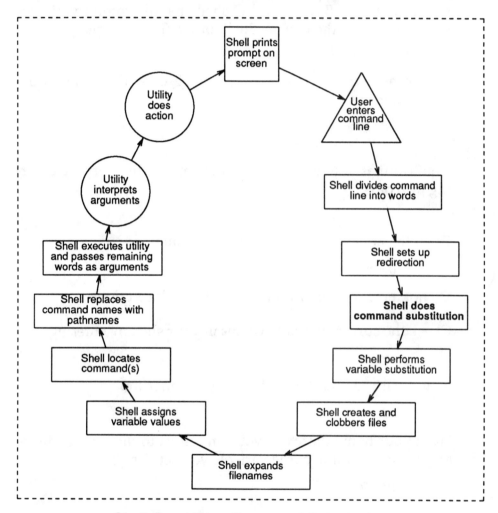

Shell Completes Command Substitution

J1   **Setting Bourne Shell Variables with Command Substitution**

As before, you can set the value of a variable to be the output of a utility. The Bourne and C shells handle setting variables differently. Use the Bourne Shell for the first example.

J2   First, change directories to one of the obscure directories of the system such as

    cd */tmp*

Confirm that you are indeed in the correct directory by entering **pwd** or **ls**.

J3   From the Bourne shell command line, enter:

    d=`pwd`

Do not include spaces, and be sure to use backquotes.

Check the current variable values in your shell by entering:

    set

Now return to your home directory by entering:

    cd

From your home directory you can return to the remote directory using the value of the variable you set. Enter

    cd *$d*

Again confirm you are in the other directory by entering **pwd** or **ls**.

The shell evaluated the variable *d*, which you had set earlier to the directory path. The value was given as an argument to the **cd** command.

If you were originally using a C shell and started a Bourne shell with **sh**, leave the Bourne Shell by entering:

> Ctrl-d

J4   Setting C Shell Variables with Command Substitution

If you are not in the C shell, start a C shell by entering:

> **csh**

J5   Again go to a remote section of the universe such as */tmp* by entering:

> **cd** */tmp*

As before, when using the C shell you set the value of variables using the **set** command. Enter

> **set** *d* = `pwd`

Check the value of the *d* variable in your C shell by entering:

> **set**

Change directories back home by entering:

> **cd**

Confirm your home location by entering **pwd** or **ls**.

Return to your remote directory by entering:

cd *$d*

Confirm you have safely returned by entering **pwd** or **ls**.

J6   **Working on Files at a Distance**

In both shells you can also access files in different directories using variables. Enter

vi *$d/filename*

where *filename* is the name of a new file to be located in the */tmp* directory.

The shell evaluated the variable *d* and replaced *d* with its value in the command line. You can now edit the file. It is located by its absolute path.

Objective K
Preventing the Shell from Interpreting Characters

Many characters have special meaning to the shell. There are times you will want to tell the shell not to interpret the special meaning. For example, look through the file *years* for the line that has *Bob Danny* in it by entering:

grep *Bob Danny years*

As the shell executes this command line, three arguments are passed to the utility: *Bob Danny* and *years*. **grep** is programmed to interpret the first as the target and all remaining arguments as filenames. When **grep** could not locate the file *Danny*, it sent the error message to standard error.

The problem was that the shell interpreted the space between *Bob* and *Danny* as the delimiter between words on the command line, dividing the line into four words, (1) **grep**, (2) *Bob*, (3) *Danny*, (4) *years*. You can hide the space by entering the following:

grep "*Bob Danny*" *years*

The shell now divides this command line into only three words, (1) **grep** (2) *Bob Danny*, and (3) *years*.

The space between *Bob* and *Danny* was not interpreted as a delimiter by the shell because it was "hidden" inside quotation marks. Some refer to this process as "protecting" terms from the shell, or "escaping" the shell. Essentially, the use of the quotation marks preserves the integrity of what is enclosed so that it can be passed on, in its entirety, to the utility and acted on by the utility, not by the shell.

Objective L
Prohibiting Variable Evaluation

L1   The shell interprets the asterisk * to be expanded to all filenames in the current directory. The shell also evaluates variables that begin with a dollar sign.

As another example, enter the following:

echo * $HOME

The output is the filenames and the value of the **HOME** variable.

You have been using the quotation marks to hide special characters from the shell.

Enter the following:

echo "* $HOME"

The double quotes protect all special characters except the **$**, which activates variable evaluation. If you are using the C shell, variable evaluation and history are not affected by double quotes. To hide *all* special characters use the single quotation marks.

Enter:

echo '* $HOME'

L2   Likewise, the **tr** utility expects two arguments for a range of characters inside brackets. In a previous step, you entered the following:

tr "[*a-z*]" "[*A-Z*]" < *filename*

Try it without the quotation marks. Enter:

tr [*a-z*] [*A-Z*] < *filename*

The **tr** utility is programmed to interpret the two bracketed arguments as the target and translated range of characters.

The shell also attaches special meaning to brackets. It matches the contents of brackets to filenames. For that reason, when you use **tr** you must tell the shell to not interpret the brackets but pass them as arguments to **tr**. When the shell interprets the command line, all characters from the first quotation mark to the second are passed uninterpreted to the utility as a single argument.

The shell must make sense out of quoted strings to interpret command lines as entered.

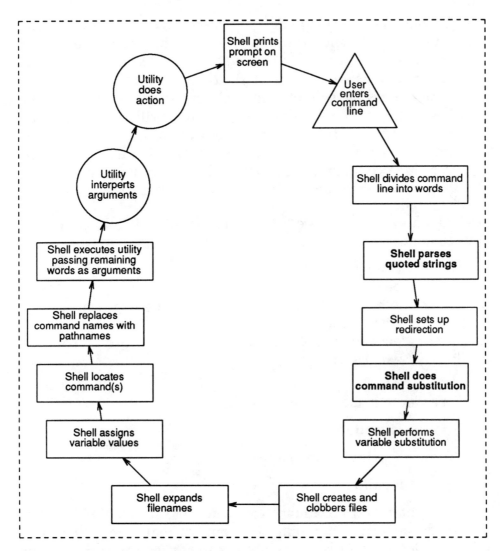

Shell Parses Quoted Strings

One of the first tasks for the shell is to determine whether or not to evaluate quoted strings. Its next task is to evaluate or parse the appropriate quoted strings.

Objective M
Issuing Commands with a Shell Script

Throughout these modules you have been entering command lines from the shell prompt. The shell has been interpreting the command lines one at a time. Both shells will also interpet commands listed in a file or shell script. Although shell programming is the subject of several other texts, we introduce the basic concept here for readers unfamiliar with the topic. Even simple scripts are useful with power utilities because they make it easier for you to manage what would otherwise be very long command lines. Scripts keep a record of commands issued, and they save retyping.

As an example, create a file called *loginfo* with the following contents.

```
echo you are in:
pwd
echo the following number of people are logged in:
who | wc -l
echo the sorted who listing is:
who | sort
```

In order to make the file *executable* enter:

```
chmod 700 loginfo
```

The shell script is now ready to run. Enter

```
loginfo
```

If a "command not found" error message resulted, either you made an error in typing, or your current directory is not included in the places the shell searches for commands. You can force a search of your current directory by entering:

```
./loginfo
```

When you enter the name of an executable file, the shell executes it. Usually it is a system executable file located in a system directory; it can also be a file that you have created. The file **loginfo** is now a command that is executed just like all the others.

There will be many times in this book when it is much easier to enter long commands into files and execute the file than to accurately type the command from the command line.

Obviously shell scripts can do much more than simply hold commands to be executed in batches, but that is the subject of other texts.

Objective N
Entering Long Command Lines

UNIX facilitates entering command lines that include several utilities. Command lines using many utilities and their options can be very long. You can issue long command lines in several ways:

- Enter the command on two or more lines, providing that you enter a backslash ⟨\⟩ before pressing each ⎡Return⎤;

- Enter the command as one line, allowing the terminal to wrap the display;

- Enter the command into a file with backslashes at the end of all but the last line, make it executable, and then run the script. This latter approach permits keeping a record of the command, enables you to use the same command at a later time to find different information, and allows you to easily modify the command to be issued.

Conclusion

This module has been an exploration of both Bourne and C shell command line syntax, as well as an examination of how the shell interprets command lines entered by users. Knowledge of the syntax, the steps, and the order of interpretation will be useful as you use power utilities.

Shell Special Characters

CHARACTER   FUNCTION

> redirect standard output

< redirect standard input

>> append standard output

| pipe the output from one command to the input of another

* expand to any number of characters, including zero

? expand to any one character

[ ] expand to any of the characters enclosed in the brackets

[-] expand to any of the characters within the range enclosed in the brackets

$ expand to the value of the variable that follows the dollar sign

& execute the command(s) in the background

; command separator, used to build a list of commands. Commands are executed sequentially, and the & applies to all.

( ) group enclosed command list and execute in a sub-shell (not discussed)

Shell Special Characters Cont'd

CHARACTER   FUNCTION

{ }   group enclosed command list and execute in current shell (not discussed)

\   do not interpret the following character as a special character

' '   single quotes, hide everything from the shell (except ! in C shell)

" "   double quotes, hide everything from the shell (except ! in C shell, $ and backquotes)

`  `   backquotes, perform enclosed command, place output here

[Ctrl-d]   end-of-file symbol

$*variable*   the shell substitutes the value of the *variable*

Module 4

Using Regular Expressions with ex

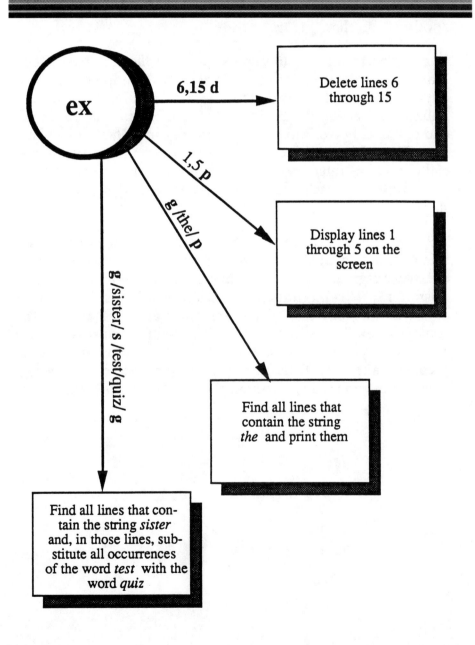

Introduction

As part of your experiences editing files you have probably had to locate specific occurrences of a word using */word*. Sets of characters that may or may not be words can be called patterns, for instance *teh*. You may have changed one pattern to another (e.g., changing *teh* to *the*).

In addition to literal patterns like *teh* and *the*, it is possible to search and substitute for special patterns. Examples of special patterns include: the word america with or without the "a" capitalized, a space at the beginning of a line, a period not at the end of a line, two or more spaces next to each other and a blank line. These kinds of special patterns are identified using special characters referred to as *metacharacters*. Patterns, whether they contain metacharacters or not, are called *regular expressions*.

This module quickly reviews the format of search and substitute commands. It then focuses on the use of *metacharacters* to construct regular expressions for use in search and substitute operations. This module introduces *regular expressions* as part of the editing process; all the examples are presented in the context of **ex** line editor commands. Regular expressions are also used by a wide variety of other UNIX utilities, such as **grep, awk** and **sed**. Thus, understanding how to construct regular expressions is an important skill for UNIX power users.

Prerequisites

Before beginning this module, you should be able to:

- use a UNIX editor— preferably **vi**, **ex** or **edit**;

- create, edit, move, copy, view and remove files;

- make directories and move around in the file system;

- use basic utilities (Module 2); and

- use the shell to issue commands (Module 3).

Objective

Upon completion of this module, you will be able to:

- interpret regular expressions;

- construct a variety of regular expressions;

- use regular expressions in commands to locate character strings; and

- use regular expressions in commands to locate and replace character strings.

Procedures

The **vi** and **ex** editors are actually two modes of the same editor. For the procedures in this module, we recommend accessing the line editor mode with the command **ex**.

If you prefer to use the visual editor, all of the **ex** commands in this module can be run from the **vi** command mode by preceding the commands with a colon (:).

Objective A
Using the **ex** Line Editor

In this section, you will use the **ex** line editor to display lines within a file, search for lines containing a specified pattern and substitute a new pattern for an old pattern within a line.

Although the commands introduced in this section may be a review for you, we recommend that you at least skim this section. If you are unfamiliar with UNIX line editor commands you should carefully read and practice the procedures covered here. This introduction to **ex** has been designed to prepare you to learn about regular expressions, not to be a complete introduction to the **ex** editor.

A1   To complete the procedures in the following section you will need a practice file. Use your favorite editor to create a file named *text* containing *exactly* the following lines ("typos" included):

> .sp
> This is the test file that
> I, Peter, am creating.
> It is different from all other test files,
> even the one created by my brother Mathew,
> and even more different than
> the one created by my brother Michael.
>
> The file Michael created is actually quite normal.
> This is because he is 12 years younger than me,
> or is that 11?
> Anyway he believes in antidisestablishmentarian.
>
> My sister Sue didn't create any test files:
> She was at work correcting social problems instead.

Now, save and store the file. If you are using the **vi** editor, instead of using **ZZ**, type, from the command mode:

> **: wq**

This action from the **vi** command mode has instructed the **ex** line editor to **write** and **q**uit the file you have just created.

A2   Invoking the **ex** Line Editor

To initiate an editing session using the **ex** line editor on the file called *text*, enter the command:

> **ex** *text*

The **ex** editor should give you one of its awe-inspiring messages— something like:

>   "text" 14 lines, 465 characters
>   :

The first line tells you the name, number of lines and number of characters associated with the file you are about to edit.

The colon

>   :

is **ex**'s prompt.

A3   Displaying a Line by Number

To instruct **ex** to display line 5 of the file, *text,* enter the command:

>   *5 p*

This instruction has two major components:

5   The address. Within **ex** a single number is used to indicate a line number; lines are counted from the top of the file.

p   The command. The **p** command is an abbreviation for **print** and results in the addressed line(s) being displayed. All **ex** commands have abbreviations that can be used instead of the full command name. The examples in this module will use the shortest acceptable abbreviations.

The general form of most **ex** instructions includes these two parts: an *address* that specifies the line or lines to be acted upon, and a *command* that specifies the type of action to be performed.

A4   Displaying the Current Line

The **ex** editor keeps track of the last line that was addressed. This line is known as the *current line*. At this point, the current line is line *5* because it was the last line you addressed. If you do not specify an address, most **ex** commands use a default address. In the case of the **print** command, the default address is the current line. Enter the command:

p

The fifth line is again displayed.

A5   Displaying a Range of Lines by Number

To have **ex** display lines 1 through 5 of the file, enter the command:

1,5 **p**

This instruction uses two numbers separated by a comma as its address. In **ex**, two numbers separated by a comma are used to indicate an inclusive range of lines, in this case all lines between and including lines *1* and *5*.

If you want to verify that these are indeed lines 1 through 5, from the **ex** prompt (**:**) type the command:

set number

This command displays numbers next to each line. If you are using the visual editor, use the colon (**:set number**).

If you wish to remove the numbers from your screen enter the line editor command:

set nonumber

A6   Identifying Lines Using the Last Line Character

To have **ex** display the lines from line 1 through the last line in the file, enter the command:

1,$ **p**

The **$** is **ex**'s *last-line* character. This character can be used in any address to specify the last line in the current file.

Most screens can only accommodate 23 lines of text. If you ask for the editor to display more than 23 lines, lines will scroll by and your screen will come to rest with only the last 23 lines in view.

A7   Copying Lines of Text

You can also copy lines of text. Enter the command:

1,3 **co $**

This command places a **co**py of lines 1 through 3 after the last line of the file.

In the examples above, the line numbers (*1,5 1,$ 1,3*) represent the *address* where the line editor can locate the text you want to affect. In this case, the **co** (for copy) is the *command* that you want to execute at that location (*address*). Lines can be moved in the same way with the **mo**ve command.

A8   Deleting Lines of Text

The editor can also be used to delete lines. To get rid of the extra lines which you just added to the end of the file, enter the command:

15,17 **d**

The **d**elete command is an important command for cleaning up files.

A9   Exploring ex's Default Action

You have seen that most **ex** commands have a default address, which is the current line. **ex** instructions also have a default action if only an address is specified. Enter the instruction:

> *4*

When no command is specified, **ex**'s default action is to print onto the screen the line(s) specified in the **address**.

The **ex** line editor accepts addresses and commands. Lines can be addressed by line number and actions performed such as print, delete, copy or move. If no address is specified, the current line is addressed. If no command is given, the line(s) are printed.

A10   Using a Contextual Address to Print a Line

Line addresses are actually just one of two types of **ex** addresses. The other type, known as *contextual addresses*, can be used to address a line when you know a *regular expression* (pattern) contained on the line but do not know its line number. Enter the command:

> */the/* **p**

The **p** in this example is optional because printing is **ex**'s default action. In this example you *addressed* (asked the computer to find) the first occurrence of a line in your file, after the current line, that contains the pattern *the*. A *contextual address* is constructed by surrounding a regular expression with two slashes.

Contextual addresses can also be used with any other **ex** command that expects an address (for example, **d** or **co**).

A11 **Performing a Command Globally**

You may have noticed that the only line printed on the screen was the first incidence of a line in your file, after the current line, that contained the specified *regular expression*. If you want to print all lines in the file that contain the pattern *the,* enter the command:

> **g** */the/* **p**

This instruction has three components:

g   The **g**lobal line address. This line address indicates that all lines in the file **(1,$)** will be examined for the specified regular expression that follows. On lines where the expression is found, the command(s) following the regular expression will be executed.

/the/ The regular expression.

p   The command list. In this case the command list consists of the single command, **p**rint.

The **g** line address *always* precedes the contextual address. The general format is:

> **g** *regular-expression command*

The **g** line address is by default all lines **(1,$)** in the file.

Line Address	Contextual Address	Command
g	*/the/*	**p**

A12 Substituting One Regular Expression for Another

It is easy to use a line editor instruction to substitute one regular expression for another. Enter the command:

   3 **s**/*creating*/*producing*/

The **s**ubstitute command requires two regular expressions separated by slashes. The action performed by the **s** command is to check the addressed line(s) for the pattern on the left (the *target* pattern), and, if it is found, substitute the expression on the right (the *replacement* pattern) for the target pattern. Thus, the above command instructs the line editor to go to line *3*, find the word *creating*, and **s**ubstitute for it the word *producing*.

A13 Using a Contextual Address for a Substitution

Contextual addresses can also be used with the substitution command. Enter the command:

   /*I*/ **s**/*am*/*was*/

This command instructs the line editor to find the first line following the current line that contains the regular expression *I*, then **s**ubstitute for the regular expression *am*, the pattern *was*.

A14 Substituting on All Lines

It is a simple extension to instruct the **s** command to act on *all* lines in the file. For example, assume that the author of the text you just entered told you that his brothers are also his friends and therefore requested that you change all occurrences of *brother* in the file *text* to the word *friend.* To accomplish the requested change, enter the command:

   1,$ **s**/*brother*/*friend*/

The **s** command checks all of the addressed line(s) for the pattern *brother* and, on lines where this pattern is found, substitutes the pattern *friend*.

Line Address	Command
1,$	**s**/*brother*/*friend*/

A15 Substituting on All Lines Containing a Pattern

It is also possible to mark all lines containing a specified pattern and, on those marked lines, replace the occurrence of some pattern with another. Enter the command (the spaces in this command line are optional):

g /*sister*/ **s**/*test*/*UNIX*/

This instruction causes **ex** to mark all lines containing the regular expression *sister*, then substitute *UNIX* for all occurrences of *test* on the marked lines.

Line Address	Contextual Address	Command
g	/*sister*/	**s**/*test*/*UNIX*/

A16 Substituting on All Marked Lines

You previously substituted a new pattern for an old one on all lines using the command:

1,$ **s**/*pattern1*/*pattern2*/

This function can also be accomplished using the **g**lobal command. This command is merely a special case of the command you just entered. For example, enter the command:

   g /*friend*/ **s**/*friend*/*brother*/

This instruction asks **ex** to mark all lines containing the regular expression *friend*, then substitute *brother* for all occurrences of that pattern. There is a short cut for this instruction. You could have entered the command:

   g /*friend* /**s**//*brother*/

The // in the substitute command is replaced by the last regular expression matched— in this case, *friend*. The above instruction has the same result as the instruction:

   1,$ **s**/*friend*/*brother*/

The main difference between the two commands is execution time. The former command takes longer than the latter and is only presented here because it is often used.

A17 Substituting for Multiple Occurrences on a Line

You may have noticed that the substitute command only works on the first occurrence of a pattern on an addressed line. If a line has more than one instance of the target pattern, only the first is affected. To have this command work on all occurrences of a pattern within a line, enter the command:

   1,$ **s**/*a*/*A*/**g**

Unlike the **g** at the beginning of the command line, which is the default address for all lines in the file (*1,$*), this **g** at the end of the substitute command is called a *flag*. The **g** flag stands for **g**lobal and instructs the substitute command to perform the replacement on all occurrences of the target pattern within the addressed line(s).

The components of the command are:

Line Address	Command	Flag
1,$	*s/a/A/*	**g**

A18 Leaving **ex**

In most cases, leaving **ex** requires the performance of two important functions. Because **ex** works on a copy of a file, not the original, it is first necessary to write all of the changes made. This is done with the **w**rite command. Next, you must quit **ex**. This is done (surprise!) with the **q**uit command. What you need to do now is quit without writing. To accomplish this, enter the command:

> **q!**

To write and quit together the command would be:

> **wq**

The **q!** command lets you exit **ex** without writing the silly changes you have made to this already silly file.

Objective B
Using Metacharacters in Searches

In the last section, you used literal patterns as contextual addresses to search for lines containing a specified pattern. In this section, you will search for lines containing non-literal patterns by using contextual addresses made up of regular expressions containing metacharacters.

B1   Again, call up *text* for editing with the command:

    ex *text*

B2   **Finding Patterns Versus Words**

Contextual addresses do not, in their simplest form, match *words*, but instead match a sequence or *string* of characters (that is, a *pattern*). The English words *the, other* and *brother* all contain the character string (pattern) *he* and are thus all valid targets for the contextual address *he*. Enter the command:

    /he

This command tells the editor to go to the next line that includes the target pattern: *he*. The English language being what it is, your cursor probably landed on *the* or *The*.

B3   **Finding a Line Containing a Word**

You can request that the editor locate the specific word *he*. Enter the command:

    /\<he\>

The \< signifies the beginning of a word; the \> signifies the end of a word. Thus this command will target the two characters *h* and *e* located between the beginning and ending of a word. It will target the word *he*.

The \< and \> characters do not work on some older versions of **ex**. If so, place a space both before and after the target pattern. Unfortunately, this trick will not work if the target word occurs at the beginning or end of a line, or is directly followed by a punctuation mark.

B4   Finding a Letter that Begins or Ends a Word

As another example, the following command will move the cursor to the next line that includes a letter *a* that is at the beginning of a word (not embedded within a word):

/\<a

The command to find the next line the includes any word that ends with an "s" in your file is:

/s\>

B5   Finding a Pattern at the Beginning of a Line

The editor can also search for patterns located at the beginning of a line. To move to the next line starting with the pattern *The,* enter the command:

/^The

The ^ (caret) is the symbol for the beginning of a line. This symbol can be used to find lines that begin with a specified sequence of characters.

B6   Matching the Beginning of a Line

Enter the following search command:

/^

Your cursor moved to the beginning of the next line; if you were to type ⬚n⬚ to move to the next occurrence, you would simply move to the beginning of the next line of text. The ^ (caret), without a specified sequence of characters, is the symbol for the beginning of a line.

B7 Specifying the End-of-Line

To locate lines in the file that end with the word *other*, enter:

/ other$

When used within a target pattern, the dollar sign (**$**) is read by the editor as signifying the end of a line *NOT* as a line address.

B8 Finding Blank Lines

The *beginning-* and *end-of-line* characters can be used together to locate blank lines. Enter the command:

/^$

The above command locates the next line containing the beginning of a line (^) and the end of a line (**$**) with nothing in between; that is, a line that begins and ends and has nothing in it.

B9 Searching for a Lower or Upper Case Letter

The metacharacters that you have been using so far are used to limit the scope of a pattern, that is, to *look for this pattern but only under the specified circumstances*. Metacharacters can also be used to expand the scope of a pattern, in effect telling the editor, *look for this pattern, and this pattern, and this pattern, etc.*

Perhaps you would like to locate a word in your file, but do not remember whether it was spelled with an upper or lower case first letter. For example, call up your *text* file for editing with **ex** and enter the command:

g */[Mm] ichael* **p**

This command displays all lines containing either the pattern Michael or michael in *text*. The brackets enclose alternative characters for the slash-search command to match. You are not constrained to a pair of upper and lower case letters.

The following command,

/[*CcBb*]*ase*

searches for the patterns *Case, case, Base* and *base*.

B10   Locating a Range of Characters

It is often useful to locate the next occurrence of a number in a file? You could enter:

/[*0123456789*]

There must be a more cryptic way.

Instead, enter the following command:

/[*0-9*]

The dash between the *0* and the *9* instructs **ex** to look for all numbers from zero up to and including nine. It sets a *range* of possible matches rather than a list of possibilities.

There is a big difference between [*09*] and [*0-9*]. The first example matches either *0* or *9*, while the second example matches any number from *0* to *9* inclusive; that is, the cursor moves to the next instance of *any* number.

B11 **Finding All Upper Case Letters**

Similarly, to locate the next line containing an upper case letter, enter the command:

/[A-Z]

This range matches any upper case letter.

B12 **Using Multiple Ranges**

You are not limited to either a list or a range between brackets, but can combine the two. For example, enter

/[13579a-z]

This matches any odd number as well as any lower case character.

What do you expect the following to not locate? Enter:

/[a-zA-Z]

B13 **Excluding Characters from a Search**

The following command will find the first instance of a character that is *not* a lower case letter:

/[^a-z]

When you place the ^ as the first character inside brackets, it asks the editor to locate any characters *other* than those specified within the brackets. The ^ allows you to specify what you do not want located.

As another example, the command to locate any character that is not a number is:

/[^0-9]

The "negation" caret, located immediately after the opening square bracket, can easily be confused with a caret outside the brackets that signifies *beginning-of-line*. To locate the beginning of a line, you enter:

/^

If someone is looking over you shoulder and you want to impress them, locate the beginning of a line that *does not* begin with a caret by entering:

/^[^^]

This command contains three carets, each with a different meaning. The first caret signifies the beginning of a line; the second caret, that follows the left bracket, is the *not* symbol. Finally, the third caret (just before the right bracket) stands for the caret character itself. So, this command says to locate a line that begins with a character other than a caret.

B14   Excluding Several Ranges of Characters

You are not limited to one identification scheme inside the brackets. For instance:

/[^0-9a-zA-Z]

will go to the next character that is not a number, lower case letter or upper case letter. There are few characters left that this command matches.

B15 ## Matching Any Character

One of the most important metacharacters available is used to match any single character. Enter the command:

   /.

Does the editor find the next dot in your file? No, the dot (.) is a special symbol that stands for any single character. This metacharacter, when used by itself, causes the cursor to be placed on the next line containing any character. Not terribly useful on its own.

B16 ## Matching Any Character Within a Pattern

The . metacharacter is most useful when it is used with other metacharacters. For example, to find the next example of a three-letter word ending in *he*, enter the command:

   /\<.he\>

This will find words like *The, the, She* or *she*, but not the word *he*.

B17 ## Matching Repeated Characters

The following command would find all words that have an *e* followed by *any* number of *t*'s, including *zero t*'s:

   */ et**

The * means *any possible number of the previous character*. This gives the * the unusual ability to match zero, one, two or fifty instances of the prior character.

To locate the word *different*, whether it is spelled correctly with two *f*'s or with 1, 3 or hundreds of *f*'s, enter:

   */ diff*erent*

It is important to remember that the * matches zero or more occurrences of the preceding character. For instance, if you were to enter the command:

/ formal*

this would find the words *formal* and *formally*, but unfortunately, it would also find *formatting*, because this last word is made up of the pattern *forma* followed indeed by zero occurrences of the letter *l*.

If you want to find all instances that included the string formal, with at least one *l*, you need to precede the * with *two* instances of that character. This instructs the editor to find the *first* instance of the character followed by zero or more of the *second* instance— in other words, one or more of the characters together.

B18 Matching Any Number of Any Characters

The . and the * characters can be used together to match any sequence of characters. Enter the command:

/s.*s

This command locates the next line containing an *s* followed by any sequence of characters followed by an *s*. Remember, the . matches any single character and the * matches any number of occurrences of the previous character. When used together, they match any number of any character. Note that the identified sequence may be a single word or cut across a series of words within a single line, because spaces are included in the definition of *any character*. The previous command will find both the pattern *sources* and the pattern *so it is*. If you are looking for a single word, you have to be a bit more specific.

B19 **Removing Magic**

The ability of the dot to match any single character is very useful, but what if you want to find a string of characters that actually does contain a dot (such as a formatting command)? Enter the command:

> /\.

The backslash (\) is the Kryptonite of special characters. It takes away the special powers of metacharacters and turns them into ordinary (mortal) characters. Thus, the above command will find the next example of a dot (period) in your file.

Similarly to find the character *, you would enter the command:

> /*

B20 **Finding Lines That Start with Periods**

To find the next line containing a period (dot) as the first character you would type:

> /^\.

This command checks the first character of each line and finds the next line that starts with a period. This sequence can be used to locate all **nroff** formatting commands in your file.

Again, all these uses of the caret character can be confusing. To locate the caret character itself, you enter:

> /\^

To locate a line that *begins* with a caret you enter:

/^\^

In both of these commands, the backslash is used to "escape" the meaning of the caret character, to hide its special meaning and use its literal meaning.

Note: As if things weren't confusing enough, the backslash character is also used to *give* a special meaning to some characters that follow it, instead of *escaping* the meaning of the character. Two examples that you have already seen are \< and \>. You will meet others soon.

B21 Deleting Blank Lines

Metacharacters are not only useful in searching for lines containing a non-literal pattern, they can also be used to perform actions on located lines. For example, to find all lines with a beginning (^) and an end ($) but no middle (i.e., blank lines), and delete them, enter the command:

g/^$/d

Line Address	Contextual Address	Command
g	/^$/	d

Objective C
Using Metacharacters with Target Patterns

So far you have been using metacharacters within contextual addresses to search for lines containing non-literal patterns. In this section you will use metacharacters within global substitution commands.

C1   Substituting for a Regular Expression

To change all occurrences of *michael*, with or without a capital *m*, to *Mike*, enter:

1,$s / [Mm] ichael/ Mike/ g

This will find all instances of either *Michael* or *m*ichael and replace them with *Mike*.

Line Address	Command	Flag
g	s/[Mm] ichael/ Mike	g

C2   Using Metacharacters in a Replacement Pattern

To see if the replacement pattern can also contain metacharacters, enter:

1,$ s/ [Mm] y/ [Mm] y/g

What happens? The pattern *[Mm]y* in the replacement pattern is interpreted literally, and not as a non-literal pattern, so that all instances of either *My* or *my* are replaced by, literally, *[Mm]y*.

> Metacharacters can *not* be used in a replacement pattern.

C3 **Removing Multiple Spaces**

The following sequence will locate every occurrence of multiple spaces, replace them with a single space and, in each instance, ask you for confirmation. Be certain to leave three spaces between the first / and the *, and one space between the fourth / and the last / (a small diamond ($\diamond$) has been inserted to mark the spaces):

$$1,\$ \ \text{s} / _{\diamond\diamond\diamond} * / _{\diamond} / \text{gc}$$

This command finds every place in the file where there are two or more spaces (note that you entered three spaces before the *) and displays each occurrence on your screen with a ˄ under the located pattern. Because you added the **c**onfirmation flag at the end of the command, you are asked to confirm that you really do want the substitution made. As each occurrence is displayed, you have the option of replacing the multiple spaces with just one space or leaving the text as entered. If you type **y** and then press RETURN the editor will substitute just one space, if you press **n** followed by RETURN the located pattern will be left as is. Excess spaces between words are usually unnecessary and can also cause unwanted formatting results. You can use this command to rid your file of such nuisances.

C4   Deleting Spaces at the Beginning of Lines

Leading spaces at the beginning of lines in a text file can cause problems. Many text formatters interpret such spaces as an indication to start a new line. The following command finds every line that begins with one or more spaces and substitutes *nothing* for the spaces. The effect is removal of the spaces. Be certain to leave two spaces between the ˆ and the * character:

> *1,$ s/ˆ ◊◊*//*

C5   Removing Spaces at the End of Lines

Trailing blanks can be very problematic to some pre-formatters, especially **tbl** and **refer**. The following command finds every line that has one or more blank spaces following the last character and removes the blank space(s). Make sure to leave two spaces between the first / and the *:

> *1,$ s/ ◊◊*$//*

C6   Isolating a Word for Search and Substitution

You know that the command:

> *1,$ s/and/or/g*

can be used to change all occurrences of the pattern *and* into the string *or*. This substitution occurs in all cases, including those instances where *and* was part of another word. The special characters we previously used to match the beginning (\<) and end (\>) of a word, within a contextual address, can take care of this problem. To affect only the *word and* and not instances where the characters *and* appear within another word, enter the command:

> *1,$* **s/\\<and\\>/ or/ g**

Objective D
Using Special Replacement Pattern Characters

In the previous section, you discovered that the metacharacters you used within contextual addresses and target patterns do not work with replacement patterns. In this section, you will use several special replacement pattern characters that do work and are very useful.

D1   Adding Characters to a Pattern

One of the many "typos" in your *text* file is that the word *antidisestablishmentarian* should have the suffix *ism*. You can use the following search-and-substitute command to make the appropriate change *and* display the changed line on the screen:

> *1,$* **s/*mentarian*\\>/&*ism*/ p**

Line Address	Command	Flag
1,$	**s/*mentarian*\\>/&*ism*/**	**p**

Note the **&** placed before the characters *ism*. The **&** symbol, when used within a replacement pattern, stands for the last pattern found, so the *ism* will be appended to the character pattern matching *mentarian\>* (resulting in *antidisestablishmentarianism*). Without the **&** symbol, this command would substitute the characters *ism* for the partial word *mentarian*.

D2   Inserting Characters Before a Pattern

The **&** character can also be used to add characters to the beginning of words. For example, to place the word *older* before the word *brother*, enter the command:

1,$ s/\<brother/ / older &/

D3   Converting from Upper to Lower Case

The following command will find any capital letter and replace it with the lower case version of itself—that's the letter *l* ("el")—not the number 1 ("one"):

1,$ s/[A-Z]/\l&/g

The pattern *[A-Z]* matches any capital letter, the expression *\l&* means: *substitute for the last pattern matched (**&**) its lower case replacement (\l).*

D4   Converting from Lower to Upper Case

The following command will find any lower case letter and replace it with the upper case version of itself:

1,$ s/[a-z]/\u&/g

The pattern [*a*-*z*] matches any lower case letter, the expression \u& means: *substitute for the last pattern matched (&) its upper case translation (\u).*

D5 Reordering Patterns Within a Line

This last exercise is a demonstration of the power of regular expressions. It is, however, a pain and is more easily accomplished using **awk**, the subject of a later module. The file, *people*, contains lines of the following form:

        1   Lurnix   computer   home   415-849-4478

Suppose you want to rearrange the fields, so that instead of having the phone number at the end, it would appear at the beginning, like this:

        1 415-849-4478   Lurnix   computer   home

To accomplish this task, you must first identify each of the three parts:

(1)   the line number,

(2)   the words, and

(3)   the phone number.

Second, a mechanism must be available for rearranging the order in which the parts are placed on each line. That mechanism is to surround each of the specified regular expressions with the delimiters \(and \) on the target side, and to place the special characters \1, \2, and \3 in their new order on the replacement side. Open the file *people*, and enter the command:

1,$ s/\(*[0-9][0-9]* *\)\([a-zA-Z].*\)\(415.*\)/\1\3 \2/

The delimiters *mark* each target pattern. The numbers preceded by backslashes on the replacement side tell the editor where to place each marked pattern. The **\1** signifies the first marked pattern, the **\2** signifies the second, and so on.

The following table displays the name, verbal description and regular expression that match each line segment.

Name	Verbal Description	Expression
line number	the beginning of the line, followed by zero or more spaces, followed by one or more numbers, followed by one or more spaces	`^◊*[0-9][0-9]*◊◊*`
words	any letter, followed by any number of any character	`[a-zA-Z].*`
phone number	the characters *415*, followed by any number of any character	`415.*`

Conclusion

In this module, you have seen how to construct and interpret regular expressions for use with the **ex** editor. Because regular expressions are used by so many UNIX utilities, you will have many opportunities to work with them in the modules that follow. Specifically, you will find them useful with **grep, awk,** and **sed**. Attached to this module are two summary tables detailing the functions of the various characters you have encountered in your work with regular expressions.

Summary of Regular Characters for

Search and Substitute Commands

CHARACTER	FUNCTION
g	**g**lobal: when placed at the *beginning* of a search, this command addresses all lines in the file. When placed at the *end* of a search statement, it causes all cases of the pattern within the lines specified to be affected. (May be used in both places to affect all occurrences of the pattern within the current file.)
s	**s**ubstitute what follows for the target pattern that precedes.
p	When placed at the end of a search, this command **p**rints the pattern found to your screen.
d	When placed at the end of a search, this command **d**eletes each line in which the pattern is found.
c	When placed at the end of a search-and-substitute command, this command requests **c**onfirmation of each change before performing the substitution. Enter *y* to confirm; enter *n* or RETURN to leave the pattern intact. It can be combined with other commands (**:g/***the***/s//***those***/gc**).

Summary of Metacharacters for Search and Substitute Commands

CHARACTER	FUNCTION
^	Match *beginning-of-line*.
$	Match *end-of-line*. Do not confuse the metacharacter with the address symbol, which stands for "last line in the file."
.	Match any single character.
*	Match any number of occurrences (including 0) of previous character.
[ ]	Match any character (or range of characters) enclosed within the brackets.
[^]	Match any character not enclosed within the brackets.
\<	Match beginning of a word or phrase.
\>	Match end of a word or phrase.
\(	Marks beginning of a pattern.
\)	Marks end of a pattern.
&	Replace with last pattern of characters encountered.
\l	Replace "target character(s)" with lower case version.
\u	Replace "target character(s)" with upper case version.
\	Remove "magic" of Special Characters (Kryptonite).
//	Match last pattern in search.
\#	Replace with the pattern that corresponds with #.

Appendix A

The following is a copy of the file *people:*

LINE #	NAME	TYPE	WHERE	TELEPHONE #
1	Lurnix	computer	home	415-666-4478
2	Lurnix	computer	work	415-666-9999
3	Peter Titus	human	home	415-999-1234
4	Peter Titus	consultant	work	415-666-4478
5	John Ramsey	human	home	415-999-1235
6	John Ramsey	consultant	work	415-666-4478
7	Peter Osbourne	Human	home	415-999-1236
8	Peter Osbourne	tech writer	work	415-666-9999
9	Mathew Clay	Human	home	415-999-1237
10	Mathew Clay	marketing	work	415-666-9999
11	Kevan Crockett	human	home	415-999-1238
12	Kevan Crockett	media critic	work	415-666-4478
13	Anne Foster	human	home	415-999-1239
14	Anne Foster	accountant	work	415-666-9999
15	Mark Calhoun	human	home	415-999-1240
16	Mark Calhoun	food service	work	415-999-2478
17	Jessica Ratliff	human	home	415-999-2356
18	Jessica Ratliff	data mgr	work	415-666-1337

Module 5

Global Searching and Printing with grep

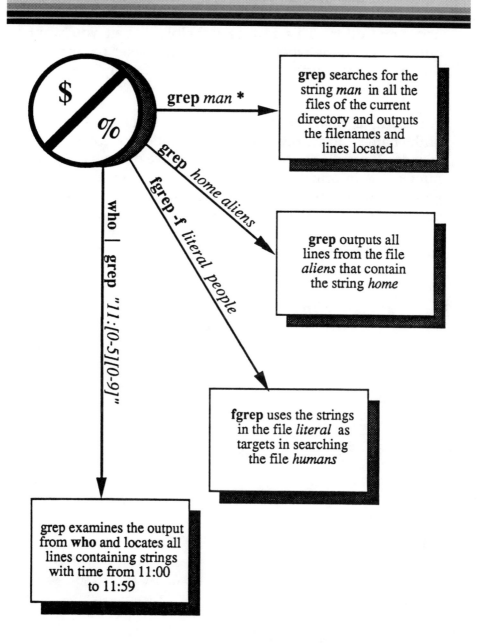

Introduction

A very useful feature provided by text editors is the ability to locate words or a pattern of characters within the file being edited. In this module you will use the **grep** utility to locate text or character patterns in files directly from the shell, *without* using an editor. This feature is helpful when you want to quickly determine whether a specific character pattern is in a file, or when you want to identify which of many files contains a specific pattern.

For example, many people maintain files that contain listings of the names, addresses and phone numbers of colleagues and friends. It would be convenient to retrieve one person's phone number or information for all people in a given area code, without calling up the file with an editor. A one-line **grep** command easily does the trick. With the **grep** utility a user can examine a whole file and search for a particular word or regular expression.

Prerequisites

Before beginning this module, you should be able to:

- create, edit, move, copy, view and remove files;

- make directories and move around in the file system;

- use basic utilities (Module 2);

- use the shell to issue commands (Module 3);

- use regular expressions (Module 4).

Objectives

After completing this module, you will be able to:

- select particular lines from one or more files;

- use **grep** as a filter within a command line that includes several utilities; and

- compare and contrast the three versions of **grep** (**grep**, **egrep** and **fgrep**).

Procedures

To best use this module you need a copy of the files named *people*, *aliens* and *info*. Create these files using Appendices A, B and C at the end of this module.

Make sure you include the numbers at the beginning of each line in these files. Having numbers on each line will make it easier to observe the actions of the **grep** utility.

To make the exercises work properly, separate each of the columns with one or more *spaces* or *tab* characters. Lining up the columns is not necessary, but it makes the files easier to read.

Objective A
The Basic **grep** Command Line

The shell utility **grep** (which comes from: **g**lobally search for regular **e**xpressions and **p**rint them) allows you to search a file for all occurrences of a word without calling up an editor.

A1   Printing Lines Containing a Specified Word

To use **grep** to print all the lines in the file *people* containing the word *human,* enter:

grep *human people*

A list of all the lines from the file *people* that contain the string *human* is printed on the screen:

5	Peter Titus	human	home	415-999-1234
7	John Ramsey	human	home	415-999-1235
13	Kevan Crockett	human	home	415-999-1238
15	Anne Foster	human	home	415-999-1239
17	Mark Calhoun	human	home	415-999-1240
19	Jessica Ratliff	human	home	415-999-2356

A2   Now enter:

grep *home aliens*

The **grep** utility is activated and told to look for the string *home* in all of the lines in the file *aliens*. It found and printed four lines:

3	E. T.	home	111-898-653-2211
4	Paul Atreides	home	919-907-324-4671
6	The Mule	home	unknown
7	Chameleon	home	ever changing

A3   Describing the Basic grep Command Line Syntax

The basic **grep** command line, as demonstrated above, is:

grep	*pattern*	*filename*

In this example, *pattern* is the target to be searched for and *filename* is the name of the file to be examined by **grep**.

A4 **Searching Through Multiple Files**

You can also use the **grep** utility on more than one file at a time by listing the file names on the command line. Enter

grep *computer people aliens*

The output that results is:

people: 3	Lurnix	computer	home	415-999-2478
people: 4	Lurnix	computer	work	415-999-9999
aliens: 5	Dora	computer	807-786-912-6870	

Each line is preceded by the name of the file from which it came. Because there were lines with the word *computer* located in both the file *people* and the file *aliens*, there are output lines from both files.

> In general, **grep** will search any files listed on the command line after a single search pattern.

A5 **Using grep on All Files in a Directory**

Look for the pattern *man* in all files in your current directory by entering:

grep *man* *

The **grep** utility searches through all the files in your current directory and locates all lines that contain the pattern *man* (The asterisk * is the *filename expansion character* that matches all filenames in the current directory). The **grep** utility labels each line of output with the appropriate file name so that you can tell which line came from which file.

A6 **Searching for Multi-word Patterns**

You can use *patterns* that contain more than one word. Enter
the following command to search through the file *people*:

   grep *"Peter Titus" people*

As you can see, the lines containing the phrase *Peter Titus* are
located and printed. The double quotes around the pattern
keep the space between *Peter* and *Titus* as part of the pattern
and hidden from the shell.

The SPACE is a special character to the shell because it is the delimiter that separates patterns as words, which may be shell
commands, utilities, options, or file names. Therefore, quotes
are necessary when you use special characters (like the SPACE
character) within a target pattern.

When you are using **grep** in a command line, you must tell the
shell not to interpret special characters by enclosing the target
pattern in quotation marks. Because these quotes usually don't
hurt, many people make it a practice to always surround the
search pattern (target) of **grep** command lines with quotes.

A7 **Listing Filenames Only**

Sometimes you may want to know only the name of the file or
files that contain a target pattern. Enter the following:

   grep **-l** *computer* *****

That is the letter *l* ("el")—not a number. With this option **grep** lists
only the names of the files that contain the target pattern, not the
lines. The **-l** option is useful for finding a misplaced file, assuming
you can recall a phrase or word that is in that file.

> The **grep** utility searches through the lines of specified files looking for specified character strings. It outputs the lines if only one file is searched, the filename and line if multiple files are searched, and only the filename if the **-l** option is invoked.

A8   When grep Comes Up Empty

Thus far, all of your commands have located target lines. What happens when the pattern for which **grep** is searching does not exist in the files that are searched? Enter the following command:

> **grep** *humorous people*

The shell prompt silently returns. Because none of the lines in the file *people* contain the pattern *humorous*, no lines were printed.

A9   Getting Line Numbers

So far the line numbers in your output were actually contained in the files *people* and *aliens*. There is an option to **grep** that will print the actual line numbers of all selected lines. Select a target pattern and one of the files in your current directory and enter:

> **grep -n** *target filename*

A10 Try the **-n** option with another of your files.

> The **-n** option instructs **grep** to include the line numbers of the identified lines in the output, as well as the actual lines.

Objective B
Using Regular Expressions

All of the search patterns you have entered thus far have been quite specific. However, there are times when you may not know all there is to know about the target pattern, or you may want a short-cut for specifying a whole group of target patterns. In these cases you can use regular expression metacharacters within **grep**'s pattern.

In a previous example, you entered the command line:

> **grep** *human people*

which called for locating the lines that contained the string *human* in the file *people*. But did it get them all? It displayed all the lines where *human* appeared, but it did not display lines 9 and 11 where the word *Human* was capitalized.

B1 **Ignoring Case**

Enter the following command line:

> **grep** "[*Hh*]*uman*" *people*

Here's what you see:

5	Peter Titus	human	home	415-999-1234
7	John Ramsey	human	home	415-999-1235
9	Peter Osbourne	Human	home	415-999-1236
11	Mathew Clay	Human	home	415-999-1237
13	Kevan Crockett	human	home	415-999-1238
15	Anne Foster	human	home	415-999-1239
17	Mark Calhoun	human	home	415-999-1240
19	Jessica Ratliff	human	home	415-999-2356

The command told **grep** to find all lines in the file *people* that include the word *Human* or the word *human*. The brackets in this command line are regular expression metacharacters. The **grep** utility matches any single character from the list of characters enclosed by the brackets.

The quotes in this command line were required to prevent the shell from interpreting the brackets as filename expansion characters.

B2 Eliminating Comment Lines

Familiarize yourself with the file *info* by scanning through it with **pg, more,** or **cat**. At times programmers need to obtain copies of programs without the comment lines. In C-Shell scripts, the comment lines begin with a pound sign (#). You can print the file *info* without lines that contain only comments. Enter

```
grep -v "^#" info
```

All lines that do *not* begin with # are printed on your screen.

As you know from the previous explanations of metacharacters, the caret ^ is the *beginning-of-line* symbol. By preceding the pound sign with a caret, you told **grep** that only a pound sign at the *beginning of a line* could qualify as a matched pattern.

The **-v** option (reverse) tells **grep** to print only those lines that do *not* contain the target string (in this case, the pound sign). Therefore, **grep** prints all lines from the file *info except* the comment lines.

B3   **Counting Lines That Are Not Matched**

You can have **grep** output a count of the lines that match the target instead of the lines themselves. Enter

   grep -c "ˆ#" *info*

A count of the comment lines is output.

As with most utilities, you can enter two or more options in one command line. Enter

   grep -cv "ˆ#" *info*

This command line counts all the lines in the file *info* that do not begin with a *#* and displays that number on the screen.

> When you use **grep** with **-c**, **grep** outputs a count of the lines, not the lines themselves.

B4   **Removing nroff Commands**

In an earlier module, you used the **deroff** utility to remove the **nroff** commands from the file *n_test_file*. The **deroff** utility removed the commands and left blank lines. The **grep** utility can be used to completely remove **nroff** commands.

Enter

   grep -v "ˆ\ . . . .*" *n_test_file*

The output is all the lines from your file that do *not* begin with a dot and two or more characters.

There are four metacharacters used in this pattern: the caret, the backslash, the dot, and the asterisk.

ˆ   the caret matches beginning-of-line.

\.   the backslash (\) removes the special meaning of the character that immediately follows. It is used in this case (\.) to allow the first period to be interpreted simply as a period.

...*   the second and third dots in this pattern are interpreted as *any single character*. The last dot and the asterisk permit any number of additional characters.

So the overall pattern means a dot at the beginning of a line followed by any two or more characters— the basic **nroff** command.

B5   Pooling Information into a Pattern

Assume you want a consultant's phone number, but you remember only the person's first name: *Peter*. You could select all lines that contain *Peter* or all the *consultant* lines, or you could combine them into one search. Enter the following command line to find the line(s) containing the name *Peter* and the title *consultant*:

> **grep** *"Peter.* consultant"* *people*

The output is the line with the word *Peter* followed by the word *consultant,* and you get the desired phone number.

In this search, you used a dot . metacharacter in the pattern to mean *any* single character. Following the dot is an asterisk *, which means zero or more of the preceding character. The preceding character is a dot, which means *any* character, so *this* combination means zero or more occurrences of any character (basically, anything at all).

The overall pattern is thus the word *Peter,* followed by a string of zero or more characters, followed by the word *consultant.*

B6   **Finding the End of the Line**

It is the morning after the annual office party where you met a wonderful co-worker. Your brain is less than efficient this morning and can only remember that the last digit of her/his phone number is a *5*. Fortunately, the number is in your office database *people* and you **grep** for it like this:

> **grep** *'5 $' people*

The lines that are printed are only those that end in *5*. The dollar sign *$* means *end-of-line*, so this command asked for lines containing a *5* immediately followed by the *end-of-line*. Without the dollar sign, a line would match if a *5* appeared anywhere, not just at the end.

You also used single quotes ' instead of double quotes " around our pattern, because, among special characters, the dollar sign has an additional significance. The double quotes will not hide the special meaning of the dollar sign from the shell; you must use single quotes.

B7   **Reviewing the grep Command Structure**

To review what you have learned thus far, the **grep** command structure looks like this:

grep	*"regular expression"*	*filename(s)*

The regular expression can be either a word or a phrase, and it can contain regular expression characters (brackets, a period, asterisk, etc.). The regular expression is followed by the name(s) of the file(s) that **grep** will search.

The quotation marks around the regular expression instruct the shell to pass the enclosed material as an uninterpreted argument to **grep**.

Objective C
Using **grep** with Other Utilities

You can combine **grep** with other utilities by using a pipe |.

C1   **Accepting Standard Input**

Find out if a particular person is currently logged onto the system by using the following command line, replacing *bill* with a real user name on your system:

who | grep *bill*

In this situation, the output from the utility **who** becomes **grep**'s input.

The **who** command creates a data line for each person who is logged onto the system. That output is sent to **grep**, which searches through it looking for the specified character string. If the target string is found, that line is printed on the screen. If *bill* (or your selected name) is not logged in, **grep** will not print anything. You can determine if *bill* is logged on more than once by entering

who | grep *bill* **| wc -l**

In this command, **grep** outputs one line for each of *bill*'s logins. The **wc** utility counts the number of lines that it receives as input, hence the number of times *bill* is logged in.

C2   Because the fourth field output by **who** is the login time of each user, you can locate those people who logged on between 11:00AM and 11:59AM by typing in this command line:

who | grep *"11:[0-5][0-9]"*

The regular expression that is searched for is *11:* followed by any number between *0* and *5*, and that followed by any number between *0* and *9*.

The dash between the numbers in the brackets of **grep**'s regular expression allows a range of characters to be specified. The brackets allow only *one* character from the range to be matched at a time.

C3   Using **grep** as a Filter

The **grep** utility can be used with other utilities as an information filter. The following command line creates a sorted phone list for last names beginning with *A* to *M*. Enter

sort +2 *people* **| grep** "^.*[*A-Z*][*a-z*][*a-z*]*◊[*A-M*]" **>** *names.A-M*

This command says to **sort** the file *people* starting on the third field (last name), and redirect the output to **grep**.

The search elements of this command are:

^   each line that begins with:

.   any single character, followed by

*   any number (including zero) of additional characters, followed by

[*A-Z*][*a-z*]   one upper case letter followed by one lower case letter,

[*a-z*]*   followed by any number of lower case letters,

◊   followed by one space,

[*AM*]   followed by one capital from A through M.

The **grep** utility takes input from **sort** and searches for all lines that meet the stated search criteria. The output is redirected to a new file, called *names.A-M*.

C4   Examine the file *names.A-M.* It is sorted by name and has only those entries whose last names start with A through M.

18	Mark Calhoun	food service	work	415-999-2478
17	Mark Calhoun	human	home	415-999-1240
11	Mathew Clay	Human	home	415-999-1237
12	Mathew Clay	marketing	work	415-949-2478
13	Kevan Crockett	human	home	415-999-1238
14	Kevan Crockett	media critic	work	415-999-2478
16	Anne Foster	accountant	work	415-999-2478
15	Anne Foster	human	home	415-999-1239

Objective D
Using **grep** in an Alias

If you are using the C-Shell, the following is applicable.

Typing the **grep** command line each time you want to take advantage of its power can become repetitive. However, **alias**es can be used to keep your more frequently used **grep** commands handy.

D1   **Creating an Alias Using who and grep**

The following **alias**, *num*, tells you how many times *bill* is logged in. Enter

    alias *num* **'who | grep -c** *bill* **'**

D2   Now to see it work, enter:

    num

You get a number back, like 0 or 1; hopefully you don't get 2.

Typing *num* caused the associated commands to be executed. The results of **who** were sent to **grep**, which, because of the **-c** option, counted the number of lines containing the string *bill*.

D3 **Passing Information to grep**

The next **alias** is more complicated. It takes a user name as an argument and checks to see if that particular user is logged in. Enter

    alias *incheck* **'who | grep "\!*"'**

D4 To run it, enter (substituting your login name or any other for the string *your_login*):

    incheck *your_login*

A line for each time your selected name is logged in appears on the screen.

When the shell encounters the **alias** *incheck*, it expands it to the command line:

    who | grep "\!*"

The **\!*** in this line is the only thing that we haven't discussed. The shell replaces this string with all arguments entered on the command line. Thus, when you type:

    incheck *carlp*

the argument is *carlp*.

After the above command line is interpreted by the shell, it looks like this:

    who | grep " *carlp* **"**

If *carlp* is logged in, **who** will say so and **grep** will select that line for output.

Objective E

Comparing **grep**, **egrep** and **fgrep**

There are actually three members of the global regular expression print family: **grep**, **egrep** (extended **grep**), and **fgrep** (fast **grep**). The rest of this module examines the differences in how they are used.

The **grep** you've used thus far is the garden variety **grep**. Its sibling **fgrep** is much faster than either **grep** or **egrep**, but **fgrep** does not recognize any regular expressions. It takes everything quite literally.

On the other hand, **egrep** does recognize nearly all the regular expressions of **grep** as well as a few even more advanced. Plain old **grep** accepts one pattern at a time, and only from the command line.

Both **fgrep** and **egrep** allow more than one pattern (or regular expression in the case of **egrep**) to be specified per search, and can read a file for pattern lists.

E1   Searching for Multiple Patterns Stored in a File

In your travels with **grep** you looked for only one pattern at a time. What if you need to search for more than one pattern? This is where **fgrep** can be used. Suppose you want the names and numbers of all the consultants and tech writers in your database.

Create a file named *boss.words* containing the following two lines:

> *consultant*
> *tech writer*

E2   **Using a Pattern File with fgrep**

Enter the following command line:

fgrep -f *boss.words people*

The output is:

6	Peter Titus	consultant	work	415-999-2478
8	John Ramsey	consultant	work	415-999-2478
10	Peter Osbourne	tech writer	work	415-999-2478

The **-f** option tells **fgrep** to use the search strings from the file *boss.words*. Each line in the string file is a separate pattern, as though it were being searched for by a separate **fgrep** command. The **fgrep** utility then searches the file *people* for instances of the strings specified in the file *boss.words* and sends those lines that contain the specified strings as output.

E3   **Using a Pattern File with egrep**

The same result occurs with **egrep**. Enter

egrep -f *boss.words people*

In these commands the search patterns for **fgrep** and **egrep** were specified in a separate file that was referenced with the **-f** option. This option is available to **fgrep** and **egrep**, but not to plain old **grep**.

Objective F
Using Metacharacters with egrep and fgrep

F1   To examine the power of **fgrep** and **egrep** using metacharacters, create a new file called *literal* with the following contents:

[Hh]uman

F2   ## Attempting to Use Metacharacters with **fgrep**

To test **fgrep**'s special powers, enter the following command line:

fgrep -f *literal   people*

No lines are printed on the screen. The **fgrep** utility is literal, meaning that it does not search for regular expressions. So, it literally searched for lines containing a left bracket followed by *Hh*, a right bracket and *uman*. Since this string does not exist in *people*, you received no output.

F3   ## Using Metacharacters with **egrep**

Enter the same command using the **egrep** utility:

egrep -f *literal   people*

The output is:

3	Peter Titus	human	home	415-999-1234
5	John Ramsey	human	home	415-999-1235
7	Peter Osbourne	Human	home	415-999-1236
9	Mathew Clay	Human	home	415-999-1237
11	Kevan Crockett	human	home	415-999-1238
13	Anne Foster	human	home	415-999-1239
15	Mark Calhoun	human	home	415-999-1240
19	Jessica Ratliff	human	home	415-999-2356

This time, the output includes all lines from *people* that contain either *Human* or *human*.

Just as **fgrep** searches for multiple *patterns* in text files, **egrep** searches for multiple *regular expressions*.

F4   **Multiple Expressions with egrep**

Create a new file called *boss.exprs* and add the following two expressions:

> M.* C.* Human

The *M.* C.* means any line that contains an *M* followed by zero or more characters, a space, and a string that begins with *C*. The string *Human* contains no metacharacter, so it stands simply for itself.

F5   Now enter the following command line to search for lines from *people* that match either expression in *boss.exprs*:

> **egrep -f** *boss.exprs people*

The output is:

9	Peter Osbourne	Human	home	415-999-1236
11	Mathew Clay	Human	home	415-999-1237
12	Mathew Clay	marketing	work	415-999-2478
17	Mark Calhoun	human	home	415-999-1240
18	Mark Calhoun	food service	work	415-999-2478

The lines matching either regular expression are printed. Four of the five lines above had a word with an *M* followed by a word beginning with a *C*. Two of the above five lines had the word *Human*.

Even though both expressions tell **egrep** to take line *11*, only one copy of the line is printed.

F6   **Special Metacharacters with egrep**

With **egrep** also comes an expanded set of metacharacters for regular expressions. All of the previous regular expression metacharacters still apply except for one: **egrep** cannot handle the use of a *hyphen* - to specify a range of characters between brackets.

The following four metacharacters are new and are effective in **egrep** regular expressions only:

+   The plus character functions much as the asterisk ***** does. The **+** means *one or more* of the preceding characters.
Example: in the expression *xy+z*, the following strings are accepted:

   xyz   *xyyz*   *xyyyyyz*

and the following strings are not:

   xz   *xyaz*   *xayz*   *xzz*

?   The **?** means zero or one of the preceding character.
Example: the expression *V?*, means *match no V or one V*.

( ) The parentheses in regular expressions add quite a bit of power. They allow you to group any sub-expression within parentheses and then use metacharacters on that group that usually only apply to single characters. For instance, you can group the string *xy* together and then say, *one or more xy*s. The regular expression would look like this:

   (xy)+

Understand that this is completely different from the expression *xy+*, which only matches one or more *y*s.

Another example is the expression *(xy.)**, which says to match zero or more occurrences of an x followed by a y followed by any character. Strings accepted by this expression include:

   xya   *xyaxyT*   *xyXxyfxyf*   "" *(nothing)*

and strings rejected include:

   xy   *xxxxy*   *xxyy*   *xyaxy*   *abC*   *xyZabc*

| The pipe | is the *or* symbol, which can be used to separate two expressions as separate search patterns. The expressions on each side of the | are treated just like separate lines in an **egrep** file— both expressions are searched for. **Example:**

egrep [*Hh*]*uman*|[*Aa*]*nimal* people

will search for lines containing either the word *human* or the word *animal*, whether or not they are capitalized.

When you specify **egrep**'s regular expression on the command line, the *or* symbol comes in extra handy for separating the different sub-expressions for which to search. In the file, however, it's just as easy to use a new line.

F7   The following table gives a summary of the different capabilities that come with each variety of **grep**:

Capability	grep	egrep	fgrep
Command line pattern	Yes	Yes	Yes
Pattern in file	No	Yes	Yes
Multiple patterns	No	Yes	Yes
Strictly literal	No	No	Yes
Especially fast	No	No	Yes
Regular expressions	Yes	Yes	No
Extended regular expressions	No	Yes	No

Conclusion

You have completed your tour of **grep** country and are now able to search for explicitly defined (as well as more loosely defined) patterns from the standard input and from files. With **egrep** and **fgrep** you are able to search for more than one pattern at once. All three utilities can be used independently; they can also be used in pipelines as filters. The possible uses of these commands are almost endless. They will come to your rescue in countless situations.

Summary of **grep** Options	
OPTION	FUNCTION
-f	file: **egrep** accepts regular expression(s) and **fgrep** accepts search string(s) from the **file** that follows the -f option. **grep** does not recognize this option.
-v	reverse: instructs **grep** to print all lines that do *not* match the pattern.
-c	count: requests a count of the number of lines in the searched file(s) that contain a match.
-l	list: requests a list of the names of only the files (not the lines) that contain a match.
-n	number: requests that the total number of lines in searched file(s) that contain a match be printed on a separate line.

Appendix A

The following database should be entered in the file *people*:

LINE #	NAME	TYPE	WHERE	TELEPHONE #
2				
3	Lurnix	computer	home	415-999-2478
4	Lurnix	computer	work	415-999-9999
5	Peter Titus	human	home	415-999-1234
6	Peter Titus	consultant	work	415-999-2478
7	John Ramsey	human	home	415-999-1235
8	John Ramsey	consultant	work	415-999-2478
9	Peter Osbourne	Human	home	415-999-1236
10	Peter Osbourne	tech writer	work	415-999-2478
11	Mathew Clay	Human	home	415-999-1237
12	Mathew Clay	marketing	work	415-999-2478
13	Kevan Crockett	human	home	415-999-1238
14	Kevan Crockett	media critic	work	415-999-2478
15	Anne Foster	human	home	415-999-1239
16	Anne Foster	accountant	work	415-999-2478
17	Mark Calhoun	human	home	415-999-1240
18	Mark Calhoun	food service	work	415-999-2478
19	Jessica Ratliff	human	home	415-999-2356
20	Jessica Ratliff	data mgr	work	415-666-1337

Appendix B

The following database should be entered in the file *aliens*:

LINE #	NAME	WHERE	TELEPHONE NUMBER
2			
3	E. T.	home	111-898-653-2211
4	Paul Atreides	home	919-907-324-4671
5	Dora	computer	807-786-912-6870
6	The Mule	home	unknown
7	Chameleon	home	ever changing

Appendix C

The following program should be entered in the file *info* :

```
#!csh
#   THIS IS A C SHELL SCRIPT
#   DATE: 18 FEB 88

#   The who utility is run, output piped to grep looking for user logins.
#   A variable number is set to be the value of the output of wc.

set number = 'who | grep $USER | wc -l'

#   The number of logins is echoed to user

echo $USER you are logged on $number time(s).
```

Module 6

Database Report
Writing with awk

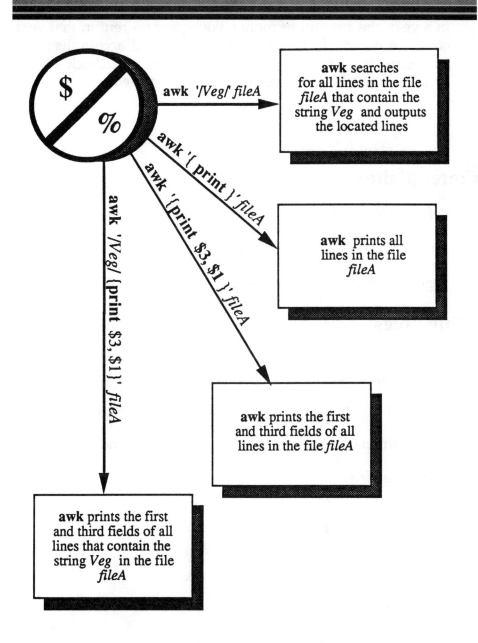

awk 'Veg/' fileA → **awk** searches for all lines in the file *fileA* that contain the string *Veg* and outputs the located lines

awk '{ print }' fileA → **awk** prints all lines in the file *fileA*

awk '{print $3, $1 }' fileA → **awk** prints the first and third fields of all lines in the file *fileA*

awk '/Veg/ {print $3, $1}' fileA → **awk** prints the first and third fields of all lines that contain the string *Veg* in the file *fileA*

Introduction

The **awk** utility is a powerful data manipulation programming language that allows you to select lines of input based on specified criteria, then to take certain actions on the data in those lines. For instance, if you had a file of all checks written in a year, the amount of money you spent on rent in that year could be determined using **awk**. You would accomplish this by instructing **awk** to select all records for rent check entries and then sum the amounts of these selected checks.

Prerequisites

Before beginning this module, you should be able to:

- use regular expressions (Module 4);

- globally Search and Print with **grep** (Module 5).

Objectives

After completing this module you will be able to use **awk** to:

- display and manipulate lines of input that match a pattern;

- perform mathematic operations on its input; and

- print reports.

Procedures

In this module you will use **awk** command lines, command files and database files to explore the power of **awk**.

Objective A
Creating and Defining a Simple Database File

The **awk** utility works on information arranged in a database file. This section defines a database file and its components.

A1   **Creating a Simple Database File**

Log onto your account and create a new directory, naming it *Awkward*. Change directories into *Awkward* and create a file called *groc_dbase* with the following content (also listed in Appendix A):

Carrots	veg	.39	1	n
Milk	Dairy	.89	2	n
Newsweek	Sundry	1.50	1	y
Cheese	Dairy	1.39	1	n
Sandwich	Deli	1.89	2	y
Onions	Veg	.29	6	n
Chicken	Meat	2.89	2	n
Fish	Meat	1.79	3	n
Floorwax	Hshld	2.65	1	y
Melon	Fruit	.98	3	n
Celery	Veg	.79	1	n
Napkins	Hshld	.49	6	y

A2 **Defining a Database File**

A database file is a file containing information about a number of items.

For example, the file you just created contains information about items on a grocery list. In database jargon, information that describes one item or object is called a *record*. The following record is the first line in the database file *groc_dbase*:

Carrots   veg   .39   1   n

This record includes five pieces of information relating to a particular item: the item's name, type, unit price, quantity and tax status. Database files are composed of individual records. Records consist of *fields*. A field contains one piece of information about the item.

The top line of the following chart lists the name of each field in the database file *groc_dbase*. The second line lists the value of each of these fields for the first record.

Name	Type	Unit Price	Quantity	Tax Status
Carrots	veg	.39	1	n

Both fields and records must be delimited. Each record must be separated from the next by a *record separator*. The default record separator is the new-line character so that each line of a file is considered to be one record.

In this database file each record contains five fields. Each field in a database file must be separated from its neighboring fields by a *field delimiter*. The default field delimiter for **awk** is one or more spaces or tabs. This example uses multiple spaces to line the fields up for easier reading. However, a single space or tab is sufficient.

Objective B
Understanding awk's Basic Usage

The **awk** utility works on input data in the form of a database file. In this section you will use several forms of the **awk** command to select and print records from the database file *groc_dbase*.

B1 ## Getting awk to Act Like grep

One common action performed on database input is to print all records containing a specified piece of information. This is exactly what the **grep** utility does.

To instruct **awk** to search through the file named *groc_dbase* and print all lines containing the string *Fish*, enter the following command line:

```
awk '/Fish/ {print}' groc_dbase
```

Every line in the file *groc_dbase* that contains the pattern *Fish* was selected and output. By default, the output is connected to the screen when no other destination is selected. This search and print action is one example of **awk**'s general function. It selects records from its input. The records are chosen based on certain criteria, then **awk** takes specific actions on the data in those lines.

The components of the command line you just entered are:

awk   Instructs the shell to execute the **awk** utility.

/Fish/   The "target string" or *pattern* part of the **awk** program is delimited by slashes. This is the

same as addresses for other utilities.

{print}   The action part of the program is enclosed in curly braces. The **print** statement is one of many actions available with the **awk** utility. Unless told otherwise, **print** outputs each entire record that contains the pattern (in this case, each record is a line).

' '   The single quotes around the **awk** program are necessary to prevent the shell from interpreting any special characters before the program is passed to **awk**.

groc_dbase   The name of the file that **awk** reads for its input.

B2   Examining the awk Command

The generic **awk** command is:

awk '*pattern {action}*' *filename*

Command		Pattern	Action		Input-file
awk	'	*/Fish/*	**{print}**	'	*groc_dbase*

The **awk** utility examines each line to determine if it matches the specified pattern. If the pattern matches, the specified action is performed on that line. After performing (or not performing) the action, the next line is checked and the cycle repeats.

B3   **Not Specifying the Action**

In the previous example you specified both the pattern for selection and the action to be taken. The pattern and the action are each optional, although one or the other *must* appear on every **awk** command line. For example, enter the command line:

> **awk** '/*Meat*/' *groc_dbase*

The **awk** utility selected every line from the data file that contains the pattern *Meat* and displayed those lines on the screen:

```
Chicken     Meat 2.89  2      n
Fish        Meat 1.79  3      n
```

The *default* action is print, so if you want **awk** to print the whole record you can simply not specify an action.

B4   **Not Specifying the Pattern**

There is also a default pattern that is invoked when none is specified.

Enter the command line:

> **awk** '{print}' *groc_dbase*

Without a pattern specified in a command line, every record (line) of the file *groc_dbase* is printed. If no pattern is included in the program, **awk** considers all records a match.

Thus far you have seen one type of pattern (simple string matching) and one type of action (printing the whole record). The **awk** utility can be used to select input based on more complex regular expressions, as well as logical and mathematical relations.

Objective C
Printing Specific Fields

In this section you will use **awk** to output specified fields from selected records.

C1 **Printing the First Field**

To print the first field of each record of the file *groc_dbase*, enter the following:

> **awk '{print $1}'** *groc_dbase*

The resulting output is the data in the first field of all records:

```
Carrots
Milk
Newsweek
Cheese
Sandwich
Onions
Chicken
Fish
Floorwax
Melon
Celery
Napkins
```

In this case, **awk** went through all the records in the file *groc_dbase* and output the first field of each.

Command		Pattern	Action		Input-file
awk	'		**{print $1}**	'	*groc_dbase*

Because no pattern was specified in the command line, **awk** examined all records in the file.

C2   **Selecting Several Fields**

You are not limited to printing just one field. It is also possible to print several specific fields. Enter the command line:

awk '{print $3 $1}' *groc_dbase*

The resulting output is the data in the third field and then the data in the first field from all records in the file *groc_dbase*:

```
.39Carrots
.89Milk
1.50Newsweek
1.39Cheese
1.89Sandwich
.29Onions
2.89Chicken
1.79Fish
2.65Floorwax
.98Melon
.79Celery
.49Napkins
```

C3   **Printing All Fields**

It is also possible to instruct **awk** explicitly to print all of the fields in a record. Enter the following command line:

awk '{print $0}' *groc_dbase*

The output includes the entire *groc_dbase* file. This same action could have been accomplished by including a **{print}** statement *without* the **$0** variable. The ability to request the printing of all fields explicitly is a useful feature in many circumstances.

C4   **Spacing the Output**

The output resulting from the above command line is cramped, with no spaces between the fields. Including commas solves the problem. Enter:

awk '{print $3, $1}' *groc_dbase*

Each comma instructs **print** to put in a blank space, so that the third field (now printed in the first column) is separated from the first field, printed in the second column:

> .39 Carrots
> .89 Milk
> 1.50 Newsweek
> 1.39 Cheese
> 1.89 Sandwich
> .29 Onions
> 2.89 Chicken
> 1.79 Fish
> 2.65 Floorwax
> .98 Melon
> .79 Celery
> .49 Napkins

C5   **Using Predefined Variables**

The command lines you just used included **awk** variables. A variable is a name for which a value can be assigned. In the example above, $1 is assigned to whatever value is in a record's first field. Likewise, $2 represents the value in the second field, $3 the third field, etc. As you have seen, $0 represents the entire record. Because **awk** is programmed to recognize these as variable names associated with a specific value, they are *preset* variables or *predefined* variables. In addition to using preset variables, you will soon create your own variables.

C6 **Selecting Specific Records**

With **awk** you can use most of the regular expressions that are used with other utilities to specify selection of records.

C7 **Selecting lines by field value**

The **awk** utility can be instructed to make selections within records based on the value in a field. Enter the following:

>   **awk '***$3** == **2.65***' groc_dbase*

This command instructs **awk** to print all records for which the value of the third field is exactly 2.65. The == is the relational "equal to" operator.

C8 Conditions other than equality can also be tested.

Enter the following:

>   **awk '***$3** < **2.65***' groc_dbase*

All records that have a value in the third field less than 2.65 are selected. The < is the relational "less than" operator.

C9 **Selecting lines ignoring case**

Regular expression syntax is understood by **awk**. Enter the following:

>   **awk '***/[Vv]eg/* {**print**}*' groc_dbase*

The following output is produced:

Carrots	veg	.39	1	n
Onions	Veg	.29	6	n
Celery	Veg	.79	1	n

The pattern /[*Vv*]*eg*/ refers to both *Veg* and *veg,* so lines containing either string are selected.

Objective D
Creating and Using **awk** Command Files

Thus far you have entered all **awk** commands from the shell command line. In this section you will create a file that contains an **awk** program, and then enter a shell command to have **awk** read the file for its program.

D1 Creating a Command File

The first step in using **awk** with a program file is to create an ordinary file containing the instructions to be followed. Use an editor to create a file called *print_dairy* that contains the following line:

```
/Dairy/ {print $1, $3}
```

The components of this command are:

Command		Pattern	Action		Input-file
		IDairyl	{print $ *1,* $*3*}		

When the program is not called from the command line but from inside a *command file,* you do not include the command (**awk**), nor surround the program with single quotes, nor include an input-file as you must when entering the program from the command line.

D2   **Executing a Command File**

To run the program, enter the following command line from the shell:

awk -f *print_dairy groc_dbase*

The output from this program is the first and third fields from all records in *groc_dbase* that contain the string *Dairy*. The results are exactly the same as if you had entered:

awk *'/Dairy/* **{print $1, $3}'** *groc_dbase*

Command files are a less transient way of accomplishing the same functions as command lines. Command files are just text files read by **awk**; they are not executable files.

The components of this command line are:

awk -f   The **-f** is the **awk** option that tells **awk** to read a file for its program.

print_dairy   The filename argument immediately follows the **-f** option, indicating which file **awk** should read for instructions.

groc_dbase   The instructions that **awk** read in the file *print_dairy* are applied to the input file *groc_dbase*.

Keeping **awk** programs inside files, rather than entering them from the command line, is particularly useful as the programs become longer and the risk of mistyping increases. Command files also make it possible to run the same **awk** command over and over, and to keep a record of what commands you have run.

D3   **Selecting lines by position**

Another way of selecting records in a database is not by content, but rather by position in the database.

Create a new command file named *findNR* and include the following **awk** command:

```
NR == 6 { print }
```

Have **awk** run the program on *groc_dbase* with the command line:

```
awk -f findNR groc_dbase
```

The following output results:

```
.   Onions    Veg        .29  6    n
```

Examining the file *groc_dbase* reveals that the line selected is the sixth line, the sixth record in the file.

Earlier in this module you used some of the **awk** predefined variables including *$0, $1, $2,* etc. The variable *NR* is another predefined variable recognized by **awk**, and its value is the Number of the Record currently being processed.

Because the notation **==** is the relational "equal to" operator, *NR* == *6* translates to: *if the current record is the 6th record*.

The whole program means: *if the current record is the 6th record, then perform the specified action (in this case, **print**).*

Objective E
Improving Program Readability

In this section, you will make your **awk** programs easier for a human reader to understand.

E1   **Formatting awk Program Files**

The **awk** utility has syntax rules that must be followed so that **awk** will interpret your programs correctly. These rules specify to a certain extent how your **awk** programs are to be laid out. For example, **awk** syntax requires that action statements be surrounded by curly braces.

Within the constraints imposed by these syntax rules, you have considerable freedom in formatting the code in a command file. For example, **awk** ignores multiple spaces and tabs in most situations. Good programmers take advantage of this freedom to make programs easier for human readers to understand.

As an example, compare the following ugly piece of code:

```
/Dairy/{print $1,$3}
```

with the following easier to read version:

```
/Dairy/ {
        print $1,  $3
        }
```

These two pieces of code will produce the same results, yet programs written in the form of the second example are much easier to read and modify. The formatting suggestion illustrated by this example is that each action associated with a given pattern (condition) should be on a line by itself using multiple spaces to indent the action(s).

In this example, the pattern */Dairy/* was followed by the open-ing curly brace on the *same line* to associate the following action(s) with the pattern. This is necessary because a pattern on a line by itself signals **awk**'s default action, which is to print the whole record if the pattern is present.

Modify your *print_dairy* program so that it looks like:

```
/Dairy/ {
      print $1, $3
      }
```

To verify that it performs identically, run the modified pro-gram again:

```
awk -f print_dairy groc_dbase
```

E2   Improving Readability with Variables

You have been using predefined **awk** variables as you have been completing this module. You can also define your own variables in the **awk** language. One of the important uses of user-defined variables in **awk** is improving program readabil-ity.

For example, copy the file *print_dairy* into another file called *print_dairy2* and modify it so that it reads as follows. Arrows indicate changed lines.

```
/Dairy/ {
               name = $1    ←
               price = $3    ←
               print name, price    ←

      }
```

Run this program by entering:

> **awk -f** *print_dairy groc_dbase*

The only new piece of syntax in this example is the =, which is **awk**'s *assignment* operator. It assigns to the variable on its left the value of the expression on its right.

In this example, the variable name is being assigned the value of the first field (*$1*); the variable price is being assigned the value of the second (*$2*). The print statement simply calls for printing the contents of these two variables. Using variables makes this program much easier to understand.

The value assigned to the variable on the left can be a predefined variable as in this example (*$1*), a constant, a user-defined variable or and arithmetic statement. This example also demonstrates that multiple actions can be specified by simply listing them, one per line, in a group that is surrounded (delimited) by curly braces.

Compare the new version of the program:

```
/Dairy/ {
          name = $1
          price = $3
          print name, price
     }
```

with the one written earlier that accomplishes the same thing:

```
/Dairy/ {print $1, $3}
```

Although the original version is shorter, it is harder to read. Using variable names such as *name* and *price* tells you at a glance what the program does. Variable names in **awk** are arbitrary names that *you* choose. Choose names that make sense— to assign the value held by *$1* to a variable called *x* would not be a marked improvement.

E3 **Including Words in Print Statements**

Thus far you have been using **awk**'s **print** statement to print the value of variables (either predefined or user-defined). You can also print one or more regular words. For example, clarity is improved by including a line like the following for each record in your *groc_dbase* file:

    cost is #.##

(where #.## is the item's price)

Create a file called *quoting* that contains the following lines.

```
{
        price = $3
        print cost is price
}
```

Run this program by entering the following:

    awk -f *quoting groc_dbase*

All that **awk** output was the contents of field 3. It did not print the phrase *cost is*. Within a **print** statement, **awk** assumes that all character strings are *variables* to be evaluated.

Thus, **awk** attempted to find the current value of the variables *cost* and *is* and to display their values. Because only *price* was actually a variable with an assigned value, its value was the only one printed for each record.

Quotation marks are the key to determining whether a string of characters should be interpreted as a variable or as a literal string.

E4   **Quoting Words Within Print Statements**

To print the words instead of multiple nothings, modify your file *quoting* to be:

```
{
        price = $3
        print "cost is " price     ←
                      ◊
}
```

For readability, a space, indicated by a diamond ◊, is included following the phrase. The output reads *cost is* 3.49, rather than reading *cost is*3.49. Run the program by entering:

awk -f *quoting groc_dbase*

E5   **Using Variable Names as Words**

With **awk** literals are enclosed in quotation marks, but variables are not. For example, enter:

awk '{*item* = **$1; print** *item*, *item*}' *groc_dbase*

Examine the output.

As demonstrated in this example, you can include multiple actions on a single **awk** command line by separating the actions with semi-colons. The output of this command simply prints the value of the variable *item* twice for each record.

E6   To print the string, enter:

awk '{*item* = **$1; print** "*item* ", *item*}' *groc_dbase*
                              ◊

The comma follows the quotation marks, so that the phrase *item*, enclosed in quotes, is separated from the variable *item*.

The output has the word item followed by the contents of the variable *item*. In the first case, the variable *item* was set equal to the value in field 1. The action statement then requested printing of this variable twice. In the second example, the variable name was quoted, which resulted in the literal string *item* being printed.

> The **print** statement prints whatever is enclosed in double quotes (") whether a sentence or even a single character. If a string of characters is not in quotes, **awk** treats the string as a variable to be evaluated.

Objective F
Performing Arithmetic Operations

Thus far you have selected records, printed specified fields and assigned values to variables. In this section you will use **awk** to perform arithmetic operations on fields and variables.

F1   Subtracting a Constant from a Numeric Field

Suppose that your supermarket is having a 10 cents off sale on all items. You could display a version of your grocery list with the prices of all items reduced by 10 cents. To accomplish this, create a command file called *sale* containing the program:

```
{
        print $1, $2, $3 - .10, $4, $5
}
```

Note that you do not quote the .10. When **awk** encounters a number, it interprets the number as a variable with a value set equal to itself.

Run the *sale* program on your *groc_dbase* file by entering:

awk -f *sale groc_dbase*

The output is your database file with all prices reduced by 10 cents:

```
Carrots veg 0.29 1 n
Milk Dairy 0.79 2 n
Newsweek Sundry 1.40 1 y
Cheese Dairy 1.29 1 n
Sandwich Deli 1.79 2 y
Onions Veg 0.19 6 n
Chicken Meat 2.79 2 n
Fish Meat 1.69 3 n
Floorwax Hshld 2.55 1 y
Melon Fruit 0.88 3 n
Celery Veg 0.69 1 n
Napkins Hshld 0.39 6 y
```

The program read the value of field three, subtracted 0.10, and printed the result.

The - (hyphen) is **awk**'s subtraction operator. You have just used this operator to subtract a constant from a field variable within a print statement.

F2   Create another **awk** command file to reduce prices by thirty five cents and run it on the *groc_dbase* file.

F3   **Subtracting a Constant from a Variable**

User-defined variables could improve this program's readability.

Modify your *sale* program to read:

```
{
        name = $1    ←
        type = $2    ←
        price = $3    ←
        quantity = $4    ←
        taxable = $5    ←
        print name, type, price - .10, quantity, taxable    ←
}
```

Run this program on the *groc_dbase* file by entering:

awk -f *sale groc_dbase*

The program first set the value of a new variable *price* equal to the value in field *3*. In the print statement, the value of the *price* variable was reduced by 10 cents before printing. The print subtracted a constant from the variable.

The subtraction operator can be used within a print statement to subtract a constant from either a predefined or user-defined variable.

F4   **Subtracting One Variable from Another**

It is good programming practice to assign constants to user-defined variables for the same reason that it is best to assign fields to user-defined variables: assignment makes their meaning more apparent.

Modify your *sale* program to read:

```
{
        name = $1
        type = $2
        price = $3
        quantity = $4
        taxable = $5
        sale = .10    ←
        print name, type, price - sale, quantity, taxable    ←
}
```

Run this program by entering:

awk -f *sale groc_dbase*

In this version a new user-defined variable is added—*sale*. This variable is given a value, which can be easily changed as the store manager grows more desperate. The sales prices are now accomplished by subtracting one variable from another.

The subtraction operator can be used within a print statement to subtract one variable (even user-defined) from another variable.

F5 Using Subtraction in a Variable Assignment

Performing mathematical operations outside of print statements also improves program readability. Modify your *sale*
program to read:

```
{
        name = $1
        type = $2
        price = $3
        quantity = $4
        taxable = $5
        sale = .10

        saleprice = price - sale      ←

        print name, type, saleprice, quantity, taxable     ←
}
```

In this case, the subtraction is accomplished by creating a new
user-defined variable, *saleprice,* which is given the value of the
price variable minus the *sale* variable.

Now run this program on *groc_dbase*:

awk -f *sale groc_dbase*

The subtraction operator can be used within a print statement
or within a variable assignment.

F6 **Using Addition in a Variable Assignment**

So much for fantasizing about sales. The manager decides that inflationary trends must be aided by raising all prices by 10 cents. Your goal is to display a version of your shopping list database file with the prices of all items raised by 10 cents.

Create a new command file named *inflation* containing the following program:

```
{
        name = $1
        type = $2
        price = $3
        quantity = $4
        taxable = $5
        inflation = .10     ←

        newprice = price + inflation    ←

        print name, type, newprice, quantity, taxable    ←
}
```

Now run this program on *groc_dbase*:

awk -f *inflation groc_dbase*

The **+** is **awk**'s addition operator. Like the subtraction operator, this operator can also be used to add a variable to another variable or a constant, within both print statements and variable assignments.

F7   Multiplying Two Values

The total price spent on each item can be computed by multiplying the unit price by the quantity. To get the product of these two fields, create a new program named *total* containing the following lines:

```
{
        name = $1
        price = $3
        quantity = $4

        total = price * quantity

        print name, total
}
```

Run this program on your *groc_dbase* file:

awk -f *total groc_dbase*

Each item's name and total price are output. The * (asterisk) is **awk**'s multiplication operator.

Like the addition and subtraction operators, the multiplication operator * can be used to multiply a variable by another variable or a constant, within both print statements and variable assignments.

F8   **Dividing One Value by Another**

Returning to fantasy land, suppose that the store manager decides to cut all prices in half. To get the result of dividing the unit price (field 3) by 2, modify your *sale* program to read:

```
{
        name = $1
        price = $3

        saleprice = price / 2    ←

        print name, saleprice    ←
}
```

Run this division program on your *groc_dbase* file by entering:

awk -f *sale groc_dbase*

Each item's name and newly halved price should be displayed on your screen:

```
Carrots  0.195
Milk  0.445
Newsweek  0.75
Cheese  0.695
Sandwich  0.945
Onions  0.145
Chicken  1.445
Fish  0.895
Floorwax  1.325
Melon  0.49
Celery  0.395
Napkins  0.245
```

> The division operator in **awk** is the / character. Like the other operators, the / operator can be used to divide a variable by another variable or a constant, within both print statements and variable assignments.

F9   ## Keeping a Running Total

In many situations keeping track of the total of all items selected is useful. One way of accomplishing this goal would be to print out each item's name, the total amount of money spent on this item (price * quantity purchased), followed by a running total of the total amount spent up to and including that item.

Create a new file called *running* and enter the following program:

```
{
        name = $1
        price = $3
        quantity = $4      ←

        total = price * quantity     ←
        running = running + total     ←

        print name, total, running     ←
}
```

Run this program using:

awk -f *running groc_dbase*

The output includes one line for each item with the item's name, total cost (price times quantity purchased), and the current running total:

```
Carrots  0.39  0.39
Milk  1.78  2.17
Newsweek  1.50  3.67
Cheese  1.39  5.06
Sandwich  3.78  8.84
Onions  1.74  10.58
Chicken  5.78  16.36
Fish  5.37  21.73
Floorwax  2.65  24.38
Melon  2.94  27.32
Celery  0.79  28.11
Napkins  2.94  31.05
```

F10 Examining How a Running Total Is Accumulated

The line

```
running = running + total
```

keeps the running total.

When **awk** processes the very first record, the variable *running* is created. A new variable has the value zero at the time of its creation; therefore, this statement reads: *create a new variable, and assign to it the sum of zero plus the value of total.*

When the program processes the next record, the variable *running* now has a non-zero value, so the statement now translates: *assign to the variable running the sum of its present value plus the value of total.* This process continues until the file ends and there are no more records to process. The value in *running* increases as each *total* is added.

F11 **Adding and Assigning in One Step**

There is a simple shortcut for accumulating a running total as the value of a variable. Open your file *running* and locate the line:

    running = running + total

Change it to read:

    running += total

Save the file and run it again with:

    awk -f *running groc_dbase*

The result is the same.

The operator **+=** means: take the value held by the variable on the left, add to it the value specified on the right, and assign the result of the sum to the variable on the left.

Thus, **a** = **a** + *1* is equivalent to **a** += *1*.

Objective G
Using the **printf** Function to Format Output

Thus far you have used **print** to output data. The **awk** utility has another function borrowed from the C programming language, named **printf**, which can also be used to print output. The **printf** command gives the programmer much more control over the final result.

G1 **Printing strings**

Create a new command file called *taxes* and include the following:

```
$5 == "y" { price = $3;
                taxedprice = price + price * .065;
                printf "%s %s\n", $1, taxedprice
         }
```

Run this tax calculating program by entering:

awk -f *taxes groc_dbase*

The output is:

```
Newsweek 1.5975
Sandwich 2.01285
Floorwax 2.82225
Napkins 0.52185
```

The program selects all records with a "*y*" in field five indicating that the item is taxable. It then calculates a *taxedprice* equal to *price* plus 6 1/2 percent of *price*.

The new construct is the **printf** statement containing the following elements:

printf "%s %s\n", $1, taxedprice

printf   The formatting statement begins with **printf**.

"%s %s\n",   These symbols enclosed in double quotes are the *format* string. These format specifiers tell **printf** how to format the output. Every variable to be printed must have a format specification. The percent sign (%) is a place holder for the variables that are named later. Whenever there is a percent sign in **printf**'s format string, **printf** expects to put a variable in there. The **s** for **s**tring, informs **printf** that the variable value should be printed as a string of characters. The **\n** at the end of the format specification tells **printf** to print a new line at that position. Unlike the **print** statement, **printf** does not produce new lines automatically— you have to tell it to do so.

$1, *taxedprice*   Data from the two variable names listed will be formatted by this **printf** statement.

This statement produces output identical to the regular **print** statement.

G2 Right Justifying the Output

Open the file *taxes* again and modify it so the **printf** statement reads:

```
printf "%20s %10s\n", $1, taxedprice
```

Run the program again.

The output has been formatted differently:

Newsweek	1.5975
Sandwich	2.01285
Floorwax	2.82225
Napkins	0.52185

The **20** in front of the **s** instructs **printf** to assign 20 spaces for the output of the variable in question (**$1**) and to right justify it (that is, to flush it against the 20th position). The **10** instructs it to right justify *taxedprice* at 10 spaces.

G3   **Aligning the Decimal**

Although the above output is better than before, it is still not correct. The prices are not arranged according to the decimal point.

Open the command file *taxes* again and change the format line so that it now reads:

>   printf "%20s %10f\n", $1, taxedprice

Run the new program again. The output is:

>   Newsweek   1.5975
>   Sandwich   2.01285
>   Floorwax   2.82225
>   Napkins   0.52185

By changing **10s** into **10f** you are instructing **printf** to print the variable *taxedprice* as a floating point numeral, which results in a much better alignment.

G4   **Truncating Numbers**

To keep the prices to just dollars and cents, modify the file so that now the formatting line says:

>   printf "%20s %10.2f\n", $1, taxedprice

Run the tax calculating program again.

The output is:

>   Newsweek   1.60
>   Sandwich   2.01
>   Floorwax   2.82
>   Napkins   0.52

By adding **.2** before the **f** we are instructing **printf** to print the floating point number with a precision of only two decimal places.

G5   **Left Justifying the Output**

The output would look much better if it were left justified instead of right justified.

Modify the file *taxes* once again, and make the format line read:

```
printf "%-20s %-10.2f\n", $1, taxedprice
```

Run it again; the output now is:

```
        Newsweek    1.60
        Sandwich    2.01
        Floorwax    2.82
        Napkins     0.52
```

The - in front of the specification instructs **printf** to left justify, that is, to start its output at the first position of the field, rather than to flush it against the last space.

For a quick reference guide to the **printf** commands we have used, look at the *Command Summary* of **awk** *Printing Commands* at the end of this module.

Objective H
Using the BEGIN and END Patterns

The **awk** utility begins its processing of a data file by scanning each line in sequence for a specified pattern and performing the requested action on the lines that contain the pattern. It is often desirable to perform some actions before and/or after the lines of a data file are processed. The special patterns **BEGIN** and **END** allow **awk** to deal with these particular situations.

H1   ## Using BEGIN in a Command File

Modify the file *running* so that it now reads:

```
BEGIN {    ←
        print "The running totals are: "    ←
        }    ←                            ◊

{

        name = $1
        price = $3
        quantity = $4

        total = price * quantity
        running += total

        print name, total, running
}
```

Run this program using:

> **awk -f** *running groc_dbase*

The line that contains the **BEGIN** statement instructs **awk** to execute the instructions that immediately follow it before even looking at the contents of the file *groc_dbase*. Only after printing the quoted sentence does **awk** do the normal processing of the records according to the instructions. The word **BEGIN** *must* be followed by an opening curly brace ({) on the same line.

H2 Using the Special Pattern END in a Program

Generally reports include totals after all records are evaluated. Modify the program *running* so that it now reads:

```
BEGIN {
      print "The name and price for each of your items is: "    ←
                                                           ◊
      }

      {

            name = $1
            price = $3
            quantity = $4

            total = price * quantity
            sum += total

            print name, total    ←
      }

      END {
            print "the total cost of all items is: " sum    ←
                                              ◊
            }
```

As in the case of **BEGIN,** the word **END** *must* be followed by an opening curly brace ({) in the same line.

Now run this program using:

awk -f *running groc_dbase*

This program is identical to the previous one except that the running total is not printed as each line is processed, but instead is printed following all record processing. Because no pattern is specified with the action that accumulates the running total (*running* **+=** *total*), this action is performed as every line is processed. After all lines have been processed, the **END** pattern is matched and its associated action, printing the running total, is performed.

Objective I
Changing the Field Separator

In this module, **awk** has been used only on files with fields separated by either spaces or tabs (white space), which is **awk**'s default field separator. There are many files, such as the */etc/passwd* file, where the fields are separated by a different character. In the case of the */etc/passwd* file the field delimiter is a colon.

I1   Attempt to print the first field of the first record of the file */etc/passwd* with the following:

> **awk 'NR == 1 {print $1}'** */etc/passwd*

The whole first record, not field, was printed.

The delimiter, or field separator, for the **awk** utility is, by default, set to one or more spaces, or the tab. Therefore, the **awk** utility does not recognize the colon as a field separator. In the command line, a different field separator can be indicated by using the **-F** option; command files use the predefined variable *FS*, for **F**ield **S**eparator, to indicate that the delimiter is neither of the default delimiters but is another character.

I2   To indicate a new field separator from the command line, enter:

awk -F: 'NR == 1 {print $1}' */etc/passwd*

Only the first field of the first record of the file */etc/passwd* was output, because the **-F:** specification instructed **awk** to recognize the colon (**:**) as the **F**ield separator in the input file.

I3   You can also use the **-F** option from the command line when the **awk** program is included in a file. Create a new file called *first.field* and enter in it:

NR == 1 { print $1 }

I4   Now run it on */etc/passwd*:

awk -F: -f *first.field /etc/passwd*

The result is the same as running the whole command from the command line. This is very useful when you have an **awk** program that you want to run on various kinds of files with different field separators. You can specify the separator as you enter the command.

I5   **Specifying Field Separators in Command Files**

When you have an **awk** program designed to work specifically on files whose field separator is other than the default, it is easier to specify the separator in the program itself.

I6   Create a file *who_where*. Enter the following program:

```
BEGIN { FS = ":" }
{ printf "%-14s %-10s %-10s %s\n", $1, $3, $4, $6 }
```

The program can examine the */etc/passwd* file and print the login names of the users in the system, their user ID's, their group ID's and their home directories.

Enter the following command line:

> **awk -f** *who_where /etc/passwd*

The */etc/passwd* file has its fields separated by colons.

Objective J
Redirecting awk's Output and Input

Thus far, you have been using **awk** as a database tool. You have always instructed **awk** to get its input from files and to direct its output to the screen. In this section you will redirect **awk**'s output to files and use **awk** as a filter between other utilities.

J1   **Redirecting Output**

To redirect **awk**'s output to a file, enter:

> **awk** *'/Meat/* **{print}'** *groc_dbase* **>** *meat.db*

This new file contains all the lines of the file *groc_dbase* where the pattern *Meat* was present. If you are using a Berkeley system, examine *meat.db* with the carnivore rally cry:

> **more** *meat.db*

Or even more offensively, on any system enter:

cat *meat.db*

J2   Obtaining Input from Other Utilities

If no filename is specified, **awk** takes its input from standard input. For example, enter:

sort *groc_dbase* | **awk** '*/Veg/* {**print**}'

The output will be:

| Celery | Veg | .79 | 1 | n |
| Onions | Veg | .29 | 6 | n |

In this case, **sort** sorted the lines of *groc_dbase* alphabetically and sent them to standard output, which was connected to the input of **awk**. Hence **awk** received sorted data, found the appropriate lines and printed them.

J3   Exploring a Command That Begs for awk's Help

The UNIX system provides a very useful system administration utility called **df** (for **d**isk **f**ree). This utility is discussed more fully in System Administration books. For now, what you need to know is that **df**, with its **-t** option, displays information about file systems, including their names and total sizes, in blocks (think of a block as a fixed size chunk of disk). Berkeley users should note that you should use **df** by itself (without the **-t** option). For that reason, we have prepared two scripts with the same purpose. Please use the one that is compatible with your system.

System V users enter the command:

> **df -t**

Berkeley users enter:

> **df**

System V users pay particular attention to the lines that look something like the following:

> total: 13566 blocks   1904 i-nodes

Berkeley users pay particular attention to the column labeled kbytes.

J4   Creating a System Administration Tool

It is useful to select each of these totals, add up the number of blocks in each file system and multiply this total by the appropriate size of each block, yielding the total number of characters (bytes) on your system.

System V Users: Create an **awk** command file named *total* and enter the following lines into it:

```
BEGIN {
     blocksize = 512
     }

/total:/ {
     blocks += $2
     }

END {
     bytes = blocks * blocksize
     print "the total amount of disk space on your system is: " bytes
     }
```

Now enter the command:

df -t | awk -f *total*

This command line uses **df -t** to produce file system information, which is piped to **awk**. From this input **awk** examines all lines. The second field of each of these lines is accumulated in a variable named *blocks*. After all lines are processed, the value of *total* is multiplied by *blocksize* to yield the total number of characters (bytes) on your system.

Berkeley Users: Create an **awk** command file named *total* and enter the following lines into it:

```
BEGIN {
      blocksize = 1024
      }
{
blocks += $2
}

END {
      bytes = blocks * blocksize
      print "the total amount of disk space on your system is: " bytes
      }
```
◊

Now enter the command:

df | awk -f *total*

This command line takes the file system information output by **df** and pipes it to **awk**. A variable named *blocks* is used to keep a running total of the value of the second field from each line of input. After all lines are processed, the value of *total* is multiplied by *blocksize*, yielding the total number of characters (bytes) on the system.

This command is just one example of how **awk** can be used as a system administration tool.

Conclusion

You can now use **awk** to select lines of input and to perform actions on the selected lines. As you have seen, **awk** is useful for manipulating databases and creating tools. While there is certainly more to learn about this powerful utility, you are now well on your way to being an **awk** guru. Attached to this module are three charts summarizing the **awk** commands, operators and variables you have encountered.

Summary of **awk** Commands

COMMAND

-f *filename* When used in the command line, instructs **awk** to look for its program in the file *filename*.

'   ' When used in the command line, delimits the **awk** program and prevents interpretation by the shell.

/pattern/ Instructs **awk** to look for *pattern* in the current record and to perform the specified action(s). Practically any pattern recognized by **sed** or **grep** is recognized by **awk**.

/pattern|pattern/ Same as above, but because of the pipe (|) separating them either of the two patterns mentioned will trigger the specified action(s).

{ Begin a block of actions.

} End a block of actions.

; Separate two actions within a block.

BEGIN Instructs **awk** to perform the following block of actions before processing the database.

END Instructs **awk** to perform the following block of actions after processing the database.

Summary of **awk** Operators		
Type of Operator	Operators	Function
Logical	*a || b*	Evaluates to true if either *a* or *b* is true.
	a && b	Evaluates to true if both *a* and *b* are true.
	! *a*	Evaluates to true if *a* is not true.
Assignment	*a = b*	Assigns to *a* the value held by *b*.
	a += b	Assigns to *a* the value that results from adding the value of *b* to the value of *a*.
Arithmetic	+	Addition operator.
	-	Subtraction operator.
	*	Multiplication operator.
	/	Division operator.
Relations	*a == b*	Evaluates to true if *a* equals *b*.
	a < b	Evaluates to true if *a* is less than *b*.
	a > b	Evaluates to true if *a* is larger than *b*.

Summary of **awk** Predefined Variables

VARIABLE FUNCTION

$#** The value of **$# is the content of the #th field of the current record.

$0 The value of **$0** is the content of all the fields of the current record.

NF The value of **NF** is the number of fields in the current record.

NR The value of **NR** is the record number of the current record.

FS The value of **FS** is the value of the field separator; default separators (delimiters) are one or more spaces, or a tab.

RS The value of **RS** is the value of the record separator; the default is a new line.

Summary of **awk** Printing Commands

COMMAND	FUNCTION
print *variable*	Prints the value held by *variable*, (for example, *cost*) followed by a new line.
print "*string*"	Prints the string enclosed by the double quotes, followed by a new line.
print *variable1, variable2*	Prints *variable1* and *variable2* separated by a blank space (for example, *price quantity*) followed by a new line.
printf "*string*"	Prints the string enclosed by the double quotes.
printf "\t*string*\n"	Prints the string enclosed by the double quotes, preceded by a tab and followed by a new line.
printf "*string* %s\n" , *variable*	Prints the string enclosed by the double quotes: includes replacing % with the value held by *variable*, and starting a new line.
printf "%10s" , *variable*	Prints the value held by *variable*, right adjusted to 10 spaces.
printf "%-10s" , *variable*	Prints the value held by *variable*, left adjusted to 10 spaces.

Summary of **awk** Predefined Variables
(continued)

VARIABLE	FUNCTION
printf "%20f" , *variable*	Prints the value of *variable* as a floating point number, right adjusted to the 20th space.
printf "%20.2f" , *variable*	Prints the value of *variable* as a floating point number, rounded to the second decimal point, right adjusted to the 20th space.

Appendix A

The following database should be entered in the file
groc_dbase:

Carrots	veg	.39	1	n
Milk	Dairy	.89	2	n
Newsweek	Sundry	1.50	1	y
Cheese	Dairy	1.39	1	n
Sandwich	Deli	1.89	2	y
Onions	Veg	.29	6	n
Chicken	Meat	2.89	2	n
Fish	Meat	1.79	3	n
Floorwax	Hshld	2.65	1	y
Melon	Fruit	.98	3	n
Celery	Veg	.79	1	n
Napkins	Hshld	.49	6	y

Module 7

Stream Editing with sed

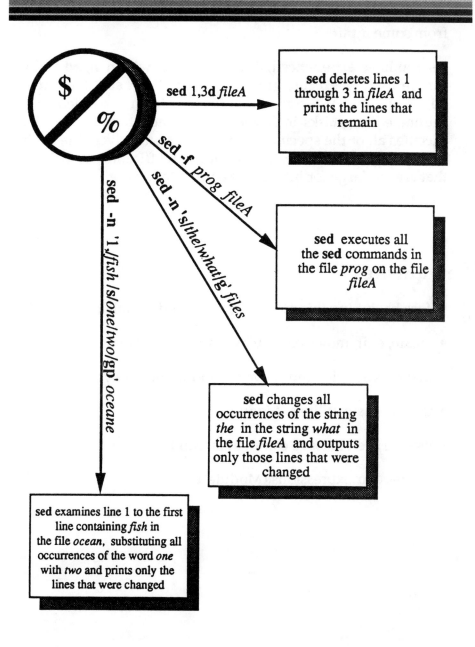

sed 1,3d *fileA*

sed deletes lines 1 through 3 in *fileA* and prints the lines that remain

sed -f *prog fileA*

sed executes all the **sed** commands in the file *prog* on the file *fileA*

sed -n 's/the/what/g' *files*

sed changes all occurrences of the string *the* in the string *what* in the file *fileA* and outputs only those lines that were changed

sed -n '1,/fish/s/one/two/gp' *oceane*

sed examines line 1 to the first line containing *fish* in the file *ocean*, substituting all occurrences of the word *one* with *two* and prints only the lines that were changed

Introduction

With most editors you interactively give a command, observe its results, then issue the next command. There are occasions, however, when seeing the result of each command is not necessary; for example, if you want to delete all blank lines from some input.

As you have experienced, line commands within **vi**, **ed** and **ex** can be used to execute global changes. With **sed**, the **stream editor**, you can use commands to execute an expanded set of routine editing tasks in fewer steps. In addition, because **sed** executes all of the specified editing tasks on a given line before continuing on to the next, you can use it efficiently to edit files that are too large for interactive editors to handle.

Prerequisites

Before beginning this module, you should be able to:

- create, edit, move, copy, view and remove files;

- make directories and move around in the file system;

- use the basic utilities (Module 2);

- use the shell to issue commands (Module 3), and;

- use regular expressions (Module 4).

Objective

After completing this module you will be able to:

- use **sed** commands to edit input; and

- use files containing **sed** commands to execute many editing changes at one time.

Procedures

In this section you will use several **sed** commands. Before using **sed** you will need to create several data files on which to practice and a directory in which to work.

Objective A
Creating Example Files

A1   Create a new directory named something like *Sed_riting* with the command:

   mkdir *Sed_riting*

This is the directory you will use to store your **sed** data and command files.

A2   Make *Sed_riting* your current directory with the command:

   cd *Sed_riting*

For the exercises in this module you will be using the files *records* and *gdbase*. Use your favorite editor to create these files using Appendices A and B as references.

Objective B
Using Line Addresses to Edit

All lines in files are numbered and can be identified by the line number.

B1   Deleting a Line by Number

The file named *gdbase* contains 12 lines of text. To have **sed** read this text as input, delete the second line and output the remaining lines, enter the command:

> **sed '2 d'** *gdbase*

The **d** is **sed**'s deletion command. The number *2* instructs **sed** to execute the specified command on line *2*. The instructions for **sed** are enclosed in quotation marks so the shell passes it as is to **sed**. The original file *gdbase* is unaltered; **sed** reads it, makes whatever changes are requested and passes the changed copy on as output, by default, to the terminal.

B2   Deleting a Range of Lines by Number

It is also possible to specify a range of lines on which **sed** should execute the specified command. Enter the command:

> **sed '2,10 d'** *gdbase*

A comma between two addresses instructs **sed** to execute the specified command on all lines between and including the first and second addresses.

B3   Making a Substitution

The **sed** utility will also replace all occurrences of a pattern or word with a new pattern. For example, enter the following:

> **sed 's/***Dairy***/DAIRY/g'** *gdbase*

This command instructs **sed** to get its input text from the file *gdbase* and to write its output with all instances of *Dairy* replaced by *DAIRY*.

No address is specified in this example. When no address is specified within a **sed** instruction the command, by default, targets all lines. In this case, because the command is to substitute one pattern for another, only the one line that contained the specified pattern was changed, but all were examined.

B4   **Quitting After a Specified Line**

The *records* data file contains 11 lines of data about various record albums. The following command will display the contents of this file up to the fifth line.

Enter:

> **sed '5 q'** *records*

This command instructs **sed** to read each line of input and write it as output until the fifth line is reached. After the fifth line is processed (the target line), **sed** completes its requested action: to **quit**. Thus, only the lines up to and including the fifth line are read and output.

The quit command is different from the other **sed** commands you have met so far: it accepts only one address. It makes sense to delete all lines between and including lines two and five, but it would be difficult to quit at all lines between and including lines two and five.

B5 Examining sed's Basic Syntax

The following are the **sed** command lines that you have encountered so far:

> **sed** *'2* **d'** *gdbase*
> **sed** *'2,10* **d'** *gdbase*
> **sed** *'s/Dairy/DAIRY/g'* *gdbase*
> **sed** *'5* **q'** *records*

The general form of these examples is:

> **sed** *'address1, address2* **command'** *file(s)*

The portion of this command line entered between the quotes is the **sed** instruction. The **sed** instruction is generally surrounded by single quotes to protect any special characters from being interpreted by the shell.

Most **sed** instructions include two parts: an address component and a command component. The *command* specifies what should be done. The *address* specifies the lines on which the command should be executed. The space between the last address and the command is optional and is used to improve readability.

The following table breaks into components each of the **sed** command lines you have used .

utility	address1	address2	command	flag	file(s)
sed	*2*		**d**		*gdbase*
sed	*2,*	*10*	**d**		*gdbase*
sed			*s/Dairy/DAIRY/*	**g**	*gdbase*
sed	*5*		**q**		*records*

There are three important features to note about these examples and **sed** instructions in general.

- All **sed** instructions begin with the utility name **sed**;

- All **sed** instructions include a command to be executed;

- Most **sed** instructions include either two addresses separated by a comma, a single address or no address.

Two addresses separated by a comma indicate that the command should be executed on all lines starting with the first address and concluding with the line that is the second address.

A single address instructs **sed** to execute the command on the specified address only.

No address specifies that the command should be executed on all lines in the input.

Objective C
Using Contextual Addresses

In the previous section you used line numbers as **sed** addresses. In this section you will enter several new **sed** commands that will illustrate the power of the other type of **sed** address, the contextual address.

C1 Quitting After a Specified Pattern

You used **sed**'s **q**uit command to instruct **sed** to quit processing a file after a specified line. It is also possible to instruct **sed** to quit processing after a specified pattern is encountered.

To display the contents of this file up to the first line containing the pattern *Manilow* enter the command:

> **sed** '/*Manilow*/ **q**' *records*

Instead of specifying a line number as the target line for **sed** this command specifies the line containing the pattern /*Manilow*/. A contextual address is a pattern surrounded by slashes. This command instructs **sed** to read each line of input and write it as output until a line containing the pattern *Manilow* is processed. After the line containing the pattern *Manilow* is processed **sed q**uits.

C2 Substituting on Lines Containing a Pattern

Suppose you want **sed** to replace the word "archaic" with the word "contemporary," but only on those lines where the word "beetles" also appears in the file *records*.

Enter the following:

> **sed** '/*beetles*/ **s**/*archaic*/*contemporary*/**g**' *records*

The components of the command line are:

sed   execute the **sed** utility

/*beetles*/   the pattern of the contextual address part of the **sed** utility delimited by slashes

s/*archaic*/*contemporary*/
              substitute for the search pattern that follows (*archaic*) this replacement pattern delimited by slashes (*contemporary*).

g   execute the command on each of its occurrences within each line in which the pattern of the contextual address (*beetles*) is found.

,   ,   single quotes telling the shell to pass everything in between to the **sed** utility. These quotes thus mark the beginning and end of instructions for **sed**.

records   the name of the file that you want **sed** to act upon.

In summary, this command line uses the contextual address */beetles/* to instruct **sed** to execute the specified substitution command only on lines containing the pattern *beetles*.

Only one address is specified; the command locates two lines containing the specified pattern *beetles,* then attempts to make the substitution. Only one line contains the string *archaic;* only one line is output.

No substitution was executed on the Wagner line, even though the word *archaic* does appear there. This line does not match the contextual address; there is no action.

> A line number will always match one and only one line, while a contextual address can match from zero to all lines in the input.

C3   Using More Than a Single Contextual Address

Contextual addresses can be used either with a line address or another contextual address to specify a range of lines to be targeted.

The following command line will replace the pattern *Meat* with the pattern *Animal* on all lines starting with the seventh line and ending with the first line containing the pattern *Fish*.

Enter the command:

sed '7,/Fish/ **s**/Meat/Animal/' gdbase

This command uses both line and contextual addresses.

The following table lists the elements of the command line you just entered:

utility	address1	address2	command	file(s)
sed	7	/Fish/	s/Meat/Animal/	gdbase

In this example the first address is a line address, the second is contextual.

Two contextual addresses separated by a comma can also be used to specify a range of lines on which the command should be executed.

C4 Using a Regular Expression to Delete Blank Lines

Thus far you have used only literal patterns as contextual addresses. In addition, **sed** accepts the full range of regular expressions within contextual addresses and within the substitute command.

For example, the regular expression ^$ can be used within a contextual address, with the delete command, to delete all blank lines from some input.

Select or create a file containing several blank lines, and enter the following command (replacing *file* with the name of the file you have selected):

sed '/^$/ d' *file*

As mentioned in the regular expression module, when the ˆ is used as part of a regular expression it signifies *beginning-of-line*. The **$** signifies *end-of-line*. Thus, a blank line is indicated by a *beginning-of-line* followed by an *end-of-line* with nothing in between.

Objective D
Giving **sed** Multiple Instructions

In the previous exercises, you gave **sed** only one instruction at a time. In this section you will give multiple instructions to **sed** in two ways.

D1   **Entering Multiple Command Line Instructions**

There are times when more than one edit is needed on a given document. For example, you can change all occurrences of *Veg* to *VEG* and *Meat* to *MEAT* in your *gdbase* file.

Enter the command:

sed   -e 's/*Veg***/***VEG***/' -e 's/***Meat***/***MEAT***/'** *gdbase*

The **-e** option placed before *each* command on the line tells **sed** that there is more than one edit command on the command line.

D2   **Creating a Command File**

The **-e** option is useful for entering commands to make two or three changes at one time, but if five or ten different **sed** commands are needed, the command line becomes impossible.

You can include several commands in a file and have **sed** act on all of them in one pass. Using **vi**, create a new file called *modify.rec* and enter the following lines:

```
s/rock/raunch/g
/disco/d
```

D3   **Running a Command File**

To have **sed** execute the instructions contained in the command file on the data file named *records*, enter the command:

sed -f *modify.rec records*

The **-f** option tells **sed** that its instructions can be found in the file named as an argument to the option.

This particular **sed** command file instructs **sed** to change *rock* to *raunch* and to delete all lines with the word *disco* in them.

Objective E
Adding Text to a File with **sed**

Thus far, you have deleted and modified lines of input text. In this section, you will add text with **sed**.

E1   Creating a Command File for Inserting Text

Like **vi** and other interactive editors, **sed** provides a mechanism for inserting text before a specified location in its input. Create a new file named *db_changes*, and enter the following code:

```
1i\
As a result of changes in supply, \
The following are the new prices for groceries:
/Carrots/s/39/69/
/Milk/s/\.89/1.19/
/Fish/s/1\.79/2.68/
/Celery/s/79/89/
```

The 1i\ tells **sed** to find line number *1*, then insert the text which follows above that line. The ⊠ says that the text is continued on the following line. When there is more than one line of text to be added in this way, each line must end with a backslash. The last line to be added has no backslash.

The remainder of the script contains the changes to be made: *find Carrots substitute for 39 the string 69,* etc. Because the period has special meaning in the search portion of the command, the backslash (\) is used, to insist that "sometimes a period is only a period."

E2   Redirecting sed's Output to a File

The **sed** utility can follow the instructions in a command file and have the shell redirect **sed**'s standard output to a file. Enter the following command line:

```
sed -f db_changes gdbase > gdbase_rev
```

Examine the resulting file *gdbase_rev*. The **sed** command file *db_changes* inserts a line of text and revises the prices of several items.

E3   **Adding Text After a Line with sed**

Earlier, **sed** inserted text preceding a line; **sed** will also append text after lines.

Create a command file for **sed** giving it the name *add_item* and include the following:

> */Fish/a*
> *Waxpaper* TAB *Hshld* TAB *1.48* TAB *1* TAB *y*
> */Napkins/a*
> *Rice* TAB *Veg* TAB *.79* TAB *1* TAB *n*

The **a** command tells **sed** to append text after the contextual address given. The new *Waxpaper* entry will be listed after the *Fish* line. The *Rice* entry will be listed after *Napkins* in the revised data file.

The difference between **a** and **I** is that one appends a new line *after* the addressed line and the other inserts the text as a line *before* the addressed line.

E4   Have **sed** execute the changes specified in the command file *add_item,* by entering:

> **sed -f** *add_item gdbase* **>** *dbase.rev2*

The components of this command line are:

sed   executes the **sed** utility

-f   informs **sed** that a file should be read for instructions

add_item   indicates the name of the command file to be read by **sed**

gdbase   is the name of the database file to be read for
                  input

>   redirects output to a file

dbase.rev2   is the name of the file to be created to receive the
                  output of **sed**

Objective F
Reading and Writing Files

In this section, you will use **sed**'s read and write commands to read files in at specified addresses and to write selected lines out to specified files.

F1 Before you employ **sed**'s read command, create a file to read named *comment.file* and enter the following three lines:

```
**********************************************************
I know this is a bit high-brow, but I like it anyway.
**********************************************************
```


F2 ## Reading in a File at a Specified Address

To read the file named *comment.file* into the file *records* at the contextual address */classical/*, type the following:

> **sed** '/*classical*/ **r** *comment.file*' *records*

The entire contents of the file *comment.file* are added after every line that contains the word *classical*. The read command is used to add text to input. It is most useful when you wish to add a large amount of text.

As with most other **sed** commands, it can be used with either single line or contextual addresses or ranges of addresses. The read command requires an argument to specify the name of the file that should be read.

F3   Writing to Files

You can also use **sed** to write selected portions of a file into another file. Enter the following:

> **sed** *'1,7* **w** *wfile' records*

Examine the new file *wfile*. The above **sed** command line instructs **sed** to apply the **write** command to lines 1 through 7 of the file *records*. Like the read command, the **write** command takes an argument that specifies the filename where output should be written.

Both the **write** command and output redirection can be used to write **sed**'s output to a file. The difference in usage is that the **write** command can *write selected portions* of **sed**'s input to a file, whereas output redirection creates a file of all selected lines. Both can be used at once. With **w** you can have a portion of the input lines written to a file; then with the **>** you can have all targeted lines sent to another file.

Objective G
Exploring How **sed** Works

In this section, you will enter several **sed** command lines and execute several **sed** command files in order to examine how **sed** functions.

G1   **Exploring the Major Actions Performed by sed**

The **sed** utility is a *filter*. Like all filters it performs three major actions. It reads lines of input, executes a command on this input and writes lines as output.

Create a file named *explorer* and enter the following line into it:

        s/Veg/Vgtbl/g

Run this command file with the command:

        sed -f *explorer gdbase*

In this example, **sed** reads all input lines, executes the specified command (substitution) and writes each line as output.

G2   **Exploring How sed Buffers Its Input**

Obviously, **sed** reads input, executes commands and writes output. But where is the input while the command is being executed? Modify your *explorer* file to contain only the following line:

        2,4 **d**

Have the shell run this command file by entering the command:

        sed -f *explorer gdbase*

In this case, line 1 and all lines after line 4 are written as output.

To accomplish this task, **sed** takes the following steps:

- First, line 1 is read into **sed**'s main buffer called the *pattern space*.

- Second, **sed** determines whether the line in the pattern space has an address that is specified in the instruction. In the case of line 1, there is no match, so the specified command is not executed on the text in the pattern space.

- Third, the contents of the buffer (pattern space) are simply written to the standard output and deleted from the buffer.

And on to line 2.

- Line 2 is read into the pattern space.

- **sed** determines whether the line in the pattern space has an address that is specified in the instruction. In the case of line 2, there is a match, so the specified command is executed on the text in the pattern space. In this case, the specified command is to delete the contents of the pattern space.

- Next, the contents of the pattern space are written to the standard output and deleted. However, in this case, because of the delete command, the pattern space is already empty. Nothing is there to be written and deleted.

Lines 3 and 4 are treated the same as line 2 because they are addressed in the instruction. The remaining lines are treated as line 1 because they are not addressed by the instruction. In summary, **sed**'s basic operating procedure is to go through the following cycle.

- copy a line of input into the pattern space;

- if the address specified with the command matches the address of the line in the pattern space, then execute the specified command on the pattern space; and

- write the contents of the pattern space to the standard output and empty the contents of the pattern space.

G3   Testing How Multiple Commands are Executed

The last example looked at **sed**'s operating procedure when a single instruction was specified. How does **sed** handle multiple instructions? Is the first instruction followed on all lines before the second instruction is followed, or are all instructions followed on the first line before the second line is processed?

Modify your *explorer* file to contain the following two lines:

```
s/Veg/Vgtbl/g
q
```

If the first instruction is followed on all lines before the second instruction is followed, then all lines in the file will be displayed with *Veg* replaced by *Vgtbl* before **sed** quits. On the other hand, if all instructions are followed on the first line before the second line is processed, then **sed** will quit after processing the first line of the file.

G4   Have **sed** follow the instructions in the command file with the command:

```
sed -f explorer gdbase
```

The output contains only the first line, indicating that all instructions are followed on the first line before the next line is processed. The **sed** utility is called a stream editor because it edits the file line by line, in a stream.

The following figure illustrates the steps taken by **sed**. Examine this diagram and trace the following steps on the diagram as you read them:

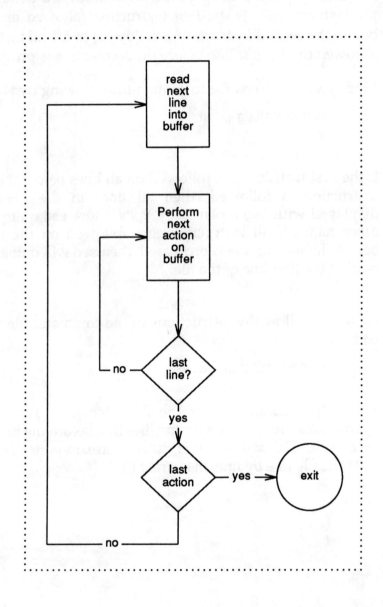

In summary, when **sed** operates on a file, it:

- reads a single line from the input stream into its buffer (pattern space);

- executes all specified commands on that line; and

- reads the next line.

> **sed** does not read the whole file into a work space; it executes all edits on one line before reading the next one.

G5 **Making Explicit Requests for Printing**

The **sed** utility will print lines on request.

Enter the following print command:

    sed *'1,2* **p'** *gdbase*

The letter **p** is used to specify the **print** command. In the output, the two addressed lines are each printed twice. The remainder of the file's lines are printed once only. A review of **sed**'s operating procedure with the print command contains an explanation.

- A line of the specified file is brought into the pattern space of **sed**.

- If the line is within the specified address range (in this case, if it is the 1st or 2nd line of the file), the specified command is executed on the contents of the pattern space. The command could have been substitution, which would have changed the line. In this case however, the action requested is **print**. The action is taken on lines 1 and 2, which are the specified addresses in this command, so they are printed.

- By default, the content of the pattern space is then written to the standard output, resulting in a second printing of lines 1 and 2.

The next line of the specified file is then brought into the pattern space, and the whole process is repeated.

G6   Summarizing **sed**'s Basic Operating Procedure

In summary, **sed** operates in the following way:

- copy a line of input into the pattern space;

- determine if the command's contextual or line address matches the contents of the pattern space;

- sequentially execute all commands if the address matches;

- write the contents of the pattern space to the standard output (regardless of whether or not there was a match and the command has been executed);

- empty the contents of the pattern space.

Objective H
Executing Substitute Commands

One powerful use of the stream editor is to make substitutions on all target lines as the lines pass through the **sed** buffer or pattern space. This section examines how the substitute command works and uses several additional features that expand its power and usefulness.

H1 Exploring How the Substitute Command Works

The basic role of the substitute command is to replace one pattern with another. For example, enter:

sed '**s**/*Dairy*/*DAIRY*/**g**' *gdbase*

This command instructs **sed** to get its input from the file *gdbase* and write its output, with all instances of "Dairy" replaced by "DAIRY."

Because no address is specified in this example, the command should be executed on all lines. But the command only appears to be executed on the two lines continuing the pattern *Dairy*. The reason is that the substitute command is to "check all lines matching the specified address for the first pattern and, if that pattern exists, replace it with the second pattern." Thus, all lines are checked for a pattern, but a substitution is made only if the pattern matches.

The **g** at the end of the substitute command is the **g**lobal flag which instructs **sed** to make the specified substitution on all occurrences of the pattern within the line. Otherwise, it would only work on the first occurrence of the pattern in each line. The flag modifies how the substitute command works.

utility	address	command	flag	file(s)
sed		s/*Dairy*/*DAIRY*/	**g**	*gdbase*

The substitute command also has two other flags.

H2 Printing with the Print Flag

The following pages describe how the print flag works on System V. On Berkeley systems the output is different, with respect to double printing.

The substitute command also accepts a flag that requests printing. Enter the command:

> **sed** '**s**/*beetles*/*bugs*/**p**' *records*

Given this command line, the **sed** utility cyclically executes the following steps:

(a)   **sed** reads the first line into the pattern space.

(b)   If the address applies (in this case, all lines), the command is executed, if possible. If the substitution is successful, the print command *flag* is executed. First the pattern space is printed, and then *the pattern space is emptied*. If no substitution takes place, the pattern space is neither printed nor emptied.

(c)   The pattern space is printed. If there was a successful substitution, the pattern space is empty.

There is no double printing. Step (b) specifies that the pattern space be printed and emptied *only* if a substitution took place; (c) specifies that the pattern space be printed—but the pattern space is empty if there has been a substitution. Hence, single printing results.

Substituting With and Without the Print Flag

Compare the output of the command:

> **sed** '**s**/*beetles*/*bugs*/**p**' *records*

with that of the following command:

> **sed** '**s**/*beetles*/*bugs*/' *records*

The second example is the same but without the **print** flag.

H4   Suppressing sed's Default Output

Thus far all the commands you used printed every line in a file at least once, and sometimes twice. If you are editing a file, having the same line appear more than once is not terribly useful (and sometimes quite annoying). Enter the following line:

sed -n '*1,5* **s**/*beetle*/*Beatle*/**p**' *records*

Obeying this command, **sed** prints only those lines affected by the substitution command. The **-n** option tells the **sed** utility to not print the pattern space. The result is that only the lines affected by the **p**rint flag of the command are actually printed.

The following is an explanation of how **-n** works on System V machines:

(a)   **sed** copies the first line into the pattern space.

(b)   If the address matches, **sed** attempts the substitution. If the substitution is successful, the pattern space is printed and then emptied (as specified by the **p**rint flag).

(c)   The **-n** option tells **sed** to suppress printing the pattern space which is normally done at this point.

Hence, the **-n** option affects the third step of the **sed** procedure.

H5   Suppressing All Output

Keeping the previous example in mind, enter the following command line (which omits the **p**rint flag):

sed -n '*1,5***s**/*beetle*/*Beatle*/' *records*

Without the **p**rint flag, **sed** does not print the pattern space after each substitution is made.

With the **-n** option, step (c) does not print it either. Therefore there is no output, even if **sed** did execute a command on the line.

> When you use the **-n** option, you must use either the print command or the **p**rint flag.

H6   Combining Flags

Earlier, you used the **g** flag to have all occurrences of a pattern on an addressed line replaced with a new pattern. You have also used the **p** flag to cause changed lines to be printed. It is possible to combine these flags.

To replace all occurrences of the pattern *archaic* with the pattern *contemporary* and have only changed lines printed, enter the following:

sed -n '*/beetles/* **s***/archaic/contemporary/***gp**' *records*

The elements of the above substitution command are:

utility	option	address	command	flag
sed	**-n**	*/beetles/*	**s***/archaic/contemporary/*	**gp**

H7   Sending Up a Write Flag

The **w** command can also be used as a flag, just as you used **g**. Using **w** as a flag also **w**rites the output of **sed** to a file, but only after the requested changes have been made. Enter the command:

sed '**s***/rock/raunch/***w** *wfile*' *records*

Examine the contents of the new file *wfile*.

The command you just entered says:

- first replace *rock* with *raunch,* then

- write the result to the file *wfile*.

All changed lines are written to *wfile*.

In both uses of the **w** command, if the file already exists, **w** writes over it. To avoid overwriting, create a new file each time you perform this type of task.

H8 Using Metacharacters in Substitutions

In an earlier example, you used regular expression metacharacters within contextual addresses. The **sed** utility accepts the full range of regular expressions in its search pattern addresses. However, you will soon see that the use of regular expressions is quite limited in the replacement pattern portion of **sed** commands.

As an example of regular expression usage in the search pattern, examine the file *records*. You will notice that it includes the word *Beetles* using both upper and lower case *b*. Because **sed** is case sensitive, it will not find *beetles* if you tell it to search for *Beetles*.

To get around case sensitivity, enter the following command line:

> **sed** '**s**/[*Bb*]*eetles*/*Beatles*/' *records*

The expression [ ] tells **sed** to match any characters enclosed within the brackets. In this example, **sed** replaces occurrences of both *B* and *b* followed by *eetles*.

Objective I
Using Advanced Print Features

In this section you will use the print feature with **sed** to select only those lines that contain the target pattern, or do not contain the pattern.

I1   ## Printing Only Lines Containing a Pattern
Assume you want a list of all the classical albums in the file *records*. Enter the following line to accomplish this task:

      sed -n '/*classical*/ **p'** *records*

This command uses the contextual address /*classical*/ to select all records containing that pattern. Then, the combination of the **-n** option and the print command tell **sed** to print only the selected lines, not the pattern space.

I2   ## Printing Only Lines Not Containing a Pattern
A list of all records *except* the classical ones can also be created. You could replace the word "classical" in the above command line, first with "disco" and then with "rock and roll," etc.—but if you have more than three or four categories, you might as well do the whole thing by hand.

Enter the following (C-Shell users, please note that the backslash (\) is necessary to hide the ! from the Shell):

C-Shell users:

      sed -n '/*classical*/ **\!p'** *records*

Bourne Shell users:

      sed -n '/*classical*/ **!p'** *records*

The exclamation point is **sed's** "not" operator, which causes the command immediately following to be applied to all the lines that are *not* in the address. Because the address is still */classical/*, **sed** executes its command (in this case, printing) on all lines that do *not* contain the specified string. The ! must always be placed between the address and the command.

The *not* operator for **sed** is the !. It acts on the address, not the command, instructing **sed** to select all records that do not fit the target.

I3   Printing All Lines That Are Not All Lines

The following command line does not include a specific address but includes the *not print* operator. Enter

sed -n '\!p' *records*

There is no output. **sed's** default address is every line. This command said to select and print all lines that did not meet the selection criteria. All lines were selected, none were left, no lines were printed.

Objective J
Grouping and Selecting Lines

J1   Bringing the Next Line into the Pattern Space

To prepare for the next step, create a file named *text* and enter text such as the listing on the top of the next page.

As you enter the following, make sure all headings are preceded by the *.SH* line. They are macro calls for formatting.

```
.SH
How Important is Education?
.LP
As more and more money is spent on equipment
that is
underutilized, the importance of a
training budget
is becoming apparent.
.SH
What is Good Education?
.LP
Every student has a different background.
Good Education assists those with little background
and doesn't limit those with more experience.
```

It is often useful to locate and act on each line that is the line following a selected pattern. For example, all section headers in the file *text* have been placed after the *.SH* lines. To locate and print out the section headers, the program must address all lines starting with *.SH*, get the *next* line and print it.

Create a command file named *after* and enter the following:

```
/^\.SH/ n
```

The ^ is the regular expression metacharacter that means, *beginning-of-line*.

Have **sed** follow the instructions in this command file by entering the command line:

```
sed -f after text
```

The lines in the file *text* are simply displayed on the screen. The **sed** utility with the next option works by printing the contents of the pattern space and then overwriting the pattern space with the next input line. Thus, a **-n** option alone has no visible effect. There is no apparent difference between using it and not using it. When used in conjunction with other features, however, it is quite useful.

The general strategy mentioned in the previous section for obtaining a print of the section headers is to address all lines starting with *.SH*, get the next line and print it.

J2   Modify your *after* command file to contain the following, which uses the print command with the next command:

```
/^\.SH/ n
p
```

Run the command file again with:

sed -f *after text*

Lines that match the regular expression (address) */^\.SH/* are displayed only once. All other lines are printed twice.

The key to understanding why this happens is that both the next command and the **p**rint command have addresses associated with them.

The address for the next command is all lines that contain the string */^\.SH/*. The address for the **p**rint command is all lines. With this in mind let's look at how this command works.

J3   **Examining the Command Line**

In the previous example, the steps taken by **sed** for each line in the file *text* are:

- First, a line is read into the pattern space.

- Second, the line is examined for the contextual address:

    (1) If it matches, then the next command is executed. This sends the pattern space to the standard output and overwrites the pattern space with the next line.

    (2) If the line does not match the address / ^\.*SH/, the next command is not executed and **sed** continues to the second command in the file.

- Third, the pattern space is printed by the **p** command.

- Fourth, the pattern space is printed again by the default printing action and the pattern space is emptied.

Thus, under most circumstances, lines matching the regular expression are printed once (by the **n** command), while all other lines are printed twice (once by the **p** command and once by the default printing action). The exception to this normal procedure occurs in the case of two *consecutive* lines that match the contextual address. In this case, the second line is never checked against the address. Hence, it is treated like a non-matching line (printed twice).

J4   **Substituting on Lines Outside of a Range**

Continue the exploration by entering the following line.

```
sed -n '3,6 \!s/rock and roll/noise pollution/p' records
```

In this case, **sed** finds every line that is *not* in lines 3 through 6 and executes the substitution command on those lines, if possible. The result is that the phrase *rock and roll* is replaced with *noise pollution* on all lines other than 3 through 6.

J5 Grouping Multiple Commands

The objective is to convince **sed** that **n**ext and **p**rint are both commands associated with the same address.

Modify your command file so that it contains the following:

```
/^\.SH/ {
n
p
}
```

Run this command file with:

sed -f *after text*

Each line following *.SH* is displayed twice, while all other lines are displayed only once.

The curly braces **{}** are **sed**'s grouping operator. Thus, the lines you entered above can be read as, "For every line matching /^\./SH/ pass the line on to be written to the standard output, overwrite the pattern space with the next line and print the contents of the pattern space."

Thus, all lines following those matching the address are printed both by the default action and by the print command. All other lines are only printed once by default. (Again, in the case of two consecutive address matches, the second line is treated like a non-matching line.)

J6   Grouping Commands to Print the Next Line

That output is getting closer to the goal. The only task remaining is suppression of the default printing.

Enter the command:

> **sed -n -f** *after text*

Only the lines after the contextual address are printed. The **-n** option in the command line tells **sed** to not print the pattern space. The **-n** thus suppresses the default printing so that only lines after the contextual address are printed. This is a result of the grouping of the next and print commands in the command file.

J7   Grouping an Address Within an Address

It is possible to instruct **sed** to execute a command only on lines 50 through 55 that contain a specific pattern such as *the*.

Create a new file called *within* and enter the following **sed** commands:

```
50,55 {
/the/a\
this is a test
}
```

Run this command file against one of your larger test files.

The line "this is a test" is appended after each line between 50 and 55 that contains the pattern *the*.

The **sed** utility identifies lines that match this address, then executes the grouped instructions that follow. Because the group begins with an additional address, this address also has to be matched for the command that follows to be executed.

J8   **Quitting to Save Time**

Modify *within* to include a quit statement.

```
50,55 { /the/a\
this is a test
}
55q
```

Run the command again on the same file as before.

The output appears exactly the same, but the execution time is probably a little faster.

Remember that **sed** examines each and every line in a file. Thus, the first version of our command file directs **sed** to examine all lines in the file after line 55, even though no more commands are to be executed. Our second version tells **sed** to stop processing after line 55 and ignore the rest of the file. This property is particularly useful with a very large file.

Objective K
Reviewing the General Form of **sed** Command Lines

Having examined all of the pieces of a **sed** command line, we can look at the basic structure of the entire line.

sed *-options address1, address2* **command** *arguments(s) file(s)*

The components displayed in *italics* are optional, while the components displayed in **bold** are required.

sed accepts three options:

-e   This option precedes expressions; it may be omitted if you are only using one expression.

-f   This option precedes the name of a command file containing instructions.

-n   This option suppresses the default printing to standard output.

Most **sed** instructions can include either two addresses separated by a comma, a single address or no address. Addresses can be line addresses or contextual addresses.

Two addresses separated by a comma indicate that the command should be executed on all lines between and including the first and second address.

A single address instructs **sed** to execute the command on the specified address only.

No address specifies that the command should be executed on all lines in the input.

All **sed** command lines must include a command. This command may accept arguments. For example, the **write** and **read** commands each take a filename argument.

The **s**ubstitute command may accept flags, such as **g**lobal and **p**rint.

sed can access input from either a specified list of files or from the standard input.

Conclusion

The **sed** utility is an extremely powerful stream editor allowing you, from the shell, to select and modify lines from files. This command can be invaluable in database applications as well as within shell scripts. At this point you are a capable **sed** programmer. The UNIX *Programmers' Manual* entry on **sed** should now be reasonably understandable. Good luck and enjoy.

Summary of **sed** Commands

sed COMMAND	FUNCTION
s	Substitute in pattern space (must be followed by a target regular expression and a replacement pattern).
g	If used as a flag for the **s** command it will execute substitutions on all occurrences of the pattern in the target address.
p	Print pattern space.
d	Delete pattern space.
l	Insert a line before the pattern space.
a	Add a line after the pattern space.
{ }	Group the commands included.
w	Write the pattern space to the following file.
r	Read into the pattern space from the following file.

sed OPTION	FUNCTION
-n	Do not print pattern space.
-e	What follows is one of at least two commands.
-f	Find the **sed** command(s) in the following file.

Summary of Metacharacters for **sed** Commands	
CHARACTER	FUNCTION
^	Match beginning of line.
$	Match end of line. Do not confuse with the address symbol which stands for "last line in the file."
.	Match any single character.
*	Match any number of occurrences of previous character (including 0).
[ ]	Match any character (or range of characters) enclosed within the brackets.
[^]	Match any character not enclosed within the brackets.
!	Match all lines not covered in the address.
\(	Marks beginning of a pattern.
\)	Marks end of a pattern.
&	Replace with last character pattern encountered.
\	Remove "magic" of Special Characters (Kryptonite).
//	Match last pattern in search.
\#	Replace with the pattern that the # stands for.

Appendix A

The following is a copy of the file *records:*

Abbey Road, the beetles, archaic rock and roll, one of their last.
Live Bullet, Bob Seger, contains "Turn the Page" rock and roll.
Deja vu, Crosby, Stills and Nash, One of their best, Free and Easy.
Who are you? The Who, rock and roll, Sister Disco, Guitar or your Pen.
Barry Manilow, The Las Vegas Years. Boy, this is a different selection.
Rachmaninoff, Variation on a theme of Paganini, in C minor. classical.
Aqualung, Jethro Tull, rock and roll, title track is outstanding.
Chipmunk disco, the Chipmunks, better than some others.
Stop Making Sense, Talking Heads, Live album, outstanding rock and roll.
War Cry of the Valkyrie, Wagner, Heavy and archaic classical.
Beetles, White album, rock and roll, Dear Prudence.

Appendix B

The following database should be entered in the file *gdbase*:

Carrots	veg	.39	1	n
Milk	Dairy	.89	2	n
Newsweek	Sundry	1.50	1	y
Cheese	Dairy	1.39	1	n
Sandwich	Deli	1.89	2	y
Onions	Veg	.29	6	n
Chicken	Meat	2.89	2	n
Fish	Meat	1.79	3	n
Floorwax	Hshld	2.65	1	y
Melon	Fruit	.98	3	n
Celery	Veg	.79	1	n
Napkins	Hshld	.49	6	y

Module 8

Manipulating Columns of Data with cut and paste

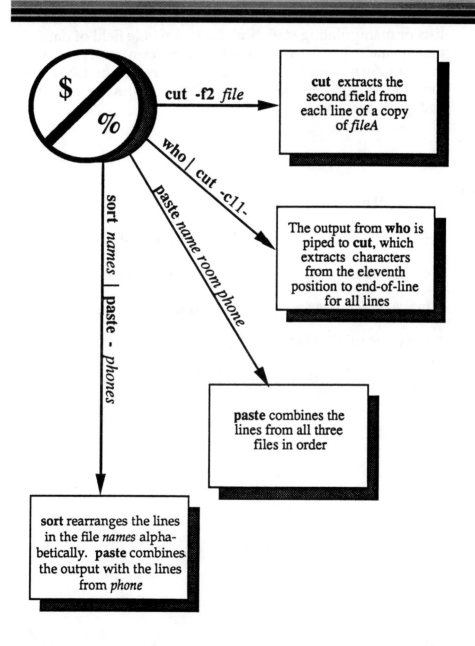

cut -f2 *file*

cut extracts the second field from each line of a copy of *fileA*

who | cut -c11-

The output from **who** is piped to **cut**, which extracts characters from the eleventh position to end-of-line for all lines

paste name room phone

paste combines the lines from all three files in order

sort names | paste - phones

sort rearranges the lines in the file *names* alphabetically. **paste** combines the output with the lines from *phone*

Introduction

In system administration, education, business and engineering environments, it is often useful to maintain data in rows and columns. Manipulation of files containing such arrays of data is essential in many tasks, for example, maintaining mailing lists or manipulating statistical data. A whole field of database management has been developed to efficiently organize and extract information from data files. Several of the UNIX utilities that are especially useful with database files are **cut, paste, sed, grep, awk** and **join**.

Prerequisites

Before beginning this module, you should be able to:

- create, edit, move, copy, view and remove files;

- make directories and move around in the file system;

- use basic utilities (Module 2);

- use the shell to issue commands (Module 3).

Objective

After completion of this module you will be able to:

- remove and add columns of information from one or more files;

- rearrange, transpose and recombine fields of data.

Procedures

The exercises in this module begin with an exploration of selecting fields and characters from a file using **cut**, and then investigate putting lines from two or more files together with **paste**.

Objective A
Creating Example Databases

The utilities **cut** and **paste** work mainly on information arranged in a database. For the exercises in this module, modify the databases you created in Module 2. If you skipped Module 2, just create these two files now with a text editor.

A1   Update *names.tmp* to include the two additional lines indicated by arrows:

> 101 `Tab` Bill `Tab` Z.
> 102 `Tab` John `Tab` M.
> 106 `Tab` Mary `Tab` L.
> 107 `Tab` Santa `Tab` C.
> 108 `Tab` Dana `Tab` M.   ←
> 109 `Tab` Leslie `Tab` A.   ←

A2   Change *numbers.tmp* to include two new lines:

> 101 [Tab]555-9136
> 102 [Tab]666-8888
> 106 [Tab]591-1191
> 107 [Tab]511-1972
> 108 [Tab]317-6512   ←
> 109 [Tab]777-2222   ←

Remember to use the [Tab] character to separate the fields in each record. It may be helpful to think of fields as columns and each record as a row within the database.

In the file *names.tmp* each of the lines has three *fields*: the first field is a room number, the second is the first name, and the third is the first initial of a last name.

In the file *numbers.tmp* there are two fields: the first field is, again, a room number; the second field is a phone number.

A field is any string of characters or numbers separated from other strings by a specific character selected to perform the function of **delimiter**. The default delimiter for **cut** and **paste** is the [Tab] character. Using other characters as the separator will be addressed later in this module. One of the advantages of the [Tab] separator is that the following is only three fields:

> *Albert Levy* [Tab]1423 Roslyn Avenue [Tab]555-7777

The use of the [Tab] for field separation instead of the [Space] bar permits the space character to be used within fields to enhance readability.

A3   **Using cut to Select a Field from a File**

The **cut** utility can be used to extract information from a file or from the output of a previous program. It can "cut out" the information.

A4   As you know from completing Module 2, the simplest use of **cut** is to extract one field from a file.

A5   From the shell, enter the following command line:

> **cut** *-f2 names.tmp*

The output is:

> Bill
> John
> Mary
> Santa
> Dana
> Leslie

which is each of the entries from the second column (field) in the file *names.tmp*.

Objective B
Examining How **cut** Works

The **cut** utility follows specific instructions. For example, you just entered the command:

> **cut** *-f2 names.tmp*

The following was communicated:

cut   The command **cut** tells the shell to execute the **cut** utility.

-f   The option **-f** tells **cut** that it must extract fields.

2   The number that follows the **-f** tells **cut** which field to extract.

names.tmp   The last argument tells **cut** which file(s) to use as input.

Once **cut** has all this information it opens the specified file and starts reading the first line, character by character, until it finds the first Tab character. All the characters read until that first Tab constitute the first field. Because the instructions were to locate the second field, **cut** discards the first and continues. It reads all the characters until the second Tab. Because the second field is the one specified, **cut** retains it and, disregarding the remainder of that line, goes on to the next. **cut** repeats the same process on the second and on all other lines until there are no lines left in the file to process. It then sends the selected text to output.

As usual, **cut** does not actually change the file that it reads for input. It outputs a copy of only the field or fields that you specify.

B1 ## Selecting a List of Fields

More than one field can be extracted from each line. From the shell, enter the following command line:

> **cut -f***1,3 names.tmp*

The output from **cut** is:

```
101    Z.
102    M.
106    L.
107    G.
108    M.
109    A.
```

The first and third fields are displayed.

The command you just entered:

cut -**f**1,3 names.tmp

consists of the following components:

Command	Option	Argument to the Option	Input File
cut	**-f**	1,3	names.tmp

To extract multiple fields from a file you must specify in the command line a list of fields separated by commas, not spaces.

B2   Enter the following:

cut -**f**1,2,3 names.tmp

Alter the order by entering:

cut -**f**1,3,2 names.tmp

The output remains in the same order that the columns were in the file (1,2,3). **cut** does not reorder fields, but leaves them in the original order. Reordering can be accomplished by using the **awk** utility, the subject of a later module.

B3   **Selecting a Range of Fields**

Selecting specific fields is easy when you are listing only three fields, but it would be tedious if you wanted ten or twelve fields. A range of fields can be specified. Enter the command:

cut -**f**1-3 names.tmp

The output includes fields 1, 2, and 3.

```
101   Bill    Z.
102   John   M.
106   Mary   L.
107   Santa C.
108   Dana  M.
109   Leslie A.
```

You can indicate a range of fields by separating the first field you want selected from the last field desired with a hyphen (–). The fields are selected first to last, inclusive.

B4   Suppose you have a database with approximately 12 or 13 columns of data; indeed, you can't remember the exact number. You know that you want a range of fields beginning at field 5 through to the last field. Rather than count the number of fields in the line, you can indicate all the rest of the fields. Enter the following:

cut -f5- *filename*

You have indicated all remaining fields by not placing a field identification number after the second - (hyphen).

Thus far you have used **cut** to separate individual fields, multiple fields, and ranges of fields from a database file.

B5   **Using cut** with Multiple Files

Like many UNIX utilities, **cut** can work on more than one file at a time. It opens all files listed as arguments and cuts whatever columns are specified.

Enter the following:

cut -f*1,2 names.tmp numbers.tmp*

The resulting output is:

```
101   Bill
102   John
106   Mary
107   Santa
108   Dana
109   Leslie
101   555-9136
102   666-8888
106   591-1191
107   511-1972
108   317-6512
109   777-2222
```

Fields 1 and 2 were selected from each file. When the input is more than one file, **cut** selects columns from the first file, followed by the selected columns from the second file, etc. Hence, the first part of the output comes from the first file; the latter output from the second.

Objective C
Using a Database File with Spaces as Delimiters

The **cut** utility can be used with other utilities in a pipeline. You can instruct the shell to connect the standard output of another utility to the standard input of **cut**.

C1   The **who** command produces a list of users currently logged on to the system. It includes the port their terminal is attached to, and the date and time of their most recent login. For instance:

scott	ttyh5	Nov 23 10:05
patty	ttyi1	Nov 23 09:47
conniejo	ttyi7	Nov 23 08:43
john	ttyie	Nov 21 08:43
dave	ttyif	Nov 23 10:48

C2   Have the shell send the output from **who** to **cut** by entering the following:

who | cut -f3

The output is more than just the third field. It is all fields. The **who** utility does not separate its output fields with tabs. Fields are separated in **who** by multiple space characters. As far as **cut** is concerned, it never found the end of the first field in the line. In that situation, **cut** outputs the whole line.

There is a solution to the problem— namely selecting characters rather than fields (hope your counting skills are up to par).

Objective D
Selecting Specific Characters

Each line in a file consists of a string of characters. Clearly, they can be counted from the beginning of the line producing a character position or character number for each character.

For instance the **who** output is:

```
12345678901234567 8 90123456789
scott      ttyh5    Nov 23 10:05
pat        ttyi1    Nov 23 09:47
```

The **cut** utility has an option that lets you extract information by character location rather than by fields. **cut** can select a single character, a list of characters or a range of characters— just as it can with fields.

To inform **cut** that you are requesting information by character and not by field, you use the option **-c**.

D1   Enter the following:

who | cut -c*1*

The output is just the first letters of the login names. The **-c** option *literally* reads each number as corresponding to one character width.

D2   To extract the fields with the names of users and the times they logged in from the output of **who** (in the example above), enter:

who | cut -c*1-9,25-29*

The output is:

```
scott    10:05
patty    09:47
conniejo 08:43
john     08:43
dave     10:48
```

The command you just entered:

who | cut -c*1-9,25-29*

consists of the following components:

Command Utility	Redirect Symbol	Command	Option	Argument to the Option
who	|	**cut**	**-c**	*1-9,25-29*

The hyphen (–) between the numbers 1 and 9 means the range of characters between those character positions (inclusive). The comma separates pieces of the list. **cut** not only extracts characters in positions one through nine, but also makes the second selection that follows the comma. It outputs the characters in the column positions 25 through 29.

D3   Obviously, using the **-c** option with **cut** requires that you count the characters individually up to the column position on the line you have selected. For instance, what appears to be the third field (the date) in the example above is actually made up of the characters that occupy the 18th to the 23rd column positions in the line.

D4   Now suppose you wanted to know how long each port has been connected, but you don't really care which person is logged on to that port. Examine the position numbers for the **who** output displayed previously. The characters designating port appear from positions eleven to fifteen.

Enter the command:

who | cut -c*11-*

When you have **-c** followed by a number followed by the **-** and nothing after, it is interpreted to mean "from the column position specified by the number to the end of the line." The output should look something like this:

```
ttyh5   Nov 23 10:05
ttyi1   Nov 23 09:47
ttyi7   Nov 23 08:43
ttyie   Nov 21 08:43
ttyif   Nov 23 10:48
```

Objective E
Changing the Default Separator (Delimiter)

You have now used **cut** to extract information by either counting positions (characters) or specifying fields using **cut**'s default delimiter, the Tab.

It is useful to work with files such as */etc/passwd*, where the fields are separated by a colon (:) or some other character. You cannot count characters because the length of the fields in the */etc/passwd* file vary. You have no way of knowing in which column a given field will be positioned in each line. Fortunately **cut** has an option that permits the user to change the default field separator.

E1   Let's say you want to check whether there are any empty entries in the password field of the */etc/passwd* file. Examine these two lines from */etc/passwd* :

```
frank:9QPSrGDlOpYqY:132:101::/lurnix/staff/frank:/bin/csh
patty::137:105::/lurnix/staff/patty:/bin/csh
```

The password field is the second field in the file. "frank" in the first line has a password, whereas "patty" in the second line does not. Enter the following:

cut -d':' -f2 /etc/passwd

The **-d** option tells **cut** that whatever character follows is the new field separator (**d**elimiter). If the new separator is a character that already has special significance to the shell, then it has to be enclosed in single or double quotes. If the delimiter is not a special character, the quotes are not needed. It is good practice to use them anyway.

This command tells **cut** to use a colon as the field separator and the /etc/passwd file as input. The **-f2** option says to **cut** out the second field.

The output will look something like this:

```
uz9e38Bbrb.86
Dsq2XvQQQtMSQ
tBixAe/LDb8Rk
YBzgOja0iTwvA
I/8I4u9SZF2C2
vRAqNCLW7KWeo
NuOosqbx9D5dU
TmVO/AFC0LeTU
6rBzROFRg4s2I
WAEv424P2rIF6
L35r7Sa4pU7fI
DjE4G.8KGsSeE
VOID
VOID
wzvHOA6672N/I
```

Because there are no blank lines in the output, you know that no accounts are set up to permit logging into the system without a password.

The command you just entered:

cut -d':' -f2 */etc/passwd*

consists of the following components:

Command	Option	Argument to the Option	Input File
cut	**-d**	**':'**	*/etc/passwd*
	-f	*2*	

The arguments to the option, such as 2-5 for ranges, work when the delimiter is changed. Select a range of fields for the password file and experiment to see what kind of output you can produce.

E2   Using Lines Without Separators

An earlier example showed that when **cut** is invoked with the **-f** option and there are no field separators in the line, then **cut** outputs the whole line. This can occasionally be very convenient.

Create a file called *record* that contains the following lines of text. Make sure there are no [Tab] characters in the first line. Use the [Tab] as a delimiter in the other lines.

NAME+CITY+PHONE
John [Tab]New York [Tab]555-9999
Peter [Tab]Chicago [Tab]555-8989

From the shell enter the following command:

cut -f2 *record*

The output should be:

> NAME+CITY+PHONE
> New York
> Chicago

The header line is included in the output, which can be useful in certain situations.

E3   There is also an option that will suppress lines that contain no separators. Enter the following:

> **cut** *-f2* **-s** *record*

The **-s** option requests that **cut** output only lines that include at least one of the requested fields and **s**uppress all others.

The output should look like this:

> **New York**
> **Chicago**

The command you have just entered:

> **cut** *-f2* **-s** *record*

consists of the following components:

Command	Option	Argument to the Option	Input File
cut	-f	2	record
	-s		

In summary, **cut** can be used to select fields separated by any character, or select ranges of characters from one or more files. The **cut** utility can be used as a filter, reading from standard input and writing to standard output. It is useful in selecting portions of database files for output to other utilities.

Objective F
Putting Files Together by Column

You can, as you did in Module 2, **paste** two files together by entering:

paste *names.tmp numbers.tmp*

The resulting **paste**d file is:

101	Bill	Z.	101
102	John	M.	103
106	Mary	L.	104
107	Santa	C.	105
108	Dana	M.	106
109	Leslie	A.	108

The **cut** utility is used to cut out selected data; **paste**, as the name implies, is used to put things together. It can be used to combine the lines of a file or the lines of two or more different files. The **paste** utility is very useful when you want to put together information located in various files.

F1   To easily demonstrate some of the properties of **paste** create a few new files in your directory. Use **cut** to create two files: *names, phones,* and use an editor to create a third file: *city.* Enter

cut *-f2 names.tmp* **>** *names*

The resulting output is field 2 of the file *names.tmp* written into a new file, *names*.

> Bill
> John
> Mary
> Santa
> Dana
> Leslie

Create a second file by using **cut** to output the second field of the *numbers.tmp* file into a new file *phones*. Enter:

> **cut** *-f2 numbers.tmp* **>** *phones*

The output in file *phones* is:

> 555-9163
> 666-8888
> 591-1191
> 511-1972
> 317-6512
> 777-2222

Use an editor and create a new file called *city* with the following contents:

> New York
> Chicago
> San Francisco
> Detroit
> Los Angeles
> Denver

F2   **Pasting a File**

When **paste** combines fields from files, it uses a specific character as a delimiter between these fields in the output created.

Just as with **cut**, the default delimiter is the Tab, but it can be
changed. Although **cut** and **paste** divide and combine files by
fields, the way they handle options is quite different.

F3   To **paste** the files *names* and *city*, enter the following:

   paste *names city*

The output is:

   Bill   New York
   John   Chicago
   Mary San Francisco
   Santa Detroit
   Dana Los Angeles
   Leslie Denver

The **paste** utility put together the first line of the first file with
the first line of the second file. Next, it combined the second
line of the first file and the second line of the second file, and so
on until the end of the file.

F4   **Working With One File**

Try the following command:

   paste *names*

The resulting output is:

Bill
John
Mary
Santa
Dana
Leslie

Not exactly earth shattering.

In this case, **paste** works very much like **cat**; that is, it takes each line from a specified file and writes it to the standard output.

You can **paste** together the lines of a single file. Enter:

paste -s *names*

The output now is:

Bill   John Mary Santa   Dana Leslie

In the first command line you entered, **paste** *names*, the *names* file was output unaltered. In an ordinary file, lines are separated by a "new-line" character that printers, terminals, etc., read to mean "start a new line of output." When **paste** has two files for input, it replaces the new-line characters with its own separator character (the ⎡Tab⎤ character), except when it is working on a line from the last file. The entries from the last file keep their new-line character so that a new line is started.

Without the **-s** option, **paste** treats a single named file as if it were the last file in a list, so each line in the file is treated as the last, and its new-line character is not replaced. When **-s** is specified, every new-line character, except the very last in the whole file is replaced by **paste**'s separator, the Tab. The **-s** option tells **paste** to substitute the delimiter for each new-line character from the input file.

F5 You can examine the output of **paste** to see that it replaced the end-of-line character with a Tab. Because the default field separator for **cut** is a Tab, you can enter the following command line:

> **paste -s** *names* | **cut** *-f3*

The name Mary appeared on the screen. Hence, **paste** must be using Tab characters (the default delimiter) to replace the new-line characters.

Another way is to enter:

> **paste -s** *names* **>** *pastednames*

Examine the file with the visual editor. From the command mode of *vi*, enter:

> **:set list**

The control character **$** tells you where the end of each line is located, and the control character ˆI indicates where each Tab character is located.

Objective G
Changing the Default Separator

You can also change the default separator for **paste** to a different character. Like **cut**, the option to change the default separator is **-d**.

G1 Using Special Characters as Separators

With **paste** you specify the character(s) to be used as the field delimiter(s). For instance, if you want to specify the **+** character as the delimiter rather than the Tab character you enter:

> **paste -s -d'+'** *names*

If you want to return to using the Tab character enter:

> **paste -s -d'** Tab **'** *names*

Here the Tab will simply appear as a tab-width space in the command line you are entering on your screen. To make the process appear more visible in the command line, enter:

> **paste -s -d'\t'** *names*

As with **cut**, it is a good policy to place a single quote before and after the character that immediately follows the **-d** option. In some cases, as with the above, this is a must.

G2 **paste** recognizes the following escape sequences:

tab   **\t**

new-line **\n**

backslash ****

empty   **\0**

> For each of the characters listed above (**t, n, 0**) to be read as a "special character" and have its special meaning, it MUST be preceded by a backslash.

For instance, enter the following:

paste -s -d't' *names*

When not preceded by the backslash, each of the above characters reverts to its regular meaning. Regular characters always have the same meaning whether preceded by a backslash or not.

G3   Specifying a List of Separators

Another difference between the **-d** option of **paste** and that of **cut** is that **paste** can receive a list of separator characters.

For example, enter:

paste -s -d'+-' *names*

The output is:

Bill+John-Mary+Santa-Dana+Leslie

The **-d** option is followed by a list of those characters that you want **paste** to use as delimiters, in the order you want them used. You can, of course, mix regular characters with special characters.

As usual, it is good practice to enclose the characters in single quotation marks, although it is not strictly required in all cases.

G4   For instance, enter:

paste -s -d'+-\t' *names*

The output is:

Bill+John-Mary   Santa+Dana-Leslie

where the space between Mary and Santa is a [Tab].

The following is a short description of how **paste** uses delimiters with the **-d** option. This option is especially useful when you use **paste** in conjunction with other utilities that may use a variety of delimiters.

- **paste** takes the first character that appears in the **-d** option list and uses it to replace the new-line character that separates the first and second lines of the file, hence a plus is entered between Bill and John;

- **paste** uses the second character in the list to replace the new-line character separating the second from the third line in the file, hence a minus is entered between John and Mary;

- The third character in the list, a tab, is used to replace the new-line between the next two lines, hence the tab between Mary and Santa;

- when **paste** exhausts the list, it goes back to the beginning and starts using the first character, then the second, then the third, and so on, until there are no lines left in the file, hence:

Santa+Dana-Leslie.

Objective H
Pasting Multiple Files

H1   Enter the command:

paste *names phones*

The output is:

```
Bill   555-9136
John  666-8888
Mary  591-1191
Santa 511-1972
Dana  317-6512
Leslie 777-2222
```

The two files have been pasted together, line 1 with line 1, line 2 with line 2, in the order of the file list in the command line.

H2 To paste together three files, enter:

paste *names phones city*

The output is:

```
Bill   555-9136   New York
John  666-8888   Chicago
Mary  591-1191   San Francisco
Santa 511-1972   Detroit
Dana  317-6512   Los Angeles
Leslie 777-2222  Denver
```

The **paste** utility is quite versatile; it can paste together the lines in two to twelve files. The order is important.

H3 You can change the order of the files, and the output will change accordingly. And as with **cut**, you can redirect the output of your **paste** command to a new file.

Enter

paste *names city phones* **>** *phone.list*

The output is:

Bill	New York	555-9136
John	Chicago	666-8888
Mary	San Francisco	591-1191
Santa	Detroit	511-1972
Dana	Los Angeles	317-6512
Leslie	Denver	777-2222

H4 As before, examine the file *phone.list* with the visual editor. From the command mode of *vi*, enter:

    :set list

The **$** is the end-of-line character and **ˆI** indicates that the default delimiter, Tab character, now separates the fields.

Objective I
Summary of the paste Process

- **paste** takes the first line of the first file and replaces its new-line character with the separator character (in the examples above, this is the default delimiter, the Tab character). "*Bill* \n" becomes "*Bill* \t".

- It then takes the first line of the second file and appends it to the above. "*Bill* \t" becomes "*Bill* \t*New York* \n".

- If there is a third file, it replaces the new-line character of the above with the separator. "*Bill\tNew York\n*" becomes "*Bill* \t*New York* \t".

- It then takes the first line of the third file and appends it to the above. "*Bill\tNew York\t*" becomes "*Bill\tNew York\t555-9136* \n".

- If there are no more files, it leaves the new-line character of the last file's first line in place; and

- **paste** repeats the above process until all lines of all files are exhausted.

Notice that the new-line characters of the lines belonging to the last file are left in place. By last file, we mean the last file that has lines left in it, not the last file mentioned in the command line.

I1   Delete the last two lines in the file *city* and the last line in the file *phones*.

I2   Enter the command:

paste *names phones city*

Your output then is:

```
Bill    555-9136    New York
John  666-8888    Chicago
Mary  591-1191    San Francisco
Santa511-1972    Detroit
Dana 317-6512
Leslie
```

Examine the control characters using the **:set list** option from within the visual editor.

Files do NOT have to be of equal length to be processed correctly.

Objective J
Pasting Standard Input

J1   Thus far you have used **paste** with explicitly named files. **paste** can also work with standard input. You must inform **paste** that it will be getting at least some of its input from the standard input by entering a minus sign (-) where the filename would otherwise appear.

Earlier you entered the command:

paste *names phones city*

and obtained the following output:

```
Bill    555-9136   New York
John   666-8888   Chicago
Mary  591-1191   San Francisco
Santa511-1972   Detroit
Dana  317-6512   Los Angeles
Leslie 777-2222   Denver
```

J2   Enter the following:

cat *names* | **paste** *phones city -*

Why was there no change in the output?

The minus sign is used as an option to **paste** that indicates where to place the data that comes from the standard input.

For another example:

sort *names* | **paste** *- phones city*

Objective K
Changing the Separator for Multiple Files

K1   As in the case of pasting a single file's lines, you can also change the default separator when pasting two or more files together. The option for this is (surprise, surprise) **-d**, and it behaves exactly as you might expect.

From the shell enter the following:

> **paste -d':'** *names phones city*

It will produce:

```
Bill:555-9136:New York
John:666-8888:Chicago
Mary:591-1191:San Francisco
Santa:511-1972:Detroit
Dana:317-6512
Leslie
```

Remember, you deleted data from two of the files.

The new-line character has been replaced with a colon (the delimiter you selected with the **-d**) in all instances *except* after the last entry (field) of each file.

K2   As was the case with a single file, you can also specify a list of multiple separators with multiple files.

Enter

> **paste -d':+'** *names phones city*

This will produce:

> Bill:555-9136+New York
> John:666-8888+Chicago
> Mary:591-1191+San Francisco
> Santa:511-1972+Detroit
> Dana:317-6512+Los Angeles
> Leslie:777-2222+Denver

Objective L
Combining cut and paste

L1   Multiple separators are especially useful when you combine **paste** and **cut**. It permits you to redefine fields in a file at your convenience. Enter

> **paste -d':+'** *names phones city* | **cut -d':'** *-f1*

The output is:

> Bill
> John
> Mary
> Santa
> Dana
> Leslie

In this case the separators are : and + for **paste**, and : for **cut**. If you change the **cut** field separator to + the first field is quite different. Now enter:

> **paste -d':+'** *names phones city* | **cut -d'+'** *-f1*

The first field extracted by **cut** is now:

Bill:555-9136
John:666-8888
Mary:591-1191
Santa:511-1972
Dana:317-6512
Leslie:777-2222

cut extracted the first field (**-f1**) that was separated by the **+** delimiter, which you indicated with (**-d '+'**).

Conclusion

You have used **cut** and **paste** by themselves and together to manipulate files by fields and by characters. You can change the character used as a field separator (delimiter) and select input and output. You can combine the output of one command with the input of another, work with a variety of input files and produce customized results.

Summary of **cut** Command Options

OPTION	Argument to the Option	FUNCTION
-f	2	instructs **cut** to extract the second field.
-c	9-25	instructs **cut** to extract characters found in **c**olumns beginning with nine through and including twenty-five.
-s		instructs **cut** to suppress all lines (records) that do not include a delimiter character. The **-s** must be used with either the **-f** option and its argument or the **-c** option and its argument.
-d	':'	instructs **cut** to replace the default delimiter with a colon (:). Any character can be used, but it must be enclosed in single quotes.

Summary of **paste** Command Options

OPTION	Argument to the Option	FUNCTION
-s		instructs **paste** to substitute its own default delimiter (the Tab) for the new-line character found in the input file(s), then place this substitute in the new output being created— except in the last line of the last file. In order for the **-s** option to take effect, a **-d** option and its argument must come immediately after it in the command line.
-d	':'	instructs **paste** to replace the default delimiter with a colon (:). As with **cut**, any character can be used, but it must be enclosed in single quotes. Unlike **cut**, the **paste** utility can be instructed to use several delimiters in sequence, in both the input and output files.

Module 9

Using Relational Files with join

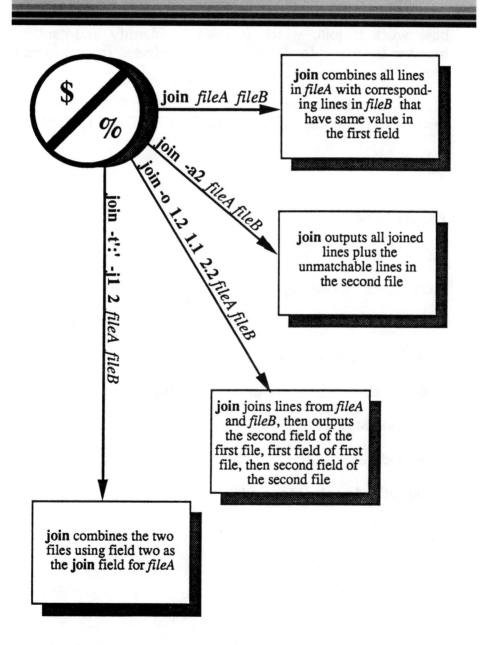

join *fileA fileB*

join combines all lines in *fileA* with corresponding lines in *fileB* that have same value in the first field

join -a2 *fileA fileB*

join outputs all joined lines plus the unmatchable lines in the second file

join -o 1.2 1.1 2.2 *fileA fileB*

join joins lines from *fileA* and *fileB*, then outputs the second field of the first file, first field of first file, then second field of the second file

join -t':' -j1 2 *fileA fileB*

join combines the two files using field two as the **join** field for *fileA*

Introduction

In previous modules you used **cut** to extract specific fields from a file, **paste** to put together lines from separate files, **grep** to locate records, **sed** to make stream editing changes, and **awk** to manipulate data values. The other essential utility for database work is **join**, which is used to identify and "splice" together lines or records appropriately selected from different files.

The ability to **join** correct records from separate files is critical to designing and maintaining a relational database application.

Prerequisites

Before beginning this module, you should be able to:

- create, edit, move, copy, view and remove files;

- make directories and move around in the file system;

- use basic utilities (Module 2);

- use the shell to issue commands (Module 3);

- use **awk** (Module 6);

- use **sed** (Module 7);

- use **cut** and **paste** (Module 8).

Objective

Upon completion of this module you will be able to:

- use the **join** utility separately and in combination with the other power utilities to develop and maintain a simple relational database application.

Procedures

The **join** utility works on files that are arranged in fields and records (columns and rows).

If you completed the exercises in Module 2, you created two data files: *names.tmp* and *numbers.tmp*. But that was then, this is now. As in all bureaucracies, this week there are new room assignments, new phone assignments, and new employees.

Objective A
Increasing the Example Files

Either create or update the *names.tmp* file to look like the following. The new lines are indicated by arrows.

       101 [Tab]Bill [Tab]Z.
       102 [Tab]John [Tab]M.
       106 [Tab]Mary [Tab]L.
       107 [Tab]Santa [Tab]C.
       108 [Tab]Dana [Tab]M.
       109 [Tab]Leslie [Tab]A.
       103 [Tab]Judy [Tab]C.   ←
       105 [Tab]Doug [Tab]M.   ←
       104 [Tab]Linda [Tab]W.   ←

Likewise, create or add the following additional room and phone numbers to the *numbers.tmp* file.

101 [Tab]555-9136
103 [Tab]666-8888
104 [Tab]591-1191
105 [Tab]511-1972
106 [Tab]317-6512
108 [Tab]777-2222
109 [Tab]333-4444   ←
102 [Tab]511-1984   ←
110 [Tab]316-1566   ←

Objective B
Identifying Relationships in Database Files

The file *names.tmp* indicates which room each person is assigned. It *relates* each person to his or her room. The file *numbers.tmp* relates each room to its phone number. The purpose of database files is to reveal relationships.

Clearly there are some rooms without occupants, and some rooms that have occupants but lack phone numbers.

B1   Examining Relationships between files

Look back at the two database files you just updated. Most of the rooms listed in the two example files have both occupants and phones. By examining the contents of the two files, humans can easily determine the correct phone number for *Leslie*.

First, her name is located in the *names.tmp* file. Associated with her name is her room number, 109. Examination of the *numbers.tmp* file reveals that room 109 has a phone with number *333-4444*. The identical value (*109*) is in the first field of a row in each of the files. Recognizing that, the remainder of each of the lines can be related. Leslie has a phone number of 333-4444.

The **join** utility operates the same way.

The complete relationship of "person to room to phone" could be examined if we created a new composite file that included each room number on the same line as the appropriate person's name and phone number.

Objective C
Combining Selected Records with join

Have **join** combine the appropriate lines of the two example files by entering:

> **join** *names.tmp   numbers.tmp*

The output is:

    101 Bill Z. 555-9136
    106 Mary L. 317-6512
    108 Dana M. 777-2222
    109 Leslie A. 333-4444

Look back at the input files. This output is not a complete join of related records. The input files include: 102 John and 102 511-1984, but the join of those lines was not included in the output.

The **join** utility goes through the lines in the files sequentially. To work properly, the lines in the input files must be in sorted order. The input files are not sorted, so **join** missed a related set of data.

C1   Sorting Data Files

Use **sort** to create ordered versions of the example files.

> **sort** *names.tmp* **>** *ord.names*

> **sort** *numbers.tmp* **>** *ord.numbers*

C2   Joining Sorted Files

These new sorted files have a common field for joining in the first field. You can now **join** the files. Enter

> **join** *ord.names ord.numbers* **>** *room_nam_ph*

Examine the two input files and the output file you just created. The output is the result of joining the two sorted input files.

- Both input files have an identifying number in the first field.

- Both input files are sorted in order, by that first field.

- The output from **join** includes only those lines that have the same value in the first field in *both* files. All other lines in both files are omitted.

- The output is a *joined composite*. The first line of output consists of: 101, the value that is common in the first field of both files. The remainder of the output line is Bill Z. from the first file, and 555-9136 from the second file.

If there is no join for a line in the input, there is no output. For example, the output from the last command line does not include Santa C. Although his name is related to a room number in one file, the room is not listed with a phone number in the other. (Either he is a new employee, or he is no longer an employee.)

In its basic form, the **join** utility does not create a joined record unless all of the files have a record with the common value in the first field. If 11 files contain information about room 107, but the twelfth file does not have the number 107 as a value in the first field, **join** does not output anything for that record.

In these two files **join** used the field containing room numbers as its common field and joined the appropriate lines, just as you did.

C3 Joining Files With Missing Information

The function of **join** is to connect fields from separate files if, and only if, the files are related to each other through the presence of a common value in the join field. There will be times when you will want files joined and the output to include the data that could not be joined.

You can have **join** output records of data with missing information. Enter:

    join -a1 *ord.names ord.numbers*

The output is:

```
101 Bill Z. 555-9136
102 John M. 511-1984
103 Judy C. 666-8888
104 Linda W. 591-1191
105 Doug M. 511-1972
106 Mary L. 317-6512
107 Santa C.
108 Dana M. 777-2222
109 Leslie A. 333-4444
```

With this command **join** outputs the joined lines as well as the lines in the *first* file that are unpairable (107 Santa C.).

To obtain information about records in the other file, enter

join -a2 *ord.names ord.numbers*

In this case, the output is:

```
101 Bill Z. 555-9136
102 John M. 511-1984
103 Judy C. 666-8888
104 Linda W. 591-1191
105 Doug M. 511-1972
106 Mary L. 317-6512
108 Dana M. 777-2222
109 Leslie A. 333-4444
110 316-1566
```

With this command **join** outputs the joined records and the unmatchable records of the second file (110 316-1566).

C4   All of the unmatchable records from either file can be output. Enter

join -a1 -a2 *ord.names ord.numbers*

This output is the complete database, joined where possible:

```
101 Bill Z. 555-9136
102 John M. 511-1984
103 Judy C. 666-8888
104 Linda W. 591-1191
105 Doug M. 511-1972
106 Mary L. 317-6512
107 Santa C.
108 Dana M. 777-2222
109 Leslie A. 333-4444
110 316-1566
```

Objective D
Determining the Output Order

Thus far each time you joined the files, the order of the fields in the output was the same as the input files. You can change the output order.

Enter the following to specify where fields are presented in the output:

join -o *1.2 2.2 1.1 ord.names ord.numbers*

The output is now rearranged into a new order.

Bill 555-9136 101
John 511-1984 102
Judy 666-8888 103
Linda 591-1191 104
Doug 511-1972 105
Mary 317-6512 106
Dana 777-2222 108
Leslie 333-4444 109

Although the order of the fields output by **join** is changed by this command, the field used for joining remains the first field. The new portion of this command line is:

-o *1.2 2.2 1.1*   This argument is passed to join, instructing **join** to output three fields: *1.2 (first name), 2.2 (phone number);* and *1.1 (room number).*

D1   Determining File and Field Numbers

Both the files and their fields are given identification numbers. Files are give numbers corresponding with the order they are entered in the command line; fields are numbered according to the order in the file. In the command line you just entered, *ord.names* is file *1* and has three fields; and *ord.numbers* is file *2* with two fields:

	File 1: *ord.names*	File 2: *ord.numbers*
Field Number	Field Name	Field Name
1	*room number*	*room number*
2	*first name*	*phone number*
3	*middle initial*	

The first field of the output (first name) comes from the first file's second field (*1.2*). The second output field (phone number) is the second file's second field (*2.2*). The last field of output (room number) is the first field from the first file (*1.1*).

Creating a table such as this is very useful when working with **join**.

Objective E
Creating Example Files with Colon Delimiter

Thus far you have used **join** with files that included the [Tab] as field delimiter. Often other characters are more useful.

Create the following two files using the colon for field delimiter. The first file relates class number to class name and is called *classes*.

```
10:Introduction to Unix
11:Shell Programming
12:System Administration
13:C Language Programming I
14:C Language Programming II
```

The second file includes one line for each course completed by the student, relating course number to student name. Create a file called *completed* with contents something like the following. The names you use are not important, but the course numbers must be in order and have the same values as in the previous file: *10, 11, 12, 13,* and *14.*

> 10:Mel Mayfield
> 10:Joan Heller
> 10:Lillian Frank
> 10:Phil Barnhart
> 10:Gene Eakins
> 11:Phil Barnhart
> 11:Joan Heller
> 11:Mel Mayfield
> 11:Gene Eakins
> 12:Mel Mayfield
> 13:Walter Mitchell
> 13:Mel Mayfield
> 14:Mel Mayfield
> 14:Walter Mitchell

As students enroll in courses the course number and name can be added to the *completed* file. Because **join** works with sorted files, the data should either be entered with other entries of the same course number, or the file should be sorted before the following command lines are entered.

Objective F
Changing the Delimiter Character

A listing of all courses taken by each student is a useful report. Enter the following:

join -t*:* **-o** *1.2 2.1 2.2 completed classes* | **sort** *+1*

Both files have colons separating the fields. The **-t** option instructs **join** to use a different field separator. In this case it calls for the colon. The resulting output is the three selected fields from the joining of two files that used the colon for field delimiter. The output consisting of one line for each student, for each course taken, is sorted by the value in the second field:

```
Phil Barnhart:10:Introduction to Unix
Phil Barnhart:11:Shell Programming
Gene Eakins:10:Introduction to Unix
Gene Eakins:11:Shell Programming
Lillian Frank:10:Introduction to Unix
Joan Heller:10:Introduction to Unix
Joan Heller:11:Shell Programming
Mel Mayfield:10:Introduction to Unix
Mel Mayfield:11:Shell Programming
Mel Mayfield:12:System Administration
Mel Mayfield:13:C Language Programming I
Mel Mayfield:14:C Language Programming II
Walter Mitchell:13:C Language Programming I
Walter Mitchell:14:C Language Programming II
```

F1   Examining the Command Line

You just entered the following command line, which changed separators, determined output order, and sorted:

join -t: **-o** *1.2 2.1 2.2 completed classes* | **sort** *+1*

join   Execute the **join** utility

-t: Use the colon instead of the ⌨Tab for the field separator.

-o *1.2 2.1 2.2* Output the results in the following order: file 1's field 2, then file 2's field 1, followed by file 2's field 2.

completed Give the argument *completed* to **join** as the first file name to open for input.

classes Likewise, pass the argument *classes* to **join** as the second file name to open for input.

| Connect the standard output from **join** to the input of **sort** through a pipe.

sort Execute the **sort** utility.

+1 Start sorting *after* the first field (therefore on the second field, which is last name).

The following table summarizes the components and functions of the command line:

join -t: **-o** *1.2 2.1 2.2 completed classes* | **sort** *+1*

Command	Option	Argument to the Option	Input	Redirect
join	**-t**	*:*	*completed*		
	-o	*1.2 2.1 2.2*	*classes*	
sort	**+**	*1*	standard input	

F2   Changing the Delimiter of the Input

The output from the **who** utility consists of fields separated by one or more spaces.

Run **who** on your system and examine the format of the output. It looks something like:

```
scott        ttyh5      Nov     23     10:05
patty        ttyi1      Nov     23     09:47
conniejo     ttyi7      Nov     23     08:43
john         ttyie      Nov     21     08:43
dave         ttyif      Nov     23     10:48
```

In a file such as this one that uses white space (tabs and/or spaces) between fields, the number of spaces between two fields varies depending on the information. If the login name is short, more spaces are included before the *tty*.

You can use **sed** to exchange the spaces for a specific character delimiter between fields. Enter

who | sed 's/ */+/g'

There are two spaces before the asterisk. They instruct **sed** to search for: one space, followed by zero or more spaces. **sed** utility can be used to change delimiters from variable white space to a specific character.

F3   Joining a File and Standard Input

Create a file called *friends* containing your login and the login names of several friends. Make sure the file is sorted in alphabetical order.

You can use **join** to create a join composite of the output of the **who** command and your *friends* file. The output of this join tells you which of your friends are logged on at the moment.

F4   Enter the following:

> **who | sort | sed 's/ */+/g' | join -t+ -** *friends*

The **join** utility produced a join composite of your friends' logins with their **who** output line. If you received information about a friend, he or she is logged on.

This command line instructs the shell to:

who	Execute the **who** utility.
|	Connect the output of **who** to the input of **sort**.
sort	Execute the **sort** utility.
|	Connect the output of **sort** to the input of **sed**.
's/ */+/g'	Pass as an argument to **sed**. Instruct **sed** to find all strings of one or more spaces and replace them with a + character.
|	Connect the output of **sed** to the input of **join**.
join	Execute the **join** utility.
-t+	Pass as an argument to **join**. Instruct **join** to use the + as the field separator.

-           Pass as an argument to **join**. Informs **join** to read standard input for the first files to join. (The output from **sed**.)

friends   Identifies the second file to be used by **join**.

Objective G

Changing the Field to be Joined

In the examples used thus far, the first field was used as the field to be joined. For each file, you can specify a different field for joining.

The following is an example password file. Each system keeps a password file called /etc/passwd. The fields in the /etc/passwd file are separated by colons. The fourth field is the number of the user's group.

```
tammy:7HRtmKLyY:631:101::/lurnix/tammy:/bin/csh
mike:4DffTWMgh:462:101::/lurnix/mike:/bin/csh
lela:F2kkURvTp:136:103::/lurnix/lela:/bin/csh
bob:8FRthKLyS:540:101::/lurnix/bob:/bin/csh
mary:9QPSrGDIO:73:102::/lurnix/mary:/bin/csh
stephany:8RgGvVSSL:246:102::/lurnix/stephany:/bin/csh
```

Look at the first two entries above (tammy and mike). The value in the fourth field (group) is *101*. Both users belong to group *101*. Generally the system administrator sets up group membership placing users who need to share files in the same group. *Data Entry, Management, System Administrators, Operators, Specific Application Users, etc.* are common groups.

G1   Examine the password file on your system using **pg** or **more** with a command such as:

more */etc/passwd*

Locate the fourth field and write down several of the group values used on your system.

G2   Create a new file called *groups* containing the group numbers and what each group probably is, separated by a colon. If you do not know what each group is, and do not care to bother the system administrator, make up a job description for this exercise. The following is an example *groups* file.

101:Administrators
102:Data Entry
103:Programmers

With the *groups* file completed, you can have **join** create a listing of all users on your system who are in each group. Because the group is the fourth field, you must sort on the fourth field and instruct **join** to use that field for joining.

G3   Enter the following

sort *+3* **-t***:* */etc/passwd* | **join** **-t***:* *-j1 4 - groups*

The output consists of a join of the *groups* file with the */etc/passwd* file sorted by users group affiliation.

101:bob:8FRthKLyS:540::/lurnix/bob:/bin/csh:Administrators
101:mike:4DffTWMgh5po:462::/lurnix/mike:/bin/csh:Administrators
101:tammy:7HRtmKLYiCv:631::/lurnix/tammy:/bin/csh:Administrators
102:mary:9QPSrGDIOYqY:73::/lurnix/mary:/bin/csh:Data Entry
102:stephany:8RgGvVSSL:246::/lurnix/stephany:/bin/csh:Data Entry
103:lela:F2kkURvTp:136::/lurnix/lela:/bin/csh:Programmers

The command you just entered was:

sort *+3* **-t***:* */etc/passwd* | **join** **-t***:* **-j***1 4* **-** *groups*

In this example, there are two new instructions:

-j*1 4*   This argument instructs **join** to join lines from the first file using its fourth field as the join field. The *1* indicates the first file; the *4* specifies the field to be used for joining.

-   The join utility is used here in a pipeline getting one file of input from the output of **sort**. The minus sign is entered into the command line as an argument to **join**. It takes the place of the filename of the first file to be joined. The minus sign is interpreted by join to mean *read from standard input for that file.*

G4   Additionally, you could instruct **join** to output only selected fields, varying the order. The following table summarizes the fields and field numbers for *groups* and the first part of */etc/passwd*.

	File 1: */etc/passwd*	File 2: *groups*
Field Number	Field Name	Field Name
1	*login*	*group number*
2	*password*	*group name*
3	*user i.d.*	
4	*group number*	

The next command line instructs **join** to output three fields: *group number, group name,* and *login*. Because this command is long, it is displayed here on two lines. As was discussed in Module 3, the backslash 🛇 is included at the end of the first line to instruct the shell not to interpret the newline character that is generated when you enter a Return key.

```
sort +3 -t: /etc/passwd           \
| join -t: -o 2.1 2.2 1.1 -j1 4 - groups
```

The output depends on the contents of your *groups* file and your system's */etc/passwd* file; it will be something like:

```
101:Administrators:bob
101:Administrators:mike
101:Administrators:tammy
102:Data Entry:mary
102:Data Entry:stephany
103:Programmers:lela
```

The addition of the output option (**-o** *2.1 2.2 1.1*) instructed **join** to output fields in the order:

File	Field	Field Name
2	1	group number
2	2	group name
1	1	login name

G5 **Entering Long Command Lines**

Command lines can get very long when you use **join** and the other powerful utilities with their many options. As was pointed out in Module 3, you can issue long command lines in several ways:

- Enter the command on two or more lines, with a backslash ⟨\⟩ before pressing each ⟨Return⟩;

- Enter the command as one line, allowing the terminal to wrap the display;

- Enter the command into a file, make it executable, and then run the script following the procedure examined in Module 3. The script approach is very useful in these modules and is recommended. Be careful in naming scripts. Avoid using command names such as **join** for script names to avoid confusion with utilities.

Objective H
Examining a Single File Design

There are two basic approaches to database application design: *single-file*, and multiple file or *relational*. To explore the differences we will examine a school records database organized both ways.

H1 Designing a Single File Application

A single file database approach could have individual records for every student in one file. The fields would include all needed information about the student, courses taken, etc. For example:

> last name
> first name
> address
> city
> state
> zip code
> area code
> phone
> date accepted
> intro unix, completion date
> shell programming, completion date
> system administration, completion date
> C language programming I, completion date
> C language programming II, completion date

H2 Using a Single File Application

The user would add a record to the file for each student who enrolls. As courses are completed, dates are added in the respective fields. If a person takes only two courses, two course fields will be used, and the remainder left blank. If a person moves or takes a course a second time, the new data are written over the old.

If new courses are added to the curriculum, new fields have to be added to all records.

H3 Examining the Advantages and Limitations

When all the information is in one file, the system can quickly locate it. Only one file has to be opened; no records need to be matched from different files.

Although CPU time is saved, there are several problems with this design.

Loss of old data: When replacement data such as a new address or the date of retaking a course are added, the old data are lost or very difficult to locate in backup versions of the file. A listing of all courses taken and their dates of completion is not possible using the single file.

Disk space is wasted: A field must be included for every possible entry. In this approach every course offered by the school has a field for the date the student completed the course, even though it is clear that not all courses will be taken by every student. Addition of fields in the middle of each record is a difficult task.

If disk space is not a problem, and if the curriculum is stable and limited or if the student body is small, this approach may work.

Multiple entry fields are difficult: Assume the school decides to grant awards to the outstanding student in each term. Do we add several fields to each student's record for possible awards? How many will be certain to cover it?

Objective I
Examining a Relational Database Design

The problems associated with a single-file design are solved using the multiple file relational database approach. However, their solution is at the expense of central processor time. A relational database uses several files linked together by join fields. Every file must be join-able to at least one other file through a common field. For example, in this application the following files could be created.

File: *classes*

       1 course identification number   [*join to registrar*]
       2 course name

File: *registrar*

       1 course identification number   [*join to classes*]
       2 student identification number [*join to awards, student*]
       3 date course completed

File: *awards*

       1 student identification number [*join to registrar, student*]
       2 date of award
       3 award name

File: *student*

> 1 student identification number [*join to registrar, awards*]
> 2 last name
> 3 first name
> 4 address
> 5 city
> 6 state
> 7 zip code
> 8 area code
> 9 phone
> 10 date accepted

Objective J
Implementing a School Relational Database

This module concludes with a series of exercises developing a relational database to keep track of school records. The process begins with the creation of example data files (the last ones to enter!). The files are used by **join** and other utilities to extract appropriate data for reports.

J1 Creating Example Files

Begin by making a new directory called *School* and create the following four files. We have included some data to demonstrate how the system works. You may want to include additional data, following the same field definitions and the colon field delimiter.

File: *student*

This file relates a student identification number to each student's name, address, etc. Each record in the *student* file consists of nine fields separated by colons:

Student ID:Last Name:First Name:Address:City:State:Zip:Area Code:Phone

Enter the following example data:

```
sid-1:Selquist:Sigrid:888 Baxter Ave S.W.:Canton:OH:42910:216:555-4788
sid-2:Braucher:Lelia:3900 Eaton Road, N.W.:Canton:OH:43819:216:555-3354
sid-3:Reed:Harry:Route 5:Benton:KY:69267:502:555-8421
sid-4:Colon:Danny:Cat Arts: 153 7th St.:Louisville:KY:87503:718:555-7254
sid-5:Strand:Lyle:137 Woods Road:Canton:OH:47079:216:555-1111
```

File: *classes*

This file connects each class name to the class identification number and consists of just two fields. It is the same classes file used at the beginning of this module; if you created it then, just copy it into this directory.

Course ID:Course name

Enter the following example data:

```
10:Introduction to Unix
11:Shell Programming
12:System Administration
13:C Language Programming I
14:C Language Programming II
```

File: *awards*

This file relates students identification number with the date and award given. Three fields are in each record of the *awards* file:

Student ID:Date:Award Name

Enter the following example data:

```
sid-1:6-15-87:Outstanding Teacher
sid-2:1-15-89:Essence of Grandmother
sid-3:9-13-88:Colleague Extraordinaire
sid-4:12-22-88:Impressive Return from the Dead
sid-5:12-28-88:Teacher of Living
```

File: *registrar*

This file, which keeps track of the courses students completed, consists of three fields:

```
Course ID:Student ID:Date
```

Create the file with the following data:

```
10:sid-1:12-15-87
10:sid-2:12-15-87
10:sid-3:12-15-87
10:sid-4:12-15-87
10:sid-5:12-15-87
11:sid-1:6-5-88
11:sid-2:6-5-88
11:sid-3:6-5-88
11:sid-4:6-5-88
11:sid-5:6-5-88
12:sid-2:12-12-88
12:sid-4:12-12-88
12:sid-5:2-22-89
13:sid-4:2-22-89
13:sid-5:2-22-89
```

As a group, the example data files provide information about the students, courses taken and awards given.

J2   Using the Relational Application

The user of this database creates a new entry in the *student* file as each new student is enrolled. When a class is given, new records are created in the *registrar* file with each student's identification number, the class number, and the date entered.

New class offerings are made by adding the information into the *classes* file.

In this situation the decision to make awards was accommodated easily. A new file of *awards*, which includes the award name, date and student identification number, was created. No modification of existing files was needed.

Management, expansion, and alteration of the data are easily handled. The cost for using this approach is computing time. The machine must create new joined tables for reports. With the speed and power of most modern computers that run UNIX this is seldom a problem unless the database is extensive and very complex.

J3   Joining Files for a Basic Report

Each of the files you created for this example database reveals specific relationships between fields of data. It is important that the files used for these examples be in sorted order. Reports often need data from several files, related properly. For example, one file relates student identification number to name, address, etc. Another relates student ID to the name of the award and date received. Between them, a report of student name and awards could be created.

The *student* and *awards* files consist of the following fields:

	File 1: *student*	File 2: *awards*
Field Number	Field Name	Field Name
1	student i.d.	student i.d.
2	last name	date
3	first name	award name
4	address	
5	city	
6	state	
7	zip	
8	area code	
9	phone	

A useful report is a listing of student names (rather than ID's) and awards received.

Enter the following:

join -t: **-o** *1.3 1.2 2.3 student awards*

The resulting joined output is:

```
Sigrid:Selquist:Outstanding Teacher
Harry:Reed:Colleague Extraordinaire
Danny:Colon:Impressive Return from the Dead
Lyle:Strand:Teacher of Living
```

The **join** utility takes input from the two files, uses the colon for field delimiter, creates a join field based on the value in the *student identification number* field, then outputs three fields: **-o** *1.3 1.2 2.3* using the standard numbering scheme.

File	Field	Field Name
1	3	first name
1	2	last name
2	3	award name

J4   ## Removing Delimiter Characters

Although the data are correct, the field delimiters are still present. Include **awk** in the command line or shell script to tidy it up. (Again the following is a single command line with a backslash entered before pressing Return to allow entering the command on two lines.

```
join -t: -o 1.3 1.2 2.3 student awards        \
| awk -F: '{print $1, $2 ",", $3}'
```

The output from **join** is a new file consisting of a join of the two input files, based on the values in the first field, *student identification number*.

Sigrid Selquist, Outstanding Teacher
Harry Reed, Colleague Extraordinaire
Danny Colon, Impressive Return from the Dead
Lyle Strand, Teacher of Living

The first portion of this command is exactly like the previous command. The **awk** section is new, and accomplishes the following:

awk   Execute the **awk** utility.

-F: Instruct **awk** to us the colon as the delimiter between fields.

{print $1, $2, $3}   Inform **awk** to select fields 1, 2, and 3 from its input. Print the selected fields.

J5   Reporting on Classes Each Student Completed

When the school officials need a report on classes completed by the students, the information must be retrieved from the *classes* and *registrar* files.

The field numbers and field names for both files are:

	File 1: *classes*	File 2: *registrar*
Field Number	Field Name	Field Name
1	course i.d.	course i.d.
2	course name	student i.d.
3	middle initial	date

Proper selection of fields from the two files produces the required report. Enter the following:

join -t: **-o** *1.2 2.2 2.3 classes registrar*

Examine the resulting output confirming that the output field specifications *(1.2 2.2 2.3)* are correct:

```
Introduction to Unix:sid-1:12-15-87
Introduction to Unix:sid-2:12-15-87
Introduction to Unix:sid-3:12-15-87
Introduction to Unix:sid-4:12-15-87
Introduction to Unix:sid-5:12-15-87
Shell Programming:sid-1:6-5-88
Shell Programming:sid-2:6-5-88
Shell Programming:sid-3:6-5-88
Shell Programming:sid-4:6-5-88
Shell Programming:sid-5:6-5-88
System Administration:sid-2:12-12-88
System Administration:sid-4:12-12-88
System Administration:sid-5:2-22-89
C Language Programming I:sid-4:2-22-89
C Language Programming I:sid-5:2-22-89
```

The output is a join composite of the two files. The output relates each student to the courses and dates the courses were completed. There are two obvious problems with this output: the student identification numbers are present, not the names, and the file is not grouped such that all courses taken by each student are listed together.

J6 Sorting Output by Student Identification Number

The **sort** utility can be used to collect the appropriate records together. Enter the following:

Join -t: **-o** *1.2 2.2 2.3 classes registrar* |**sort -t**: *+1*

The output that results from this command line is sorted by the second field, student identification number:

```
Introduction to Unix:sid-1:12-15-87
Shell Programming:sid-1:6-5-88
System Administration:sid-2:12-12-88
Introduction to Unix:sid-2:12-15-87
Shell Programming:sid-2:6-5-88
Introduction to Unix:sid-3:12-15-87
Shell Programming:sid-3:6-5-88
System Administration:sid-4:12-12-88
Introduction to Unix:sid-4:12-15-87
C Language Programming I:sid-4:2-22-89
Shell Programming:sid-4:6-5-88
Introduction to Unix:sid-5:12-15-87
C Language Programming I:sid-5:2-22-89
System Administration:sid-5:2-22-89
Shell Programming:sid-5:6-5-88
```

The output now has all courses taken by each student listed together, but student numbers are still present.

J7 **Joining Records from Three Files**

Thus far *classes* and *registrar* have been joined to produce the student classes report. To replace the numbers with student names, information from a third file, *student*, must be included. Three files can be joined on different fields in sequence.

Enter the following:

```
join -t: -o 1.2 2.2 2.3 classes registrar   \
| sort -t: +1     \
| join -t: -j1 2 -o 2.3 2.2 1.1 1.3 - student
```

This command line produces a joined composite of *classes* and *registrar* then joins that output with the file *student* producing a new composite file:

```
Sigrid:Selquist:Introduction to Unix:12-15-87
Sigrid:Selquist:Shell Programming:6-5-88
Lelia:Braucher:System Administration:12-12-88
Lelia:Braucher:Introduction to Unix:12-15-87
Lelia:Braucher:Shell Programming:6-5-88
Harry:Reed:Introduction to Unix:12-15-87
Harry:Reed:Shell Programming:6-5-88
Danny:Colon:System Administration:12-12-88
Danny:Colon:Introduction to Unix:12-15-87
Danny:Colon:C Language Programming I:2-22-89
Danny:Colon:Shell Programming:6-5-88
Lyle:Strand:Introduction to Unix:12-15-87
Lyle:Strand:C Language Programming I:2-22-89
Lyle:Strand:System Administration:2-22-89
Lyle:Strand:Shell Programming:6-5-88
```

The new portions of the previous command line specified which field **join** examined for joining the first file:

-j1 2   This argument instructs **join** to use the second field (*student i.d.*) from the first input file (standard input) for joining. The second file has *student i.d.* as its first field, so no specification for which field to use is needed.

-o *2.3 2.2 1.1 1.3*   The output fields are specified by this option, using the field and file numbers described in the following table:

	File 1: *standard input*	File 2: *student*
Field Number	Field Name	Field Name
1	*course name*	*student i.d.*
2	*student i.d.*	*last name*
3	*date*	*first name*
4		*address*
5		*city*
6		*state*
7		*zip*
8		*area code*
9		*phone*

J8   Cleaning Up a Three File Join

The output is rather messy with colons still hanging around. It can be made more useful by including **awk** in the command line to select and print fields.

```
join -t: -o 1.2 2.2 2.3 classes registrar    \
| sort -t: +1    \
| join -t:-j1 2 -o 2.3 2.2 1.1 1.3 - student    \
| awk -F: '{print $1, $2 ",",   $3 ";", $4}'
```

Look closely at the **awk** portion of the command line. The commas inside the quotation marks are in italic font indicating that they are text and can be changed to any other characters. The commas following quotation marks in bold type are **awk** commands setting off the units of the command.

The output is now more readable having printed out the fields with appropriate punctuation:

```
Sigrid Selquist, Introduction to Unix; 12-15-87
Sigrid Selquist, Shell Programming; 6-5-88
Lelia Braucher, System Administration; 12-12-88
Lelia Braucher, Introduction to Unix; 12-15-87
Lelia Braucher, Shell Programming; 6-5-88
Harry Reed, Introduction to Unix; 12-15-87
Harry Reed, Shell Programming; 6-5-88
Danny Colon, System Administration; 12-12-88
Danny Colon, Introduction to Unix; 12-15-87
Danny Colon, C Language Programming I; 2-22-89
Danny Colon, Shell Programming; 6-5-88
Lyle Strand, Introduction to Unix; 12-15-87
Lyle Strand, C Language Programming I; 2-22-89
Lyle Strand, System Administration; 2-22-89
Lyle Strand, Shell Programming; 6-5-88
```

With the above command or script you can print out a listing of all students and the courses they have completed. Modification of the script would permit a wide variety of reports.

J9   Using a Shell Script to Report for One Student

One very useful way of interacting with a database is to make inquiries concerning a single student. To do so, an argument indicating which student must be passed to the script.

Create a new file called *stu_trans* with the following shell script for its contents:

```
join -t: -o 1.2 2.2 2.3 classes registrar     \
| sort -t: +1      \
| join -t: -j1 2 -o 2.3 2.2 1.1 1.3 - student     \
| grep $1     \
| awk -F:     \
'BEGIN {
print
print "Summary of Courses Taken"
print
print "Name, Course Taken; Date"
print
}
{
    f_name = $1
    l_name = $2
    courses = $3
    date = $4
print f_name, l_name ",", courses ";", date
}
END {
print
print "Student has taken", NR, "courses"
print
}'
```

J10   Make the script executable by entering:

```
chmod 700 stu_trans
```

J11   Run the script by entering the following, where *Braucher* is one of the students:

stu_trans *Braucher*

The resulting output lists the courses taken by the one student named:

Summary of Courses Taken

Name, Course Taken; Date

Lelia Braucher, System Administration; 12-12-88
Lelia Braucher, Introduction to Unix; 12-15-87
Lelia Braucher, Shell Programming; 6-5-88

Student has taken 3 courses

Most of the script is the same as previously entered commands calling for the joining of files, sorting, etc.

It is important to recognize the different uses of the **$1** in the above script. The shell interprets the **$1** to be a predefined variable set equal to the second "word" in the command line (the first being the $0 word). Commands issued in the form of **command** *argument* such as **stu_trans** *Braucher*, result in the argument becoming the value of **$1**. The first use of **$1** in the above script requests that the shell place the value of **$1** in the script as the argument for **grep**. The result is that **grep** looks for records that contain the target student's information.

The **$1** is also used in the **awk** command for the predefined variable, *field 1*. The shell does not interpret the second **$1** but passes it along to **awk** as is because it is inside the single quotation marks that surround the **awk** command. Hence **awk** can interpret it.

J12   Using awk to Calculate Tuition

Thus far we have used **awk** as a formatting tool to print fields and punctuation. The **awk** utility is a powerful data manipulator that can be used to make changes and do calculations. The following shell script uses **awk** to calculate the tuition paid by a student for all courses taken.

J13   The *classes* file currently has two fields, class number and class name. To include tuition in the database, add a third field to the records in the *classes* file, resulting in:

```
10:Introduction to Unix:650
11:Shell Programming:700
12:System Administration:750
13:C Language Programming I:750
14:C Language Programming II:800
```

J14   Copy the previous shell script to a file named *tuition* and make changes to it that are identified on the following page:

```
join -t: -o 1.2 2.2 2.3 1.3 classes registrar    \    ←
| sort -t: +1      \
| join -t: -j1 2 -o 2.3 2.2 1.1 1.3 1.4 - student    \    ←
| grep $1    \
| awk -F:    \
'BEGIN {
print
print "Summary of Courses Taken"
print
print "Name, Course Taken; Date, Tuition"    ←
print
}
{
    f_name = $1
    l_name = $2
    courses = $3
    date = $4
    tuition = $5    ←
    tot_tuition += $5    ←
print f_name, l_name ",", courses ",", date ",  $" tuition    ←
}
END {
print
print "Student has taken", NR, "courses"
print
print "Total Tuition is $" tot_tuition    ←
}'
```

J15 Make the script executable and run it with a student name argument:

tuition *Strand*

The output from the script is a listing of the student name, courses, and tuition.

The output from the script is:

Summary of Courses Taken

Name, Course Taken; Date, Tuition

Lyle Strand, Introduction to Unix; 12-15-87, $650
Lyle Strand, C Language Programming I; 2-22-89, $750
Lyle Strand, System Administration; 2-22-89, $750
Lyle Strand, Shell Programming; 6-5-88, $700

Student has taken 4 courses

Total Tuition is $2850

J16 Including Student Information in a Report

As a final exercise in this example database application, the next script collects student information and includes it in the output report. The **print** command in **awk** is a powerful tool for writing reports.

J17 Copy the previous script into a file named *invoice* and make the changes indicated on the next page.

```
join -t: -o 1.2 2.2 2.3 1.3 classes registrar     \
| sort -t: +1     \
| join -t: -j1 2 -o 2.3 2.2 1.1 1.3 1.4 2.4 2.5 2.6 2.7 - student     \
| grep $1  \
| awk -F:   \
'BEGIN {
print
print "Summary of Courses Taken"
print
print
print "Course Taken; Date, Tuition"      ←
print
}
{
    f_name = $1
    l_name = $2
    courses = $3
    date = $4
    tuition = $5
    tot_tuition += $5
    address += $6    ←
    city += $7    ←
    state = $8    ←
    zip = $9    ←
print courses ";", date ",◇◇$" tuition     ←
}
END {
print
print "Student " f_name, l_name, "has taken", NR, "courses"     ←
print    ←
print "Total Tuition is $" tot_tuition
print
print f_name, l_name    ←
print address    ←
print city ",", state, zip    ←
}'
```

J18   To run the script, enter:

Invoice *Strand*

The script creates an output table consisting of fields from three files, then formats the output including tuition, courses, and the student's address.

Summary of Courses Taken

Course Taken; Date, Tuition

Introduction to Unix; 12-15-87, $650
C Language Programming I; 2-22-89, $750
System Administration; 2-22-89, $750
Shell Programming; 6-5-88, $700

Student Lyle Strand has taken 4 courses

Total Tuition is $2850

Lyle Strand
137 Woods Road
Canton, OH 47079

The example relational database demonstrates some of the features and usefulness of the power utilities. The programs can be expanded to include many reports, calculations, and formatting of output using additional features of **awk, grep, cut, paste**, etc.

Conclusion

In this module you have used **join** to locate records in two files that have a common value in a specified field. The ability to join files in that way permits development of relational database applications. You used **join** and several other Power Utilities to create a small relational database application.

Summary of **join** Options

OPTION	FUNCTION
-a1 *filename1 filename2*	outputs *all* of the records in *filename1* and only those that are matchable from *filename2*
-a1 -a2	outputs all records of each corresponding file, joining the matchable files
-o 1.2 2.2 1.1	outputs all joined in the following filename and field order: field 2 of *filename1*, field 2 of *filename2*, and field 1 of *filename1*
-t:	use the colon instead of the Tab for the field separator
-	informs **join** to read standard input
-j1 4	instructs **join** to Join lines from the first file using its fourth field as the join field: *1* indicates the first file; *4* specifies that the fourth field is the one used for matching

Module 10

Locating
Files with find

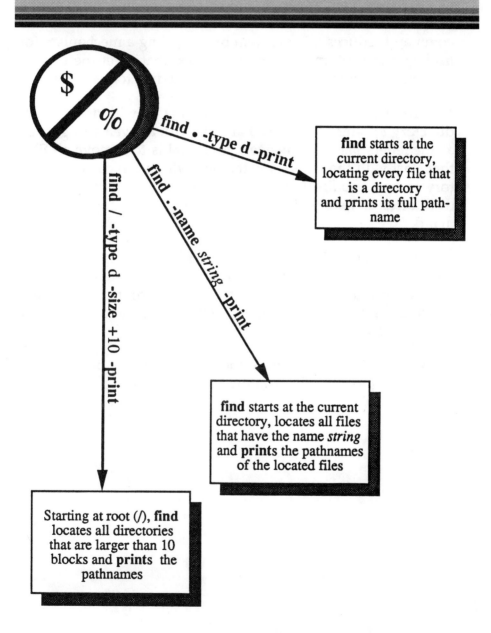

find • -type d -print

find starts at the current directory, locating every file that is a directory and prints its full path-name

find • -name string -print

find starts at the current directory, locates all files that have the name *string* and **prints** the pathnames of the located files

find / -type d -size +10 -print

Starting at root (/), **find** locates all directories that are larger than 10 blocks and **prints** the pathnames

Introduction

On UNIX systems, directories are very useful for organizing large numbers of files. However, using many directories can become a problem. Keeping files in separate directories makes it more difficult to locate or perform actions on files. The **find** command reduces this problem by providing a mechanism for finding and performing actions on files that meet the criteria and are located within or below specified directories.

You have probably used the **rm** command within a current directory to remove all files that start with a given string, such as the letters *tmp*. If, however, your goal is to remove all files that start with the letters *tmp* that are within the current directory or any subdirectories of the current directory (and subdirectories of its subdirectories, etc), you need the **find** command.

Ordinary users utilize **find** to locate files, identify large files, and perform other actions across directories. System Administrators use **find** to locate large files, identify programs that have unusual permissions, change ownership for a collection of files, and so on.

The **find** utility does not have the prettiest syntax but it is one of the most useful utilities on the UNIX system.

Prerequisites

Before beginning this module, you should be able to:

- create, edit, move, copy, view and remove files;

- make directories and move around the file system;

- use basic utilities (Module 2);

- use the shell to issue commands (Module 3);

- use regular expressions (Module 4).

Objective

Upon completion of this module, you will be able to:

- use the **find** command to search for files that meet certain selection criteria;

- use **find** with multiple selection criteria; and

- perform actions on files located by **find**.

Procedures

Many instances of the **find** command will work most smoothly if you are logged in as the super user. If you are not the super user you will be denied access to many directories because the **find** command can only search directories that are both readable and executable by you. For this reason we will recommend that some procedures in this module be completed while you are logged in as the super user. If this is not an option for you, be prepared to see error messages similar to Cannot Open Directory indicating that you do not have permission to read or execute files within the indicated directory.

Objective A
Finding Files and Printing Their Full Pathnames

The **find** command enables you to locate a file based on whether or not it meets one or more criteria.

A1   Finding a File with a Known Name

To locate a file with a specific name enter the following command replacing *filename* with the name of a file located in a directory below your current directory. Use the name of a file that is not located in the current directory to demonstrate that **find** is not limited to files within the current directory.

> **find . -name** *filename* **-print**

This command line instructs **find** to search the current directory and all of its subdirectories (and subdirectories of subdirectories, etc.) for the specified file.

A2   Examining the Syntax of the **find** Command

In general, the **find** command is used to search through one or more directories specified by a *path-list* for a set of filenames matching one or more *selection-criteria*, and then to perform some *action* on the files that match the selection criteria.

The general form of the command line used to specify these functions is:

find *path-list selection-criteria action*

The *path-list, selection-criteria* and *action* can all be varied to meet particular situations.

These three functions were specified in the above example as follows:

Command	Path-list	Selection-criteria	Action
find	.	**-name** *filename*	**-print**

find

instructs the shell to execute the **find** command.

.

tells **find** to start searching at the current directory. This is the starting point, hence **find** will examine not only the current directory, but also all of its subdirectories, and subdirectories of its subdirectories, etc.

-name *filename*

instructs **find** to act on any file with the specified name.

-print

specifies that the action is to print the full path name of each occurrence of the file(s) matching the selection criteria.

A3   **Finding All Files Owned by a User**

To locate all files on the system owned by a particular user you may need to be logged in as the super user. The **find** command can only search directories that are both readable and executable by you. Become the super user (if you can). Either way, enter the command:

find / -user *username* **-print**

replacing *username* with your login name or the login name of some other user on your system. This may take awhile if you are on a large system. You may want to interrupt the command after you have seen that it is working.

In this case, the components of the command are:

Command	Path-list	Selection-criteria	Action
find	**/**	**-user** *username*	**-print**

find   instructs the shell to execute the **find** command.

/   specifies that the root directory and every directory located below the root directory should be searched.

-user *username*   specifies that all files owned by *username* should be acted on.

-print   specifies that the full path name of each occurrence of the file(s) matching the selection criteria should be printed.

A4   **Finding Files Not Accessed in a Time Period**

The **find** command can also be used to choose all files that have or have not been accessed within a specified number of days. The following command identifies all files that have not been accessed in the last *30* days and have the name *.login*:

find / -atime *+30* -name *.login* **-print**

Access time is defined as the last time the file was updated. It is updated when you use **cat, more, cp** etc. on the file.

The portions of the command line are:

Command	Path-list	Selection-criteria	Action
find	/	**-atime** *+30* **-name** *.login*	**-print**

The new elements are:

-atime *+30*   specifies that all files that have not been accessed within the last *30* days should be acted on.

-name *.login*   specifies that all files named *.login* should be acted on.

The plus sign (+) in front of the *30* is interpreted to be *more than 30*. When we specify "all files that have not been accessed in *30* days," we are actually saying "all files that were last accessed *more than 30* days ago." If the command specifies **-atime** *30*, without the plus sign, the message would have been "all files that were last accessed *exactly* 30 day ago." A specification of **-atime** *-30*, is interpreted as "all files that were last accessed *less than* 30 days ago."

This command called for two criteria to be met. When two selection criteria are present, both criteria must be met.

Later in this module ou will see more examples of the plus and minus signs with numbers in the **find** command.

A5 Finding Files Modified Within a Specified Time

Like access time, modify time can also be used as a criterion for **find**. The following command will identify all files that (1) have been modified within the last *10* days and, (2) have the name *.login.* Enter:

> **find / -mtime** *-10* **-name** *.login* **-print**

Modify time is defined as the last time the file was written to disk. It is updated when the file is written (**:w**) from within **vi**, or modified with any other utility.

The elements of this command line are:

Command	Path-list	Selection-criteria	Action
find	*I*	**-mtime** *-10* **-name** *.login*	**-print**

These are the new components:

-mtime *-10*   is interpreted as "all files that were last modified *less than* ten days ago." The minus sign (**-**) indicates *less than.*

-name *.login*   indicates that the file must be named *.login* to be acted on.

A6 **Finding More Recently Modified Files**

The above command line can be used to generate a list of files that have been modified within a specified period of time. It is also possible to generate a list of all files that have been modified more recently than a specified file.

In the following command, substitute for *filename* the name of one of your files that has not been modified in three or four days. The identified comparison file, *filename*, must be located in the current directory or you must use the absolute path name of the comparison file. The **find** utility will look for other files of the same name. Enter

find . -newer *filename* **-print**

The elements of this command are:

Command	Path-list	Selection-criteria	Action
find	.	**-newer** *filename*	**-print**

The new aspects of this command are:

-newer *filename*   instructs **find** to select only those files with the most recent modification date (stored with each file) newer than the modification date for the comparison file *filename*.

One practical use of this example is to generate a list of files to be archived onto some backup medium. The strategy is to create or update a dummy file when you perform a backup. The modification time on this dummy file is then the same as the last time the system was backed up. The next time the system is backed up, this dummy file will have a modification date against which all other file modification dates may be compared. All files that have been modified since the last backup (and thus need to be backed up this time) are listed by the **find** command.

A7   Identifying the Most Recent Version of a File

At times users have more than one copy of a file and want to make certain they are about to print or modify the *most recent* version.

Copy a file from your current directory into a sub-directory using:

> **cp** *filename directoryname*

The comparison file *filename* associated with **-newer** in the following command must either be in the current directory or you must enter the complete path name of the selected file. Enter the following command, substituting the name of the file for both occurrences of *filename*:

> **find . -name** *filename* **-newer** *filename* **-print**

The elements of this command are:

Command	Path-list	Selection-criteria	Action
find	.	**-name** *filename*	**-print**
		-newer *filename*	

The new portions are:

-name *filename*   specifies that a match must have the name *filename*. Only files (or directories) with the name *filename* will be selected.

-newer *filename*   specifies that a match must be newer than *filename*.

Note that the name *filename* is the same for both selection criteria; you're looking for newer versions *with the same name* as the current comparison file.

> When two selection criteria are used as above, *both* must be satisfied for the file to pass the selection test.

If no files are located by **find,** the version of *filename* named by the criterion **-newer** *filename* is the most recent version of the file with that name. If path names are printed out by **find,** those versions have more recent modifications.

A8   **Finding All Set-user-id Files**

Another characteristic of files that **find** can evaluate is the permission status. The following command identifies the names of files with the set-user-id bit set. Finding such files is an important security procedure. The set-user-id bit is a special permission flag. Although exploration of the set-user-id is beyond the scope of this book, for security reasons it is important to be able to identify such files.

Enter the following:

    find / -perm *-4000* **-print**

The elements of this command are:

Command	Path-list	Selection-criteria	Action
find	*/*	**-perm** *-4000*	**-print**

The new aspect of the command is:

-perm *-4000*   indicates that files with their set-user-id bit set will be selected. The **-perm** instructs **find** to examine the permissions of the files. The minus sign in front of the *4000* instructs **find** to look at more than just the basic permission bits and to accept files that are not an exact match. The *4000* refers to the set-user-id bit in particular. The search is for files that have the set-user-id bit set, regardless of the other permissions.

Run **ls -l** on one of the filenames printed by **find** such as */bin/passwd*. Something like the following line is produced:

-rwsr-xr-x   1 root   system   14216 Nov   4   1986 /bin/passwd

Examine the permissions. In the field where the owner execution permission is usually placed, there is now an **s**. This is the indicator that told **find** that */bin/passwd* had the set-user-id bit set.

A9   **Finding All Set-group-id Files**

The set-group-id bit is similar to the set-user-id bit. Enter

   find / -perm *-2000* **-print**

The components are:

Command	Path-list	Selection-criteria	Action
find	*I*	**-perm** *-2000*	**-print**

The new portion is:

-perm *-2000*   indicates that files with the set-group-id bit set will be selected. The **-perm** instructs **find** to examine file permissions. The *2000* refers directly to the set-group-id bit.

Listing the permissions of a file located by this command demonstrates that these files do indeed have the set-group-id bit set (it is entirely possible that no files on your system have the set-group-id bit set).

The security implications of the set-group-id bit are similar to those for the set-user-id bit.

A10 Identifying All Large Directories

The **find** utility also permits selection of files based on size. Enter the following **find** command to print the names of all directories larger than ten blocks:

    find **/** **-type** *d* **-size** *+10* **-print**

The command line includes the following elements:

Command	Path-list	Selection-criteria	Action
find	**/**	**-type** *d* **-size** *+10*	**-print**

-type *d*   indicates that **find** should select *d*irectories.

-size *+10*   instructs **find** to locate all directories larger than ten blocks. The *+* in the *+10* means

-**size** *+10*, cont.　　*more than*. Blocks is the default size units for **find**'s **-size** selection criterion. The size of a block is system-specific, but generally it is either 512 or 1024 bytes (that is, characters), or a multiple thereof.

A11 Identifying All Large Files on a System

By modifying the options in the previous example, you can instruct **find** to look at files instead of directories.

Enter the following **find** command to print the names of all files of over 138 blocks in size:

> **find** / **-type** *f* **-size** *+138* **-print**

The elements of the command are:

Command	Path-list	Selection-criteria	Action
find	/	**-type** **f** **-size** *+138*	**-print**

The new portions of the command are:

-**type** *f*　　　　　indicates that the type of the entity selected by **find** must be a regular f ile.

-**size** *+138*　　　indicates that files larger than 138 blocks be identified. The + indicates *more than*, and blocks are the default size units for **find**'s -**size** selection criterion.

Objective B
Using Multiple Selection Criteria

Thus far, having more than one selection criterion in sequence in a command line requires that the file pass *all* criteria for the selection to be made. The following examples illustrate how to tell **find** to select files that pass either one or another selection criterion.

B1   ## Finding All Set-user-id and Set-group-id Files

Two of the above examples might logically be combined into one **find** command. Enter the following example:

find / \(**-perm** *-4000* **-o** **-perm** *-2000* \) **-print**

The components of the command are:

Command	Path-list	Selection-criteria	Action
find	/	\(**-perm** *-4000* **-o** **-perm** *-2000* \)	**-print**

The new element in the command line is:

\(**-perm** *—4000* **-o** **-perm** *-2000* \)

instructs find to locate files with either the set-user-id or set-group-id bit set. Parentheses are used to keep the selection criteria grouped separately from the **-print** action, which follows. The parentheses are preceded by backslashes so that they will not be interpreted by the shell. Without the backslashes, the shell would interpret the parentheses as process grouping characters.

\(-perm *−4000* **-o -perm** *-2000* **\)** cont.

> The two criteria are not placed sequentially. **-o** for
> **or** is inserted between them. With the *or* construct,
> **find** matches any file having *either* permissions flag
> set.

B2 Finding All Large Files and Directories

The **-o** (for **or**) facility of **find** can be used between any two
selection criteria.

As another example, enter the following command:

find / **\(-type d -size** *+10* **-o -type f -size** *+138* **\) -print**

The elements of the command are:

Command	Path-list	Selection-criteria	Action
find	**/**	**\(-type d -size** *+10* **-o -type f -size** *+138* **\)**	**-print**

\(-type *d* **-size** *+10* **-o -type** *f* **-size** *+138* **\)**

> instructs **find** to locate all files with either **-
> type** *d* and **-size** *+10* together *or* **-type** *f*
> and **-size** *+138* together. The selection cri-
> teria designate all files that are directories
> and are over ten blocks *or* that are regular
> files and are over 138 blocks.

> When two *selection-criteria* are not separated by an *or* operator, both must be true for a file to be selected. This is the *and* operator. This relationship is implied. The *or* operator is explicitly stated with the **-o** option.

The parentheses are used to group the selection criteria separately from the **-print**; the backslashes are again necessary to shield the parentheses from the shell.

Objective C
Performing Actions on Located Files

Each command entered thus far has specified that the filenames selected should be printed (the **-print** action). The **find** utility also executes other actions on located files.

C1 Changing the Group Membership of a Set of Files

One application of **find** is to change the group membership of a directory and all of its files and subdirectories and all of their files and subdirectories, etc. You could **cd** into each of the sub-directories individually and then enter: **chgrp** *groupname* * in each one.

The power utility **find** allows you to change the membership of all files in the directory tree by entering one command at the highest level directory in the tree of directories that you want affected.

Select a portion of your account that has a few directories and files below it. Make that your current directory. Enter the following command to change the group name of all the files in and below your current directory. You should substitute the name of a common group on your system in place of *groupname*:

find . -exec chgrp *groupname* **{} \;**

Command	Path-list	Selection- criteria	Action
find	**.**		**-exec** **chgrp** *groupname* **{} \;**

For this example, there is no selection criterion specified. All of the files in the path-list are selected for the action. Leaving the selection criterion (which is restrictive) unspecified causes no files to be ruled out, so all are selected.

-exec   instructs **find** to **exec**ute on each located file whatever UNIX command follows.

chgrp   is the UNIX command to *change the group* for the selected files.

groupname is an argument to **chgrp** indicating the name of the new group for the selected files.

{}   is the placeholder for the selected filename. Whatever filename **find** locates (after the name has passed through the selection criteria) is substituted into the execute command at the position of these curly braces.

\;   tells find where the command ends. A semicolon (;) is
                      always required at the end of the command part of the
                      -exec action. The backslash before the semicolon is
                      required to hide it from the shell. If the shell sees it
                      (when there's no backslash), it will interpret the ; as a
                      command separator.

The result of this **find** command is to locate all files in directories *in and under* the current directory, then change the group
to *groupname*.

C2   Use a similar **find** command to change the group ownerships
     of your files back to what they were originally.

C3   **Removing Temporary Files**

Users often create temporary files for various reasons. Almost
as often, users forget to remove the temporary files after they
create them. At some point, the system may be bogged down
by an excess of temporary files. Many users create temporary
files with the string *tmp* somewhere in the filename, such as
project.tmp or *tmp.project*, etc. This is an aid in periodically
removing all of the temporary files at once.

Enter the following **find** command to remove all *tmp* files in or
below the current directory. You may want to create some *tmp*
files before you try the command, so you can verify that it
works.

Enter

        find . -name *"*tmp*"* **-exec rm {} \;**

The command line consists of:

Command	Path-list	Selection-criteria	Action
find	.	**-name** *"*tmp*"*	**-exec rm {} \;**

The new elements of the command line are:

-name *"*tmp*"*   is the selection criterion. The *tmp* is expanded to be any filename that has the string *tmp* in it. The quotation marks around it are required to shield the asterisks from the shell. If the shell saw the asterisks, it would try to match all the filenames at once before executing **find**, and furthermore, the files would only be from the current directory.

-exec rm {} \;   executes the **rm** command on *filename*, where *filename* is the currently selected name from the selection criterion. The {} are used in the command line to represent this current name. Again, the \; at the end of the line is used to end the command part of the **-exec**.

C4   Executing Multiple Utilities

The previous example is quite powerful. You can, also, incorporate multiple **exec**s to make your **find** commands even more useful.

C5   Create some *tmp* files, and then enter the following (it includes the "minus eye" option for **rm**):

find . **-name** *"∗tmp∗"* **-exec ls -l** {} \; **-exec rm -i** {} \;

This example ultimately accomplishes the same task as the previous command line. The addition of **-exec ls -l** {} \; causes this **find** command to display a full listing of each file and asks for confirmation before it is removed. Unlike **-print**, this output includes the owner of the files. The addition of the inquire option allows you to choose which files are removed.

C6   **Changing the Owner of Files**

Should you find the need to rearrange the ownership of the files on your system, the following command will be an aid. Do not execute this command at this time.

The specific components of the command line are:

find . **-user** *olduid* **-exec chown** *username* {} \;

Command	Path-list	Selection-criteria	Action
find	.	**-user** *olduid*	**-exec chown** *username* {} \;

-user *olduid*   instructs **find** to select files with user ID (or owner) of *olduid*, where *olduid* is a user ID number. All files that have the user ID *olduid* are selected for the action.

-exec chown *username* {} \;

> executes the **chown** command to change the ownership of the selected file to *username*. Again, the semicolon ends the command part of the **-exec**.

This command changes the ownership of every file and directory in or below the root, previously owned by *olduid* to *username*.

C7   Searching for a Pattern in Files Below a Directory

When writing programs or manuscripts, the need often arises for a way to search all files in and below a specific directory for a certain string. A **grep** command alone will only handle the files in one directory, but a **find** command that does a **-exec grep** will get the job done. Enter the following command:

find . -exec grep *pattern* {} \; **-print**

The elements are:

Command	Path-list	Selection-criteria	Action
find			**-exec grep** *pattern* {} \; **-print**

The new portion is:

-exec grep *pattern* {} \; **-print**

> This tells **find** to perform two actions. First, the **-exec** requests that **grep** be executed and instructed to search for

pattern in the file. If (and only if) this search is successful, the second action is performed. So, if **grep** locates the indicated *pattern* in a file, the name of that file is printed because of the **-print** action. The **-print** is included so that file names are printed. (When given a single filename, the name of the file is not output by **grep**, hence **find** is told to **-print** it.)

Objective D
When **find** Complains

If you have not dreamed up dozens of ways in which you want to use **find** to enrich your life, you have probably been tangled with error messages issued by **find**. Taking a look at a few of the basic types of errors produced by **find** can make future mistakes much easier to rectify.

D1   Identifying Permission Errors

There really are not too many kinds of error messages that you are likely to encounter. The most common message you will get is:

```
find: cannot open <dir>
```

Where *dir* is the name of a directory beneath the starting point for a given **find** command. This message crops up when **find** tries to access a directory for which you do not have read permission. This can only be remedied by being logged in as super user or as someone who has read permission.

D2 Identifying Syntax Errors

Most other error messages that you are likely to encounter are syntax related. The most common of these is:

Usage: find path-list predicate-list

This message greets you when you inadvertently omit the starting path (path-list) or some form of predicate (either selection-criteria or action) from the **find** command. Every **find** command must have at least one predicate.

If you include selection criteria but omit an action, there will be no error produced; then again, there also will be no output. If you omit selection criteria but include an action, *all* files in the path-list will be affected by the action.

D3 Identifying Incomplete Statements

Finally, another error message you may encounter when **find** complains about syntax is:

find: incomplete statement

This message is generally an indication that you entered a **find** command line in which the semicolon (;) was not preceded by a backslash (\).

Conclusion

The **find** utility includes *path-list, selection-criteria* and *action*. The *path-list* for **find** can be any list of one or more directories; the *selection-criteria* can indicate nearly any aspect of a file or a directory; and the *action* section can be used to print the selected name or to execute essentially any UNIX command.

Summary of Options for **find** Commands

find OPTION (CRITERION)	FUNCTION
-name *filename*	The name of a file must match *filename*. Quotes must be used if expansion characters (**?, ***) are used.
-user *username*	The owner of a file must be *username*, which can be expressed either as a login name (e.g., john) or as the user's uid number (e.g., 58).
-atime *+N*	The file must have been last accessed more than *N* days ago.
-atime *N*	The file must have been last accessed exactly *N* days ago.
-atime *-N*	The file must have been last accessed less than *N* days ago.
-mtime	The same as **-atime**, only it refers to modification time (i.e. *+N* = more than *N*, *N* = exactly *N*, *-N* = less than *N*).
-newer *filename*	The modification time of the found file must be more recent than the modification time of *filename*.
-perm *-4000*	The file must have the user-id bit set.
-perm *-2000*	The file must have the group-id bit set.

Summary of Options for
find1 Commands (continued)

find OPTION (CRITERION)	FUNCTION
-type *d*	The item must be a directory.
-type *f*	The item must be a regular file.
-size *+N*	The size of the item must be larger than *N* blocks.
-size *N*	The size of the item must be exactly *N* blocks.
-size *-N*	The size of the item must be less than *N* blocks.
\(*criterion* **-o** *criterion* \)	Either of the two selection criteria must be true.

find OPTION (ACTION)	FUNCTION
-print	Print the name of the file that meets the selection criteria.
-exec *command* {} \;	Execute the named *command* on the file(s) that meet the selection criteria. Note that the *command* chosen can be invoked with all its options.

Command Index

Command Index

To assist you in locating commands you used while completing these modules, all commands and their page numbers are listed on the following pages. If the same command is used more than once within a few pages, only the first use is listed here.

1,$ **s/ */ /gc**	136
1,3 **co** *$*	118
1,5 **p**	117
15,17 **d**	118
1,$ **s/** *a/* *A/* **g**	123
1,$ **s/** *brother/friend/*	121
1,$ **s/** *friend/brother/*	123
1,$ **s/** *pattern1/pattern2/*	122
1,$ **p**	118
1,$ **s/** *<and\\>/or/* **g**	138
1,$ **s/** *< brother// older &/*	139
*1,$* **s/ *$//**	137
1,$ **s/^ *//**	137
1,$ **s/** *and/or/* **g**	137
1,$ **s/** [A-Z]/\\l&/ **g**	139
1,$ **s/** [a-z]/\\u&/ **g**	139
1,$ **s/** [Mm]y/[Mm]y/ **g**	135
1,$ **s/** *mentarian\\>/&ism/* **p**	138
1,$ **s/** [Mm] *ichael/Mike/* **g**	135
3 **s/** *creating/producing/*	121
5 **p**	116
alias *incheck* **'who	grep "\\!*"'**	163
alias *num* **'who	grep -c** *bill* **'**	162
awk -F: **'NR == 1 {print $1}'** */etc/passwd*	214
awk **'/Dairy/ {print $1, $3}**	188
awk -F: -f *first.field* */etc/passwd*	214
awk -f *findNR groc_dbase*	190
awk -f *inflation groc_dbase*	201

awk **-f** *print_dairy groc_dbase*	189
awk **-f** *quoting groc_dbase*	194
awk **-f** *running groc_dbase*	204
awk **-f** *running groc_dbase*	211
awk **-f** *sale groc_dbase*	197
awk **-f** *sale groc_dbase*	203
awk **-f** *taxes groc_dbase*	207
awk **-f** *total groc_dbase*	202
awk **-f** *who_where /etc/passwd*	215
awk *'$3 == 2.65' groc_dbase*	187
awk *'$3 < 2.65' groc_dbase*	187
awk *'/Dairy/* **{print $1, $3}***' groc_dbase*	189
awk *'/Fish/* **{print}***' groc_dbase*	181
awk *'{item = $1;* **print** *"item ", item}' groc_dbase*	195
awk *'{item = $1;* **print** *item, item}' groc_dbase*	195
awk *'/Meat/* **{print}***' groc_dbase > meat.db*	215
awk *'/Meat/' groc_dbase*	183
awk *'pattern {action}' filename*	182
awk *'/dairy/* **{ print $3 }***' food*	51
awk *'/[Vv]eg/* **{print}***' groc_dbase*	187
awk *'NR ==* **1 {print $1}***' /etc/passwd*	213
awk *'{***print** *$0}' groc_dbase*	185
awk *'{***print** *$1}' groc_dbase*	184
awk *'{***print** *$3 $1}' groc_dbase*	185
awk *'{***print}***' groc_dbase*	183
cat *file1 file2 > file3*	42
cat *file1 file2*	48
cat *file1*	48
cat *filename*	42
cat *meat.db*	216
cat *names*	**paste** *phones city –*	296
cat *logged_in*	70
cat *west coast > states*	42
cd *$d*	100
cd *$d*	98
cd *Sed_riting*	229
cd */tmp*	98

cd $HOME 92

cd 98

chmod 700 *loginfo* 104

chmod 700 *stu_trans* 339

comm -1 *sor_west sor_coast* 33

comm -12 *sor_west sor_coast* 34

comm -23 *sor_west sor_coast* 34

comm *sor_west sor_coast* 33

cp *filename directoryname* 358

cp *test_file n_test_file* 38

csh 96

csh 99

cut -d':' -f*2* */etc/passwd* 282

cut -f*1 numbers.tmp* 46

cut -f*1,2 names.tmp numbers.tmp* 277

cut -f*1,2,3 names.tmp* 275

cut -f*1,3,2 names.tmp* 275

cut -f*2 names.tmp* 273

cut -f*2 names.tmp* 45

cut -f*2 names.tmp* **>** *names* 285

cut -f*2 numbers.tmp* **>** *phones* 286

cut -f*2 record* 283

cut -f*2 **-s** *record* 284

cut -f*5- filename* 276

*d=***`pwd`** 98

date >> *filename* 74

date > *logged_in* 73

deroff *n_test_file* 40

deroff -w *filename* | **sort** | **uniq** | **wc -l** 54

deroff -w *n_test_file* 41

df | **awk -f** *total* 218

df -t | **awk -f** *total* 218

df -t 217

df 217

echo * $HOME 101

echo "* $HOME" 102

echo '* $HOME' 102

echo *xxx* **>** *[test.file* 90

echo *xxx* **>** *\[test.file* 91

echo *You are in the* `**pwd**` *directory* 96

echo *$project* 94

echo **$HOME** 92

echo **$PATH** 92

echo **$SHELL** 92

echo the following number of people are logged in: 104

echo the sorted who listing is: 104

echo you are in: 104

egrep **-f** *boss.exprs people* 167

egrep **-f** *boss.words people* 165

egrep **-f** *literal people* 166

egrep [*Hh*]*uman*│[*Aa*]*nimal* people 169

ex *text* 115

ex *text* 125

fgrep **-f** *boss.words people* 165

fgrep **-f** *literal people* 166

find */* **-atime** *+30* **-name** *.login* **-print** 355

find */* **\(** **-perm** *-4000* **-o** **-perm** *-2000* **\)** **-print** 363

find *.* **-exec** **chgrp** *groupname* **{} \;** 366

find */* **-mtime** *-10* **-name** *.login* **-print** 356

find *.* **-name** *filename* **-print** 352

find *.* **-name** *"*tmp*"* **-exec** **rm** **{} \;** 367

find *.* **-newer** *filename* **-print** 357

find */* **-perm** *-2000* **-print** 360

find */* **-perm** *-4000* **-print** 359

find */* **-type** *d* **-size** *+10* **-print** 361

find */* **-type** *f* **-size** *+138* **-print** 362

find */* **-user** *username* **-print** 354

find *.* **-name** *filename* **-print** 53

find *.* **-exec** **grep** *pattern* **{} \;** **-print** 370

find *.* **-name** *filename* **-newer** *filename* **-print** 358

find *.* **-user** *olduid* **-exec** **chown** *username* **{} \;** 369

g */friend* */**s**//brother/* 123

g */friend/* **s**/*friend/brother/* 123

g */*[*Mm*]*ichael* **p** 127

g /*sister*/ **s**/*test*/*UNIX*/ 122

g /*the*/ **p** 120

grep *an years so_temp* 86

grep *Bob Danny years* 100

grep *computer people aliens* 152

grep "[*Hh*]*uman*" *people* 155

grep *home aliens* 151

grep *human people* 151

grep *human people* 155

grep *humorous people* 154

grep *man* * 152

grep *pattern filename(s)* 44

grep "*Peter Titus*" *people* 153

grep "*Peter.*consultant*" *people* 158

grep *string filename(s)* 86

grep **-c** "^#" *info* 157

grep **-cv** "^#" *info* 157

grep **-l** *computer* * 153

grep **-n** *target filename* 154

grep "*Bob Danny*" *years* 101

grep **-v** "^\...*" *n_test_file* 157

grep **-v** "^#" *info* 156

grep *he test_file* 43

grep *pattern file1 file2* 44

g /^$/ *d* 134

join -t: **-o** *1.2 2.1 2.2 completed classes* | **sort** *+1* 314

join -a1 -a2 *ord.names ord.numbers* 311

join -a*1* *ord.names ord.numbers* 309

join -a*2* *ord.names ord.numbers* 310

join -o *1.2 2.2 1.1 ord.names ord.numbers* 311

join -t: **-o** *1.2 2.2 2.3 1.3 classes registrar* \
   | **sort -t**: *+1* \
     | **join -t**: **-j***1 2* **-o** *2.3 2.2 1.1 1.3 1.4*   \
   - *student* | **grep $1** \
   | **awk -F:** (list of **awk** commands) \ 341

join -t: **-o** *1.2 2.2 2.3 1.3 classes registrar* \
   | **sort -t**: *+1*   \

join -t: -j1 2 -o 2.3 2.2 1.1 1.3 \\	
1.4 2.4 2.5 2.6 2.7 - student	grep $1 \\	
	awk -F: (list of awk commands) \\	343
join -t: -o 1.2 2.2 2.3 classes registrar	333
join -t: -o 1.2 2.2 2.3 classes registrar \\	
	sort -t: +1 \\	
	join -t: -j1 2 -o 2.3 2.2 1.1 1.3 - student \\	
	awk -F: '{print $1, $2 ",", $3 ";", $4}'	337
join -t: -o 1.2 2.2 2.3 classes registrar \\	
	sort -t: +1 \\	
	join -t: -j1 2 -o 2.3 2.2 1.1 1.3 - student \\	
	grep $1 \\	
	awk -F: (list of awk commands)	339
join -t: -o 1.2 2.2 2.3 classes registrar \\	
	sort -t: +1 \\	
	join -t: -j1 2 -o 2.3 2.2 1.1 1.3 - student	335
join -t: -o 1.2 2.2 2.3 classes registrar	sort -t: +1	334
join -t: -o 1.3 1.2 2.3 student awards \\	
awk -F: '{print $1, $2 ",", $3}'	332
join -t: -o 1.3 1.2 2.3 student awards	331
join -t: -o 1.2 2.1 2.2 completed classes	sort +1	315
join -t: -o 1.2 2.1 2.2 completed classes	sort +1	316
join names.tmp numbers.tmp	307
join names.tmp numbers.tmp	49
join ord.names ord.numbers > room_nam_ph	308
loginfo	104
ls -a	82
ls -l	62
ls -l	82
ls -l	91
ls -l chap*	88
ls chapter?	88
mkdir Sed_riting	229
more /etc/passwd	320
more meat.db	215
more logged_in	70
nroff n_test_file > formatted	39

nroff *n_test_file* | **more** 39

nroff *n_test_file* | **pg** 39

nroff *test_file* | **more** 37

nroff *test_file* | **pg** 37

p 117

paste -d':+' *names phones city* 297

paste -d':' *names phones city* 297

paste -d':+' *names phones city* | **cut -d':' -f1** 298

paste -d':+' *names phones city* | **cut -d'+' -f1** 298

paste *file1 file2* 48

paste *names city phones* **>** *phone.list* 293

paste *names city* 287

paste *names phones city* 293

paste *names phones* 292

paste *names* 287

paste *names.tmp numbers.tmp* 285

paste *names.tmp numbers.tmp* 47

paste -s -d'+-' *names* 291

paste -s -d'\t' *names* 290

paste -s -d'+-\t' *names* 291

paste -s -d'+' *names* 290

paste -s -d't' *names* 291

paste -s *names* **>** *pastednames* 289

paste -s *names* 288

paste -s *names* | **cut -f3** 289

pg *logged_in* 70

*project=chap[1-4]** 94

pwd 62

pwd 104

q! 124

rm *sort* 78

rm *[test.file* 91

mail *$school* 95

vi *$d/filename* 100

grep *'5 $' people* 159

school="butch kaye jason amber brandon" 94

sed -e *'s/Veg/VEG/'* -e *'s/Meat/MEAT/' gdbase* 237

sed -f *after text* 256

sed -f *explorer gdbase* 243

sed *'1,2* **p'** *gdbase* 247

sed *'2* **d'** *gdbase* 230

sed *'2,10* **d'** *gdbase* 230

sed *'5* **q'** *records* 231

sed *'7,/Fish/* **s**/*Meat/ Animal/'* *gdbase* 236

sed *'/beetles/* **s**/*archaic/contemporary/***g'** *records* 234

sed *'s*/*Dairy/DAIRY/***g'** *gdbase* 230

sed *'s*/*Dairy/DAIRY/***g'** *gdbase* 249

sed -f *add_item gdbase* **>** *dbase.rev2* 240

sed -f *db_changes gdbase* **>** *gdbase_rev* 239

sed -f *modify.rec records* 238

sed -n -f *after text* 260

sed -n *'1,5* **s**/*beetle/Beatle/***p'** *records* 251

sed -n *'/beetles/* **s**/*archaic/contemporary/***gp'** *records* 252

sed -n *'\!***p'** *records* 255

sed -n *'/classical/* **p'** *records* 254

sed -n *'/classical/* **!p'** *records* 254

sed -n *'/classical/* **\!p'** *records* 254

sed -n *'1,5***s**/*beetle/Beatle/'* *records* 251

sed *'/chocolate/***s**/ /*coffee/***g'** *test_file* 50

sed *'/chocolate/***s**/ /*coffee/***g'** *test_file* **>** *coffee_test* 50

sed *'/classical/* **r** *comment.file'* *records* 241

sed *'/Manilow/* **q'** *records* 234

sed *'/^$/* **d'** *file* 237

sed *'s*/*[Bb]eetles/Beatles/'* *records* 253

sed *'s*/*beetles/bugs/'* *records* 250

sed *'s*/*beetles/bugs/***p'** *records* 250

sed *'s*/*beetles/bugs/***p'** *records* 250

sed *'s*/*rock/raunch/***w** *wfile'* *records* 253

sed *'1,7* **w** *wfile'* *records* 242

set *d* = `` `pwd` `` 99

set *project* = *"chap[1-4]*"* 96

:set list 289

:set list 294

set nonumber 117

set number 117
set 96
sh 94
sort > *2_sor_years* < *years* 76
sort > *so_temp* 79
sort < *years* | **uniq** > *ord_years* 81
sort < *years* 75
sort < *years* 78
sort < *years* > *sor_years* 75
sort +2 */etc/passwd* 26
sort -d *test_file* 23
sort -f *test_file* 24
sort +3 *respected* 25
sort +3 -t: */etc/passwd*   \
    join -t: -o 2.1 2.2 1.1 -j1 4 - *groups* 322
sort +3 -t: */etc/passwd* | **join** -t: -j1 4 - *groups* 320
sort *coast* > *sor_coast* 31
sort */etc/passwd* 25
sort *filename* | **uniq** 54
sort *groc_dbase* | **awk** '/Veg/ {print}' 216
sort *names* | **paste** - *phones city* 296
sort *names.tmp* > *ord.names* 308
sort *numbers.tmp* > *ord.numbers* 308
sort *test_file* > *sor_test_file* 26
sort *test_file* | **uniq** 29
sort *test_file* 22
sort *west* > *sor_west* 31
sort *years* 83
sort -r *test_file* 24
sort -t: +3 */etc/passwd* 26
tr "[7a]" "[2X]" < *years* 102
tr [a-z] [A-Z] < *filename* 102
tr "[a-z]" "[A-Z]" < *years* > *cap_years* 76
tr "[A-Z]" "[a-z]" *years logged_in* 86
tr "[13S]" "[G&n]" < *test_file* 35
tr "[a-z]" "[A-Z]" < *test_file* 35
uniq < *years* 79

uniq **-d** *sor_test_file* 30

uniq *sor_test_file* 29

uniq *test_file* 27

uniq *xyz* 84

uniq **<** *xyz* 84

uniq **-u** *sor_test_file* 29

wc **-lc** *test_file* 21

wc **-l** *test_file* 20

wc *test_file* 19

wc **-l** *filename* 62

wc **-w** *$project* 94

wc *chapter[2-5]* 89

wc *chapter[2-5]** 90

**who | sort | grep $USER   **

   | tr "[a-z]" "[A-Z]" 91

who **>** *logged_in* 69

who **>** *old_who* 87

who **>** *sort* 78

who **| comm -** *old_who* 87

who | cut **-c***11-* 280

who | cut **-c***1-9,25-29* 279

who | cut **-c***1-9,25-29* 280

who | cut **-c***1* 279

who | cut **-f***3* 278

who | grep **"***11:[0-5][0-9]***"** 160

who | sort > *alpha_users* 77

who | grep **"\!*"** 163

who | grep *bill* **| wc -l** 160

who | grep *bill* 160

who | grep **"** *carlp***"** 163

who | sed 's/ */+/g' 317

who | sort | sed 's/ */+/g' | join -t+ - *friends* 318

who | sort 104

who | sort 78

who | wc -l 62

who | wc -l 104

who 76

:wq 115

wq 124

write *login* **<** *years* 85

write *login* 85

/ˆ 130

/ˆ[ˆˆ] 130

/\ˆ 133

/ˆ\ˆ 134

/ˆ\. 133

/\<a 126

/\<he\> 125

/* 133

./loginfo 104

/ˆ 126

*/I/ **s**/am/was/* 121

/[0123456789] 128

/[0-9] 128

/[13579a-z] 129

/[A-Z] 128

/[a-zA-Z] 129

/[CcBb]ase 128

/diff*erent 131

/et* 131

/formal* 132

/he 125

/other$ 127

/s\> 126

*/the/ **p*** 119

/ˆ$ 127

/ˆThe 126

/\. 133

/\<.he\> 131

/[ˆ0-9] 130

/[ˆ0-9a-zA-Z] 130

/s.*s 132

/[ˆa-z] 129

Index

Index

$, use in **awk**   184,187, 222
$, use in **ex**   118,127, 138, 139, 144
' ', function in **awk**   182, 220
. use in **grep**   157,158
, use in **grep**   159
(and), use in **egrep**   168
, use in **find**   355
+= , use in **awk**   206
+, use in **awk**   201
+, use in **egrep**   168
, use in **awk**   195
, in **awk**   186
-123 options, **comm**   33, 34
- use in **awk**   197-9, 200
- use in **egrep**   167
-print option, **find**   353
-r option, **sort**   24
., use in **ex**   131, 132, 144
/ , **awk**   203
; use in **awk**   195, 220
< use with **tr**   35
<, use with **awk**   187
==, use with **awk**   187
=, use in awk   193
>, use in **awk**   215
>, use with **sort**   26
?, use in **egrep**   168
[], use in **grep**   155
[], use in **ex**   127-129, 144
[], use with **awk**   187
" , use in **awk**   195
* , use in **awk**   202
* , use in **grep**   152
* , use in **grep**   157, 158
*, use in **ex**   131-32, 144
!*, grep   163
( ), use in **find**   363, 375

( ), use in **ex**   139, 144
;, use with **find**   367, 375
, use in **grep**   157
(), use in **ex**   139, 144
< and **>**, use in **ex**   125, 126, 137, 144
, use in **ex**   130, 133, 144
ˆ, **grep**   156, 157

A

accepting standard input, **grep**   163
action (default) of **awk**   183
action (multiple) on one **awk** line   195, 220
actions performed by **sed**   243
adding:
    and assigning in one step, **awk**   206
    characters to a pattern in **ex**   138
    output to an existing file   73
    text after a line with **sed**   240
addition operator, **awk**   201
address (contextual), definition in **ex**   119
address nesting, **sed**   261
address, definition in **ex**   116
administration (system) tool, **awk**   217
aliases using **grep**   162
aligning decimal points, **awk**   209
altering the order of redirection in a command   76
alternative patterns, finding in **ex**   127, 144
appending output to an existing file   73
appending text, **sed**   240
arguments to a utility, multiple   86
arithmetic operations, **awk**   196, 198-203, 206
assigning options to a utility   82
assignment operator, **awk**   193
asterisk, use in **awk**   202
asterisk, use in **grep**   152, 157, 158

awk:
> BEGIN   210, 211, 220
> assignment operator   193
> calculations in database report   341
> command file execution   189
> command file   188
> command syntax   183
> command   182
> data manipulation   51
> default action   183
> default field delimiter   180
> default pattern   183
> executing a command file,   189
> **-F** option   213
> **-f** option   189, 220
> field separator   180
> format   52
> formatting output   186
> formatting program files   191
> general function   181
> line selection   51
> multiple actions on one line   195
> pattern search   181
> predefined variables   186
> **print** command   196, 181
> **printf** option   207
> printing fields   185
> printing words   194
> record separator   180
> removal of delimiter characters   332
> running a command file   189
> selecting fields   185
> subtracting a constant from a numeric field   196
> syntax   191
> variables, (user-defined)   192

B

backslash, in long command lines   323
backslash, use in **grep**   157
basic syntax, **grep**   151
basic syntax, **sed**   232
beginning of line, pattern finding in **ex**   126, 144
blank line, finding in **ex**   127, 134
brackets, use in **grep**   155
buffering input, **sed**   243
buffers, **sed**   243

C

c flag in **ex**   136, 143
calculations in database report   341
caret, **grep**   156, 157
case sensitivity, **grep**   155
case, ignoring, **sort**   24
cat   42
changing:
    default separator/delimiter, **paste**   289, 299, 300
    default separator/delimiter, **cut**   281, 299
    delimiter character, **join**   314
    delimiter with **sed**   317
    field delimiter, **sort**   25
    field separator, **awk**   213
    file ownership with **find**   369
    group membership of files, **find**   365
    output order, **awk**   186
    output order, **join**   311
    range of characters, **tr**   35
    separator for multiple files, **paste**   297
    specified characters, **tr**   35

character:
   any, finding in **ex**   131, 144
   changing, **tr**   35
   counting, **wc**   19, 21
   exclusion from a search in **ex**   129, 144
   insertion before a pattern in **ex**   139
   multiple ranges, exclusion from search in **ex**   130
   multiple ranges, finding in **ex**   129
   range changing, **tr**   35
   range, finding in **ex**   128, 129, 144
   range, selection with **cut**   279, 299
chgrp, use with **find**   365, 366
chown, use with **find**   369, 370
co command in **ex**   118
combining:
   cut and **paste**   298
   files, **cat**   42
   flags, **sed**   252
   lines, **join**   49
   records, **join**   307
   utilities   54
comm, selecting unique or common lines   33
comma in **awk**   186
command file:
   creation, **awk**   188
   creation, **sed**   238
   execution in **awk**   189, 220
   formatting, **awk**   191
   inserting text, **sed**   239
   running, **sed**   238
command line:
   editing, **sed**   50
   grep   44
   instructions multiple, **sed**   237
   interpretation   71
   join   315
command structure, **grep**   159
command substitution for directory paths   98
command syntax, see syntax

comment lines, removal **grep**   156
common lines, identifying, **comm**   33
common lines, selecting, **comm**   33
comparing redirection symbols   78
confirmation flag in **ex**   136
connecting records, **join**   307
connecting utilities with pipe   29
constants, arithmetic use in **awk**   196, 198
contextual address:
      construction in **ex**   119
      definition in **ex**   119
      multiple, **sed**   235
      use in substitution in **ex**   121
converting from lower to upper case in **ex**   139, 144
copying lines of text in **ex**   118
counting:
      characters with **wc**   21
      lines, **wc**   19, 157
      unmatched lines, **grep**   171
      words with **wc**   21
cp   38
creating:
      an alias, **grep**   162
      Bourne shell variables   94
      command file, **awk**   188
      command file, **sed**   238
      database, **awk**   179
      example database files   45
current line, definition in **ex**   117
cut:
      -c option   278, 279, 280, 299
      -d option   281, 283, 299
      -f option   273-5, 277, 299
      -s option   284, 299
      field selection from a file   45

D

d command in **ex**   118, 143

data file, fields   24

data manipulation, **awk**   51

database:

    description   325

    design relational   326

    design, single file   324

    report, calculations   341

    definition, **awk**   180

    using a relational   330

    using single file design   324

decimal points, aligning with **awk**   209

default:

    action of **awk**   183

    action of **ex**   119

    address of **p** command in **ex**   117

    delimiter, **cut** and **paste**   272

    delimiter, changing, for **cut**   281, 299

    field delimiter, **sort**   25

    input and output   80

    output, **sed**   251

    pattern, **awk**   183

    selection criterion, **find**   366

    separator, **awk**   180

    separator/delimiter (changing), with **paste**   289, 299

    separator/delimiter, **paste**   287, 300

defining a database, **awk**   180

defining variables in **awk**   192

delete:

    blank lines in **ex**   134

    blank lines, **sed**   236

    comment lines, **grep**   156

    duplicate lines, **uniq**   27

    line by number, **sed**   230

    lines of text in **ex**   118, 143

    lines without separators/delimiters, **cut**   284, 299

range of lines by number, **sed**   230
spaces at the beginning/end of lines in **ex**   137
temporary files, **find**   367
delimiter:
    changing with **sed**   317
    character changing, **join**   314
    characters, removal with **awk**   332
    default, **sort**   25
    definition   25
    field changing, **sort**   25
    field, default, **awk**   180
    field, definition, **awk**   180
    grep   153
    join   313
    paste   292
    white space   317
deroff   40
dictionary order, **sort**   23
directories (large) finding, **find**   361, 375
disk space, single file database design   325
display:
    current line in **ex**   117
    line by number in **ex**   116
    line numbers in **ex**   117
    lines in **ex**   119
    range of lines by number in **ex**   117
    range of lines in **ex**   118
division operator, **awk**   203
dot, use in **grep**   157, 158
double quotes, use in **grep**   153
duplicate lines, identifying, **uniq**   30
duplicate lines, removal of, **uniq**   27

E

editing from the command line, **sed**   50
egrep, -f option   165, 171
egrep   164

eliminating:
> blank lines in **ex**   134
> comment lines, **grep**   156
> duplicate lines, **uniq**   27
> lines without separators/delimiters, **cut**   284, 299
> spaces at the beginning of lines in **ex**   137
> spaces at the end of lines in **ex**   137
> temporary files, **find**   367

END, use in **awk**   210, 212,, 220
end of line, pattern finding in **ex**   144, 126
end of word, letter finding in **ex**   144
end-of-line character, **grep**   159
end-of-line, pattern finding in **ex**   127
error messages with **find**   371
escape sequences, **paste**   290
ex:
> instructions, general form   116
> line editor, use   114, 115
> default action   119
> definition   114

excluding characters from a search in **ex**   129, 144
excluding several ranges of characters in **ex**   130
execute:
> command file, **awk**   189, 220
> multiple commands, **sed**   245
> multiple utilities with **find**   368
> utilities   61, 67

expanding filenames with wildcard characters   88
expansion filename character, **grep**   152
expressions multiple, **egrep**   167
expressions regular, definition   112
extracting:
> characters, **cut**   278, 299
> fields, **cut**   272, 299
> multiple fields, **cut**   274
> ranges of characters, **cut**   279, 299
> range of fields, **cut**   275

fgrep, -f option   165, 171
fgrep   164

F

field:

    changing join field   319
    definition   25, 180, 272
    delimiter, **join**   313
    delimiter, **sort**   25
    delimiter, default, **awk**   180
    delimiter, default, **sort**   25
    multiple, selection with **cut**   274
    multiple, selection, **awk**   185
    range, selecting with **cut**   275
    relationship in files   306
    selecting all, **awk**   185, 222
    selecting with **cut**   272, 299
    selection from a file, **cut**   45
    separator changing, **awk**   213
    separator, **join**   313
    separator/delimiter, changing for **cut**   281, 299
    sorting, **sort**   25
    specific, selecting, **awk**   184, 222
    value, use in selecting with **awk**   187

file:

    as input to commands   74
    combining, **cat**   42
    command, creation in **awk**   188
    command, execution in **awk**   189, 220
    descriptors   68
    expansion character, **grep**   152
    finding **grep**   153
    finding, **find**   352, 374
    finding, by user, **find**   354, 374
    finding, modified within a specified time,**find**   356, 374
    finding, more recently modified, **find**   357, 374
    finding, most recent version, **find**   358
    finding, not accessed in a time period, **find**   355, 374
    finding, set-group-id, **find**   360, 374
    finding, set-user-id, **find**   359, 374

group membership changing, **find**   365
joining, **join**   307
locating large with **find**   362, 375
location, **find**   53
merging, **cat**   42
multiple search, **grep**   44, 152
multiple, with **paste**   292
names, finding **grep**   171
ownership, changing, **find**   369
pattern, **egrep**   165
pattern, **grep**   165
program formatting, **awk**   191
searching and printing lines   43
searching through, **grep**   152
selecting a field with **cut**   45
single, with **paste**   287, 288, 299
temporary removal, **find**   367
filter, **grep**   161
filter, definition   18
find:
command, general form   352
-atime option   355, 374
-exec option   365, 366, 375
-mtime option   356, 374
-name option   352, 353, 374
-newer option   357, 374
-o option   363, 375
-perm option   359-361, 374
-print option   352, 353, 374
-size option   361, 362, 375
-type option   361, 362, 375
-user option   354, 374
default selection criterion   366
error messages   371
executing multiple utilities   368
file finding   352, 374
file location   53
incomplete statements   372
multiple selection criteria   356, 363

permission errors   371
removing temporary files   367
syntax errors   372
use of minus sign   355, 374
use of plus sign   355, 374
finding:
nroff commands in ex   133
letter as the beginning of a word in ex   126, 144
letter as the end of a word in ex   126, 144
line containing a word in ex   125, 144
pattern at the beginning of a line in ex   126, 144
range of characters in ex   128, 128, 129, 144
all upper case letters in ex   128
any character in ex   131, 144
blank lines in ex   127
end-of-line character, grep   159
files modified within a specified time, find   356, 374
files not accessed in a time period, find   355, 374
files, by user, find   354, 374
files, known name, find   352, 374
files, more recently modified, find   357, 374
large directories, find   361, 375
large files, find   362, 375
line numbers, grep   154, 171
lines containing a specified word, grep   151
lines that start with periods in ex   133
patterns versus words in ex   125
patterns, grep   151
set-group-id files, find   360, 374
set-user-id files, find   359, 374
words in ex   125, 144
flag, print, sed   249
flags, multiple, sed   252
form (general) of find command   352
format (general) of awk commands   182
format specifiers, awk   207
format, awk   52
formatting output, awk   186
formatting program files, awk   191

FS variable in **awk**   213
function (general) of **awk**   181

G

g command in **ex**   120, 122, 143
g flag in **ex**   123, 143
general form of **ex** instructions   116, 352
general format of **awk** commands   182
general format of **g** command in **ex**   120
general function of **awk**   181
global substitution in **ex**   121, 122
global use of commands in **ex**   120, 143
greater than sign (**>**), use in **sort**   26
grep:
    -c option   157, 171
    command line   44
    database report writing   340
    definition   150
    -l option   153, 171
    multiple file search   44
    -n option   154, 154, 171
    use with **find**   370,
    -v option   156, 171
group membership changing, files, **find**   365
grouping an address within an address, **sed**   261
grouping commands to print the next line, **sed**   260
grouping multiple commands, **sed**   260

H

hyphen, use in **awk**   167, 197-200

I

identifying:
>   duplicate lines, **uniq**   30
>   lines using the last line character in **ex**   118
>   most recent version of a file, **find**   358
>   unique and common lines, **comm**   33
>   unique lines, **uniq**   29

ignoring case, **awk**   187

ignoring case, **grep**   155

ignoring case, **sort**   24

improving readability with variables, **awk**   192

including words in print statements, **awk**   194, 220

incomplete **find** statements   372

information passing to**grep** in script   340

input from other utilities, **awk**   216

input, definition   18

inserting characters before a pattern in **ex**   139

inserting text with a command file, **sed**   239

interacting with the shell   63

interpreting the basic command line   71

invoking the **ex** line editor   115

isolating a word for search and substitution in **ex**   137

J

join:
>   changing delimiter character   314
>   changing output order   311
>   combining lines   49
>   command line   315
>   definition   306
>   field delimiter   313
>   **-j** option   319
>   joining records   307
>   missing data   310
>   missing values   308

output, description of   308
reading standard input   319
records   305
selecting groups   320
sorting data files   308
specifying join field   319
standard input   335
syntax   316
unpairable lines   310
with **sort**   307
with passwd and groups file   320
joined composites   308
joined files   308
joining data from three files   335
joining files with missing information   309
joining sorted files   308
joining standard input/output   76
joining two files, **join**   307

K

keeping a running total, **awk**   204
kernel   61

L

large directories, finding, **find**   361, 375
large file finding, **find**   362, 375
last line character, definition in **ex**   118
leaving **ex**   124
left justifying, **awk**   210
less-than sign with **tr**   35
letter, finding (beginning or end of word) in **ex**   126, 144

lines:

   blank, removal in **ex**   134
   combining, **join**   49
   copying, **ex**   118
   counting, **wc**   19-21
   deletion, **ex**   118, 143
   deletion, **sed**   230
   duplicate, identifying, **uniq**   30
   duplicate, removal of, **uniq**   27
   moving, **ex**   118
   numbers, finding, **grep**   154, 171
   numbers, how to display in **ex**   117
   of a single file, **paste**   288, 299, 300
   ordering with **sort**   21
   pasting together, **paste**   47
   printing to screen in **ex**   119
   selection, **awk**   51
   unique or common, identifying, **comm**   33
   unique, identifying, **uniq**   29
   unmatched, counting, **grep**   157, 171
   without separator/delimiters, **cut**   284, 283, 299
   without separators/delimiters, **cut**   283
listing filenames, **grep**   153, 171
locating **nroff** commands in **ex**   133
locating a range of characters in **ex**   128, 144
locating files and printing their pathnames, **find**   53
long command lines, entering   323
lower or upper case in searches in **ex**   127
lower or upper case, **grep**   155
lower to upper case conversion in **ex**   139, 144

M

manipulating data, **awk**   51
marked lines, substitution on in **ex**   122

matching:

   any character in **ex**   131, 144

   any character within a pattern in **ex**   131

   any number of any characters in **ex**   132

   beginning of a line in **ex**   126

   repeated characters in **ex**   131, 144

membership (group) of files, changing, **find**   365

merging files, **cat**   42

metacharacters:

   definition in **ex**   112

   egrep   166

   fgrep   166

   grep   157

   in substitutions, **sed**   253

   removing meaning in **ex**   133, 144

   special, **egrep**   167

   use in **grep**   155

   use in replacement pattern in **ex**   135

   use in searches in **ex**   124, 127

   use with target patterns in **ex**   135

minus sign, use in **find**   355, 374

missing data, **join**   310

missing values, **join**   308, 309

mo command in **ex**   118

modified file finding, **find**   356, 357, 374

moving lines of text in **ex**   118

moving to the next line, **sed**   255

multiple:

   actions on one **awk** line   195, 220

   arguments   86

   command grouping, **sed**   260

   command line instructions, **sed**   237

   commands, **sed**   245

   contextual addresses, **sed**   235

   expressions with **egrep**   167

   field, selection, **awk**   185

   field, selection, **cut**   274

   file search, **grep**   44, 152

   files, **cut**   276

files, **paste**   292
options, **grep**   157
options, **wc**   21
pattern search, **grep**   158, 164
ranges of characters, exclusion from search in **ex**   130
ranges of characters, finding in **ex**   129
redirection symbols   81
selection criteria, **find**   356, 363
separators/delimiters, specifying with **paste**   291
spaces, interpretation by **awk**   191
spaces, removal in **ex**   136
tabs, interpretation by **awk**   191
utility execution with **find**   368
word searches, **grep**   153
multiplication operator, **awk**   202

N

nesting an address within an address, **sed**   261
no output, **grep**   154
not specifying the pattern, **awk**   183
NR variable in **awk**   190
nroff   37
nroff commands, locating in **ex**   133
nroff commands, removal of, **grep**   157
null output, **grep**   154
number truncating, **awk**   209

O

one word per line output, **deroff**   41
operating procedure, **sed**   248
options assignment   82
options (multiple), **grep**   157

order:
    dictionary, **sort**   23
    lines with **sort**   21
    of output, **join**   311
    of redirection   76
    of sorting, **sort**   22
output:
    definition   18
    description, **join**   308
    formatting, **awk**   186
    line numbers, **grep**   154, 171
    null, **grep**   154
    order, **join**   311
    redirection, **awk**   215
    redirection, **paste**   293
    standard redirection, **sort**   26
    suppression, **sed**   251
outputting filenames, **grep**   153, 171
ownership of files, changing with **find**   369

P

p command in **ex**   116-118, 143
parentheses, use in **egrep**   168
passing information to **grep**   163
paste:
    -d option   289, 291, 297, 299, 300
    how it works   294
    multiple files   292
    -s option   288, 299, 300
    standard input   296
pasting a file   287
pasting lines together, **paste**   47
pattern:
    default, **awk**   183
    definition   43
    files, **egrep**   165
    files, **grep**   165

finding in **ex**   127, 144
finding, **grep**   151
finding, at end of line in **ex**   127, 144
finding in **ex**   119
multiple search, **grep**   158, 164
multiple word searches, **grep**   153
reordering within a line in **ex**   140
replacement, definition in **ex**   121
replacement, special characters in **ex**   138
replacement, with metacharacters in **ex**   135
search, **awk**   181, 220
searching with **find**   370
substitution in **ex**   121-123, 143
target, definition in **ex**   121
versus words in **ex**   125
percent sign, use with **awk**   207
performing a command globally in **ex**   120, 143
permission errors, **find**   371
PID   66
pipe   29, 76
pipe, use in **egrep**   169
pipe, use in **grep**   163
piping output to another command   76
plus sign, use in **egrep**   168
plus sign, use in **find**   355, 374
predefined variables in **awk**   186
print flag, **sed**   249
print lines containing a specified word, **grep**   151
print command of **awk**   181, 183, 196, 220
printing:
a line to the screen in **ex**   116
a range of lines to screen in **ex**   117, 118
all fields, **awk**   185, 222
current line to screen in **ex**   117
fields, **awk**   184
lines to screen in **ex**   119
multiple fields, **awk**   185
only lines containing a pattern, **sed**   254
only lines not containing a pattern, **sed**   254

requests, **sed**   247
strings, **awk**   207
variable names, **awk**   195
with the print flag, **sed**   249
words, **awk**   194, 195, 220
process identification number   66
program file, creation, **awk**   188, 189, 191, 220

Q

q command in **ex**   124
question mark, use in **egrep**   168
quit after a specified line, **sed**   231
quit after a specified pattern, **sed**   233
quit, **sed**   231, 261
quitting **ex**   124
quitting **ex** without saving changes   124
quotes (single), use in **awk**   182
quotes (single), use in **grep**   159
quoting words within print statements, **awk**   195

R

range:
        character changing, **tr**   35
        characters, exclusion from a search in **ex**   129, 144
        characters, finding in **ex**   128, 129, 144
        characters, selection with **cut**   279, 299
        fields, selecting with **cut**   275
        lines, displaying in **ex**   117, 118
        multiple of characters, exclusion from search in **ex**   130
        multiple of characters, finding in **ex**   129
        substituting on lines outside of, **sed**   259
readability improvements, **awk**   191, 198, 199
reading in a file at a specified address, **sed**   241
recent version (file), finding with **find**   358

record, definition, **awk**   180
record separator, default, **awk**   180
records, **join**   305, 307
redirecting:
    input, **awk**   216
    input, **write**   85
    output to an existing file   73
    output to another command   76
    output, **awk**   215
    output, **sed**   239
    output, **sort**   26
    standard input   75
    standard output   69
regular expression addresses, **sed**   236
regular expression substitution in **ex**   121, 135, 143
regular expressions, definition   112
relational database:
    advantages and limitations   330
    design   326
    definition   304,306
    implementation   327
    reports   330
    shell script   338
    using   330
relational operators in **awk**   187
relationship of fields in files   306
relationships within records   306
remove line numbers in **ex**   117
removing:
    blank lines in **ex**   134
    comment lines, **grep**   156
    lines without separators/delimiters, **cut**   284, 299
    magic in **ex**   133, 144
    meaning of metacharacters in **ex**   133, 144
    multiple spaces in **ex**   136
    nroff commands, **grep**   157
    spaces at the beginning/end of lines in **ex**   137
    temporary files, **find**   367

reordering patterns within a line in **ex**   140
repeated characters, finding in **ex**   131, 144
replacement pattern, definition in **ex**   121
replacement pattern, with metacharacters in **ex**   135
replacement patterns, special characters in **ex**   138
replacing:
    a range of characters, **tr**   35
    regular expressions in **ex**   121, 143
    specified characters, **tr**   35
    the default separator/delimiter, **paste**   300
    the default separator/delimiter, **cut**   281, 299
    the default separator/delimiter, **paste**   289, 299
    the separator for multiple files, **paste**   297
report writing with **awk** and **join**   337
reports with **join**   333
reports, creating in relational database   330
request for printing, **sed**   247
reverse option of **grep**   156, 171
reverse sort, **sort**   24
review of command structure, **grep**   159
right justifying, **awk**   208
running a command file, **awk**   189, 220
running a command file, **sed**   238
running total, **awk**   204, 205, 206

S

s command in **ex**   121, 122, 123, 135, 143
saving changes in **ex**   124
search:
    files and printing lines   43
    for a lower or upper case letter in **ex**   127
    for a pattern, **awk**   181, 220
    for a pattern with **find**   370
    multi-word patterns, **grep**   153
    multiple patterns, **grep**   158, 164
    through multiple files, **grep**   44, 152

sed:
>> address nesting   261
>> appending text   240
>> basic operating procedure   248
>> basic syntax   232
>> buffering input   243
>> combining flags   252
>> command line editing   50
>> default output   251
>> delete blank lines   236
>> delimiter changing   317
>> how it works   243
>> line deletion   230
>> metacharacters in substitutions   253
>> multiple command grouping   260
>> multiple command line instructions   237
>> multiple commands   245
>> multiple contextual addresses   235
>> print flag   249
>> printing requests   247
>> quit   231, 261
>> reading in a file at a specified address   241
>> regular expression addresses   236
>> running a command file   238
>> standard output redirection   239
>> string substitution   234
>> substitute   249
>> substituting strings   230
>> suppressing all output   251
>> text insertion with a command file   239
>> using the next command   255
>> **write** flag   252
>> writing to files   242
> selecting:
>> a field from a file   45
>> a list of fields   274
>> a range of fields, **cut**   275
>> all fields, **awk**   185, 222
>> fields, **cut**   272, 299

filenames within a range   89
lines and printing fields, **awk**   51
lines by field value, **awk**   187
lines ignoring case, **awk**   187
multiple fields, **awk**   185
multiple fields, **cut**   274
ranges of characters, **cut**   279, 299
specific characters, **cut**   278, 299
specific fields, **awk**   184, 222
unique or common lines, **comm**   33
selection criteria (multiple), **find**   356
sending output to a new file   69
separator:
    changing, **join**   314
    changing default, with **paste**   289, 299
    changing for multiple files, with **paste**   297
    default, **cut** and **paste**   272
    default, **join**   313
    default, **paste**   287, 300
    default, **sort**   25
    default, changing, **cut**   281, 299
    field, changing, **awk**   213
    field, changing, **sort**   25
    field, definition   25
    multiple, specifying with **paste**   291
    record, default, **awk**   180
    record, definition, **awk**   180
set nonumber command in **ex**   117
set number command in **ex**   117
set-group-id files, finding, **find**   360, 374
set-user-id files, finding, **find**   359, 374
shell interaction   63
shell script in relational database   338
single file database design:
    advantages and limitations   325
    disk usage   325
    using   324
single quotes, function in **awk**   182, 220
single quotes, use in **grep**   159

slash, use in **awk**   203
sort:

       by fields, **sort**   25

       changing field delimiter   25

       data files, **join**   308

       dictionary order, **sort**   23

       -d option   23

       -f option   24

       field delimiter (default)   25

       ignoring case   24

       line ordering   21

       order, **sort**   22

       order of sorting,   22

       redirecting standard output   26

       regardless of case, **sort**   24

       reversal, **sort**   24

       syntax   22

       -t option   26

       -u option   30

       with **join**   307

space, use in **grep**   153

spaces at beginning of line, removal in **ex**   137

spaces at end of line, removal in **ex**   137

spaces (multiple), interpretation by **awk**   191

spaces (multiple), removal in **ex**   136

spacing the output, **awk**   186

special characters as separators, **paste**   290

special characters for replacement patterns in **ex**   138

special characters, **paste**   290

special metacharacters with **egrep**   167

special pattern END in a program, **awk**   212

specifying a list of separators   291

specifying field separators in command files, **awk**   214

specifying neither input nor output   80

splicing records, **join**   307

standard input:
>   **cut**   277
>   description   68
>   from other utilities, **awk**   216
>   **grep**   163
>   **paste**   296
>   in pipelines   86
>   reading with **join**   319
>   redirection   75
>   with **join**   335
standard output   68
standard output redirection, **sed**   239
standard output redirection, **sort**   26
starting processes   67
string printing, **awk**   207
string substitution, **sed**   230, 234
substitute command, **sed**   249
substitution:
>   all lines containing a pattern in **ex**   122
>   all lines in **ex**   121
>   all marked lines in **ex**   122
>   for a regular expression in **ex**   135
>   for multiple occurrences on a line in **ex**   123
>   lines containing a pattern, **sed**   234
>   lines outside of a range, **sed**   259
>   strings, **sed**   230
>   using a contextual address in **ex**   121
>   using metacharacters, **sed**   253
>   with/without the print flag, **sed**   250
subtraction, **awk**   196-200
summary of the **paste** process   294
suppressing **sed**'s default output   251
suppressing lines without separators/delimiters, **cut**   284, 299

syntax:
>   **awk**   191
>   **cut**   151
>   errors, **find**   372
>   **grep**   151
>   **join**   315, 316
>   **paste**   151
>   **sed**   151

system administration tool, **awk**   217

T

tab (multiple), interpretation by **awk**   191
target file specification   83
target pattern, definition in **ex**   121
target pattern, use with metacharacters in **ex**   135
temporary files, removing, **find**   367
text insertion with a command file, **sed**   239
three files, joining data   335
total (running), **awk**   204-206
tr, less-than sign   35
translating specified characters, **tr**   35
truncating numbers, **awk**   209

U

uniq:
>   **-d** option   30
>   identifying duplicate lines   30
>   lines, identifying, **comm**   33
>   lines, identifying, **uniq**   29
>   lines, selecting, **comm**   33
>   removing duplicate lines   27

unjoinable lines, **join**   310
unmatched lines, counting, **grep**   157, 171
unpairable lines, **join**   310

upper and lower case, **awk**   187
upper and lower case, **grep**   155
upper and lower case in searches in **ex**   127
upper to lower case conversion in **ex**   139, 144
usage error, **find**   372
user specific file finding, **find**   354, 374
user-defined variables, **awk**   192
utilities, connecting with pipe   29
utility combining   54
utility (multiple) execution with **find**   368

V

variable:
       definition in **awk**   192
       names, selection, **awk**   193
       names, words to be printed, **awk**   195
       predefined, **awk**   186
       user-defined, **awk**   192, 220

W

w command in **ex**   124
w option, **deroff**   41
wc:
       -c option   21
       counting lines   20
       counting words   21
       -l option   20
       multiple options   21
       -w option   21
white space, delimiter   317
who   277

word(s):
     command line   71
     counting, **wc**   21
     finding, **grep**   151
     multiple pattern searches, **grep**   153
     printing of, **awk**   194, 195, 220
     versus patterns in **ex**   125, 144
write flag, **sed**   252
writing changes in **ex**   124
writing to files, **sed**   242

Resources

After people complete exercises such as these modules, it is helpful to be able to locate specific pieces of information. The following references are available to assist you in looking up the "right command" or the proper syntax:

(1) **INDEX:**   page 395

The complete index permits you to quickly locate a particular explanation or example when you need it. You can access information by:

- command name such as: **sed, find, join;**

- object that is involved: *file, argument, range of lines, unique lines;*

- action to be performed: *remove, redirect, select, combine;*

- the usual index topic entries: *field delimiter, relational database,* and *command interpretation.*

(2) **COMMAND INDEX:**   page 381

All commands used in the modules and their page numbers are listed in alphabetical order in the Command Index. The page number permits you to quickly locate the explanation where the example was used in the modules.

(3) **COMMAND SUMMARIES:**   (at ends of modules)

Following each module the commands and their options are listed with explanations. This summary allows for quick review to locate the syntax and option to accomplish a desired goal.

LURNIX
The Computer Education
and Support People

PO Box 10164
1680 Shattuck Avenue
Berkeley, California 94709
800/433-9338
800/433-9337 in Ca
415/849-4478

Lurnix is a group of professional educators and computer scientists dedicated to making education efficient and enjoyable. We develop materials and deliver training. Our specialty is curriculum design. We assess student needs, identify specific content, determine the best methodology, tailor materials, deliver courses, and evaluate effectiveness of educational programs.

License and Sale of Modules

Lurnix materials, like the modules in this book, are modular for several educational reasons. After the employee's needs are determined, we can quickly combine the appropriate modules to create the most effective training program. This approach maximizes the benefit students receive from training, because the focus is on the essential content pertinent to the job. In addition to the modules in this book, Lurnix has developed nearly a hundred other modules on topics including: advanced editing, text processing, database application design and development, shell programming, system administration, C Language programming, security, communications and windows. All modules are available for license or volume sale.

Services Provided

Lurnix teaches a full range of courses on the client's site and in our Berkeley classroom. Staff members also teach specific topic workshops, consult, and assist other firms in developing their training programs and expertise.

RELATED TITLES FROM MIS:PRESS

X Windows Applications Programming

Professional programmers will find this powerful tutorial and reference work indispensable in mastering X Windows—the new vendor-independent, hardware-independent graphical windowing system developed by MIT. Loaded with source code and illustrations, this book delineates X Windows programming involving both C and UNIX. Programmers will learn to build a full-fledged X Windows application. It also includes a programming library of useful tools programmers can use over and over again.

Kevin Reichard/Eric F. Johnson   1-55828-016-2 $24.95

User Interfaces in C

C Programmers will find this powerful reference an invaluable tool in writing user interfaces for their own programs. Clearly and concisely written, this book gives in-depth information on constructing pull-down menus and windows. This book is loaded with sample programs that illustrate the important concepts programmers need to make the task of building user interfaces easier and faster. Presented in a step-by-step manner, this book takes programmers systematically from mastering lower level functions to C's most powerful tools.

Mark Goodwin   1-55825-002-2 $24.95 $49.95 w/disk

C/C++ for Expert Systems

The most lucid expert systems reference book ever written for professional C programmers, this book exposes the concepts and program components necessary to unleash the power of artificial intelligence with C/C++. Loaded with sample programs, it demonstrates how to create expert systems or shells, make programs "intelligent," introduce uncertainty of knowledge, and embed reasoning capabilities into programs. Includes LISP and Prolog utility programs in C.

David Hu   0-943518-86-5 $24.95 $49.95 w/disk

C Data Base Development

All the tools programmers need for writing C data base programs—with complete, detailed instructions on how to use them. Explains DBMS concepts, C data utilities, the C data compiler, and using C as a data definition language. Includes a billing system program as a sample data base application.

Al Stevens   0-943518-33-4 $23.95 $43.95 w/disk

Turbo C

Everything Turbo C programmers need to get the most out of this fast and powerful programming language. Covers topics and techniques including memory management, ROM BIOS functions, programming screen input/output, and writing memory-resident utility programs in Turbo C.

Al Stevens   0-943518-35-0 $24.95 $44.95 w/disk

QuickC

QuickC is the latest compiler from Microsoft. This book provides a C language development environment for both beginning and advanced users. Includes an integrated editor and debugger. The code you develop is upward-compatible with the Microsoft C compiler.

Al Stevens   0-943518-80-6 $24.95 $49.95 w/disk

Extending Turbo C Professional

This serious how-to is for professional programmers looking to master programming techniques for using Turbo C Professional in advanced and complex computer systems. Hot topics include building programs with overlays, interrupt service routines, and video windows; the latest techniques for building memory-resident pop-up programs in Turbo C; and serial input/output and modem driver functions. Also included are a library of EMS functions, tricks for programmers to extend use of the keyboard, cursor, and audio speaker, and unpublished details of MS-DOS internals.

Al Stevens 1-55828-018-9 $49.95 w/disk

Available where fine books are sold.

MANAGEMENT INFORMATION SOURCE, INC.
P.O. Box 5277 • Portland, OR 97208-5277
(503) 222-2399

Call free
1-800-MANUALS

MIS
PRES

M A N A G E M E N T   I N F O R M A T I O N   S O U R C E ,   I N C .